Five of a Kind

GW Cody

Cover design and graphics by gw Cody

ISBN 978-0-6151-3987-6

Special Thanks

This book is dedicated to family and friends. In particular to Dan and Rusty whose encouragement, support and their belief in my ability to complete the writing of this book got me through the many drafts. To Michael E., Michael M., and David A. who all passed away before I completed writing the book. To my sister who encouraged me to undertake this project. To my husband who listened to all my ideas and thoughts as I put this book together. And to the many people I have worked with who have accepted me for who I am. Without them, my success would have been limited.

Foreword

This book uses a party as the vehicle to tell the story of five friends and the beginning of each of their relationships. The individual characters tell their story of how they met their partner in the character chapters. By having each individual character tell about his relationship the story has more of an intimate touch. The party portions of the story are told from the view point of the character named Colt.

Contents

In complete darkness we are all the same

it is only our knowledge and wisdom that separate us.

Don't let your eyes deceive you.

Janet Jackson
1966 --

To Niceboy

The Gang

Summer was rapidly coming to an end. For the
last several years, five of us had gotten together for an annual
Summer Is Over party at my place. It was time to remind the
other four it was party time. Over the years, this party was
one that we all had made a commitment to attend. We always
showed no matter what. It was like a New Year's Eve,
Thanksgiving, Christmas, family kind of gathering for the
five of us. This was the one yearly event that we shared
secrets with one another, talked, and enjoyed our time
together.

      The party started out as a fluke. One year I had the
bright idea to have an end of the summer party. I invited
everyone I knew, and prepared for a large party. I bought lots
of food and beverages. The night of the party, the only ones
to show were the five of us. We had so much fun talking and

confiding in each other, we decided to make it an annual event just for the five of us.

This year I was particularly excited, because I had some exciting news to share with the gang, as we referred to one another. One important event happened recently in my life, which I had kept to myself, and I wanted to tell all four of them at once. I was anxious for the evening to arrive. I needed to make the reminder calls. With telephone in hand, I began with Sampson. I could just picture his six-foot plus slender build rapidly answering the phone.

"Hello."

"Sampson, hi, Colt. How are you?"

"I'm fine and yourself?"

"I'm okay. How's Ron?"

"He's fine. What's up?"

"Oh, a few things, but I'll tell you about them later Sampson."

"Let me guess, it's party time again, and I have to wait to hear details about Max and you until then, right?"

"You're right. It's only two weeks from today. That's the main reason for my call. I wanted to remind you of the date."

"Oh Colt, I remembered. I already told Ron I'd be gone that evening."

"Good. I wanted to be sure you'd remember."

"Colt, I wouldn't forget our annual bash. I'll be there, eightish as usual?"

"Sure, why change a good thing?" Beep. "Listen, I have another call, so I'll let you go." Beep. "Tell Ron hi, and I'll see you in two weeks, if not sooner."

"Ok Colt, tell Max hello, and take care." Beep.

"I will, you too." Beep. . . ."Hello . . . hello . . ." whoever it was hung up! Sampson was like the mother hen, always in charge of his brood. He was in a word, industrious. There was a certain system to placing these reminder calls. I usually started with Sampson, because he was most likely to be out of town. Next I usually called Derrek, because he was seldom home, the blue-eyed jock.

"Hello, this is Derrek, and we're not in right now, if you'll leave a message at the sound of the tone, we'll return your call as soon as possible." BEEWAAP.

"Yo Derrek, this is Colt. Just called to remind you of our annual party. Two weeks from tonight, Saturday. Give me a call and let me know if you'll be there. Didn't charge your cell phone last night? Talk to you later, bye."

Next in the line up of calls was Marshall, because his schedule constantly changed. His brown eyes captivated you. I hope he had turned his on cell phone.

"Hello."

"Marshall, 'tis me Colt."

"Well, hello Colt. How ya doin'?"

3

"I'm fine, and you?"

"Oh, fine real busy. The new cook at work just can't get his act together, and is a pain to deal with, but otherwise I'm fine. What can I do for you?"

"It's just time for our annual end of the summer party. I just called to remind you."

"God, has it been a year already?"

"It sure has!"

"Sure, I'll be there. I may be a little late, work is so screwed up. What day it this again?" Marshall asked.

"Two weeks from today. How's Tom?"

"Oh, he's fine. He had to go in today, so he's off at work. Well, Colt, I don't mean to be rude, but I've gotta go. I have to go into the restaurant today and do some work. I'll call you later. Bye."

"Later Marshall."

In a word, Marshall was charismatic. Marshall was the true party boy, yet he would give you the shirt off his back. Darrin was the easiest to get a-hold of, so he was last. His cell phone was always attached to his hip, so whatever location he was presently at you could always get a hold of him. However one never knew who, or how the phone would be answered. It did make it kind of a fun call to make. His slender six-foot build and blond hair could be easily found in crowd.

"Hello?"

"Hello, Colt?"

"Derrek? How weird, I just picked up the telephone to call Darrin!"

"You mean your phone did not ring?"

"No, it didn't. That is really weird."

"Yeah uh huh, it is. I was just returning your call on that. I had my cell. I forgot to turn it on. Sure, I will be there. I have it marked on my calendar."

"I'm glad. How are Jason and Clem?"

"Oh, they are both fine. How are big Max and little Max?"

"Oh, fine. Little Max is sitting here by my feet. Big Max is at work."

"So, we doing this at eight as usual? And at your place?"

"Yeah, eight, my place."

"Yea uh huh, well, Colt, I have got some contracts I need to get to today. I just wanted to take time out to return your call. I need to get goin."

"Okay. I need to call Darrin anyway. Talk at you later."

"Yeah, uh huh. Take care."

"You too."

Hearing his name mentioned Max was up and ready for a walk. Sometimes I wondered if this dog couldn't understand the conversations on the phone. A one-word description of Derrek is jovial. Derrek was the big prankster, always trying to pull some joke on everyone.

"Okay Max, out the front door for a quick walk. I still have another call to make kid." We walked outside, and Max ran to dutifully do his job in the field in front of the townhouse. He came running back, and into the house. I went to the phone to make the last call.

"Yo Ins and Outs, Darrin here, how may I help you?"

"Hello Darrin its Colt."

"Well, hi dude, what's up?"

"So you answer your cell as a business phone now? I just called to . . ."

"Tell me it's time for the end of the summer gig. Marshall called this morning in a panic, he couldn't get a hold of Tom, and his Jag wouldn't start. I took him to work, and he said you called."

"The electrical system again I'm sure."

"Correct. What else would it be?"

"You comin' then?"

"Maybe, maybe not. Depends on what you're serving this year." Darrin laughs.

"Fine, be that way, don't come."

"Oh, Colt, I'll be there. Just had to give you a hard time is all." Darrin teased.

"It'll be nice to see you again. It's been awhile. How's Mat?"

"Oh, he's ok. Hey, a customer just walked in, I gotta go."

"Okay, see you in two weeks."

"Ok, bye dude."

In a word, Darrin is assertive. He is like a hard candy with a cream center. His bark is worse than his bite. Once you get past his tough exterior, he is very soft. Marshall called me back, we talked about his car, re-confirmed the time and date and that he would be late. Other than that call, we all went about our personal lives, knowing we would see one another soon. Those two weeks lapsed rapidly.

I put together some munchies ahead of time for the party and made sure I had on hand the correct brand of liquor for each of the guests. The house was thoroughly cleaned, Max was groomed, and all was in order, looking good for the party. As the actual day drew closer, I got more excited, like a kid waiting for Christmas morning to open presents. We always had so much fun and I had big news I had kept secret.

That night "Big" Max had gone out with some friends, I was busy putting out cold cuts, cheese, chips, dips, veggies and cookies when the doorbell rang. Max ran to the door barking to see who was there. I walked to the door to welcome the first guest.

"Betchya it is Derrek, Max." I opened the door to discover I was correct.

"Well, hello Colt, you are looking good. Hi Max, how are you fella?" Derrek gave me a hug.

"Hi Derrek, come in. You look good too. I see you decided to wear your ball cap."

"Yeah, uh huh, keeps my hair from getting messy. I see you are barefoot as usual. It's a butuful evening." He leaned down and petted Max.

"Yes it is Derrek. Come on into the kitchen." We walked into the dining room and Max followed us. We sat at the table.

"I knew you'd arrive first. So, how's business?"

"Going good. I have surpassed my goals for this quarter and landed two rather large remodeling jobs."

"Great! How are Jason and Clem?"

"Fine. Jason is out tonight with friends and Clem is home alone. I almost brought him with me to visit little Max. How is big Max?"

"He's fine. He is out with friends too. You should have brought Clem. Max would have enjoyed the company of another dog. Want a beer?" I got up to get it.

"Yea uh huh, sure, I'm ready for one. I will have to bring Clem by one day next week." Derrek said.

"Here you go. Sure, bring Clem by. We can take the dogs for a walk along the canal."

"Yea uh huh, I will. Thanks for the beer. We have not gone for a long walk with the kids in awhile."

"I know. Here, have a chocolate chip cookie. I baked them particularly for you."

"Thank you, I appreciate that. How is teaching?"

"Oh, it's fine. This class isn't too bad. It's been a good start, let me put it that way." I replied.

"That is good, and so are these cookies."

"Thanks." I said.

"There is the doorbell. Any bets?" Derrek asked.

"I'll go for Sampson."

"Uh huh, my choice too Colt."

As I walked to the door I pondered what Sampson would be wearing if he was indeed the one to arrive next. Max beat me to the door. As I opened the door, I found we were correct. There stood Sampson in a very classy dress shirt and slacks. Max bounded out to greet Sampson.

"Hello Colt, Max."

"Hi Sampson, come in. Derrek's here and we were just talking about you." I said.

"Oh really. So, how are you?" He leaned down hugged me and kissed me on the cheek.

"I'm fine, and you?" We walked toward the dining room.

"Fine. Hello Derrek, and what tacky things were you saying about me?" Sampson asked.

"Hello Sampson. We were not saying anything tacky, just talking about who would arrive next." Derrek said innocently.

"Oh, sure you were. So, how ya been Derrek?"

"Oh, fine Sampson, and you?" Derrek replied.

"Busy Derrek, real busy, but fine. How's Jason?"

"Jason's fine."

"And don't I get a hug out of you?" Sampson scolded. Derrek stood and hugged Sampson.

"Yea uh huh," Derrek replied as he hugged Sampson. "How's Ron?"

"Oh, Ron's fine. Said he was going to go out for awhile tonight." Sampson responded.

"Vodka and Seven Sampson?" I interrupted.

"Yea, sure, please." Sampson replied.

"Yea uh huh, Jason said the same thing, headed out with friends," Derrek said.

While I mixed the drink, I wondered who would be next to arrive. I handed Sampson his drink.

"So, Colt, what do you have to tell me that had to wait until tonight?" Sampson inquired.

"Well, I want to wait until everyone is here, then I'll tell you all at once."

"Oh, sure, make me wait! I've only waited two weeks as it is!" Sampson sighed.

"What news Colt? You did not tell me you had any news!" Derrek said amazed.

"Like I said, I'm waiting until everyone arrives."

"Oh, come on Colt, just tell us." Derrek pleaded.

"No, I'm waiting. New outfit Sampson?" I said quickly to change the subject.

"No, not really. Just one of my favorite outfits. These are my . . ."

"Favorite colors, I know purple and black, looks good." I completed his sentence for him.

"Thank you Colt. So, where are Marshall and Darrin?"

"Come on Sampson, neither one of them ever arrives on time. Marshall said he'd be late when I called him, so I won't hold my breath." I explained.

"You're right. I was just anxious to see them, and hear this news!" Sampson quipped.

"The doorbell again Colt. Has to be Darrin." Derrek said.

"Help yourselves to munchies guys, I'll be right back." Max ran ahead of me as I walked to the door. He sat waiting for me when I got to the door. I opened the door and there stood Darrin.

"Yo dude, hi Max."

"Hi Darrin, come on in. So, how's life?"

"Awe, its ok, except for the drive out here to the plains. I see you decided to almost wear something this evening!" He leaned over and hugged me, a tight squeeze. As he squeezed me he whispered, "Aren't you getting to old to dress like this?"

"Funny, very funny Darrin. You are as old as you feel." I retorted. We walked into the dining room to join the others. Darrin and Sampson stood out, both being so tall.

"Hi Darrin." Derrek said.

"Hello Darrin." Greeted Sampson.

"Hello boys, or should I say guy and gal? Well, look at you two! Derrek in his usual jogging get up and Sampson all duded up queen that she is, and of course Colt is almost dressed." Darrin said sarcastically. "I'm wondering Derrek if the shorts and T-shirt isn't because you are one of those dingy blonds who can't tell the difference in the seasons." Hugs were exchanged as they talked.

"Dingy blond! Look who's talking Darrin, you are blond too! At least shorts and a T-shirt are summery, what is with a flannel shirt, leather vest, and leather pants?" Derrek responded, "On a night like tonight I'd prefer wearing shorts, besides I will probably go jogging after the party."

"Like I said the jogging get up. Well, Derrek, you are blonder than me. I look at is this way, fall begins tomorrow, and I can wear my leather and flannel because the weather will be getting cooler. Besides, I just got this vest

12

and shirt. I wanted to wear them out. I'm starting fall tonight." Darrin explained.

"And there is the real reason, isn't it, a new outfit," Sampson stated, "but let's watch the queen cracks."

"Oh come on now Sampson, you perform in drag, don't give me the old I'm not a queen crap." Darrin pointed out.

"JD and Coke Darrin?" I asked trying to end an argument before it started.

"I thought you'd never ask. I need a cocktail!"

"Comin' right up." I replied as I walked into the kitchen.

"I may be a queen when I perform Darrin, but I am all male when I am off stage," Sampson snapped.

"Girlfriend if that's what you believe, then more power to you," Darrin volleyed back.

"Colt, that is the door bell again!" Derrek teased.

"No, Derrek, I thought it was the microwave! Help yourselves to food." Walking to the door, I hoped Marshall had a good day and that the little tay to tay in the kitchen had ended. If not, we all would hear bitching about the restaurant, and an argument about Sampson's masculinity. With a deep breath, I opened the door.

"Hello Colt, I brought you this torte. It didn't turn out too good, but I made it special for tonight."

"Well thanks Marshall. It looks good. That was nice of you. Come on in, and I'll take that for you. Last as usual." He hugged and kissed me as he handed me the torte.

"So, what else is new? I'm always late. I can never seem to get ready on time. I guess I just like to make the grand entrance."

"Touché. How's Tom?"

"Oh, he's doing fine. And Max?"

"Doin' good."

"You're still looking tan Colt."

"Thanks, you look pretty dark yourself. Come on in, the rest of the gang is here." We walked into the dining room and heard the end of a conversation about Mat being fine. Max had stayed with the others in hopes of someone dropping crumbs and now ran up to greet Marshall.

"Well, hello Max. Hi boys, how are you?" Marshall reached down and petted Max.

"Hello Marshall." Sampson said.

"Hi Marshall." Derrek said in unison with Sampson.

"Yo dude." Darrin's typical greeting. "I see we did the old baggy T-shirt and the faded jeans."

"You wouldn't know me without them," Marshall fired back. He always had a way to put Darrin in his place, without a battle. Once again hugs were exchanged.

"How about a Manhattan?" I asked Marshall.

"I'm ready for one, thanks."

14

"What is in your hands Colt?" Derrek asked.

"It's a torte Marshall brought." I sat it down on the dining room table.

"Well, let us taste it then." Derrek said.

"Yea, I'm with Derrek let's taste it." Darrin replied.

"Go ahead and serve it Marshall," I suggested.

"No, you can Colt. I've had it with food for one day," Marshall said.

"Here. I'll settle this, let me serve it," Sampson took charge as usual. He grabbed the plate, cut the torte into pieces and served everyone. While Sampson was serving, I fixed Marshall his drink, and handed it to him.

"Thanks Colt." Marshall said.

We all took a bite of the torte at the same time and replied unanimously, "It is great!"

"Thanks. I wasn't too pleased with how it turned out, but Tom said you guys would eat anything," Marshall replied.

"That was nice of Tom," Darrin replied.

"He knows us well though, does he not?" Derrek said in defense of Tom.

"He certainly does," I added quickly.

"Sampson, I have a question for you. Remember you told me that I'd be moving several years ago?" Marshall asked.

"And . . . I suppose you want another tarot card reading since I was wrong back then," Sampson replied.

"No, no need for a reading, I am moving. Colt said you were looking for a house and I wondered if you'd be interested in ours." Marshall blurted out.

"Well, I don't know, I'd have to talk to Ron. Why are you moving?" Sampson inquired. "I told you, you would be!"

"Tom got transferred to the California, and that's why I've been working at the restaurant such long hours. I have had to train the new cook." Marshall explained.

"Uh huh, and I thought Colt had the unexpected news!" Derrek said, "When will you be leaving?"

"Before the end of the month if all works out right. Tom leaves then for sure," Marshall sighed.

"Thinking about how you two met, and how things went for awhile, I can't believe you are leaving the state!" Darrin said with a puzzled expression.

"Well, I've been with Tom for four years. I think you could say we are working out fine," Marshall replied.

"Well, Marshall, let me talk to Ron, and maybe all four of us can get together this week and discuss this further," Sampson said "With Roberta I would love to have a house with a yard so I could just open the door and let her out and not have to go on a long walk every time."

"I'd really like to sell the house to someone I knew would take care of it. I'd feel better about you and Ron having the place. I've put too much work into it." Marshall answered.

"Let me talk to Ron about it, and give you a call," Sampson responded.

"Sounds like a plan." Marshall sighed.

Marshall and Tom

Selling the house and moving out of state! When I met Tom, I would never have thought it would end up with us living together *and* moving to another state. I first met Tom over five years ago. I had just started going to a bar called the Hole. One night in July I talked Colt into going with me my first night and saw Tom for the first time while we were there. He was playing pinball and he looked at Colt and me several times, but I couldn't tell if he was looking at Colt or at me.

Being my first time in the bar I paid little attention to him, I was more interested in the bar, the music, and all the men. I guess I ran into Tom several times after that, but he never ever spoke. Then for a while, the restaurant was so busy I didn't go into the Hole at all. One night, fed up with work, I decided I was going out drinking, screw the job. My attitude was cranky and grumpy that evening. When I walked into the Hole, I saw Tom sitting at the end of the bar. I was in no mood to deal with anyone, so I went and sat at the other end of the bar alone. The bar tender brought me a drink and said it was from Tom. At the time my motto had become so many men, so little time. The offer of a drink flattered me, so I walked over to where he was to thank him.

"Hello, the bar tender said you sent me this drink."

"Yes, I did." He said. "My name is Tom."

"Thanks, my name is Marshall."

"I've seen you in here before. I have always intended to talk to you, but never managed to." Tom explained.

"I've seen you before as well. You look real familiar to me." I replied.

"You do, too. I just thought it was from seeing you somewhere else. You work around here?" He asked.

"Not too far away. I work at the Fez."

"Maybe I've seen you in there. I've eaten there a couple of times."

"I doubt that. I'm a cook. I'm never out front."

"Oh, well then I guess not."

"Want to play pinball?" I asked.

"Sure." We walked back to the pinball machines. Tom was attractive when you actually looked at him. Close up his dark hair and dark eyes were very sexy. He barely had any buttons buttoned on his shirt and he had a chest that looked like a rug. He started to play pinball and I didn't think I was ever going to get a turn.

"Damn!" He sighed. "Well Marshall, go ahead. Let's see how well you do."

"Not this good, I know." I said.

"Oh, you just say that now. You are probably a hustler!" He laughed.

"You'll see." I played the best I had ever played, but I was not as good as Tom. He took his turn and again I began to feel I was never going to be at the controls again. "You are very good!"

"Back home this was one of the only forms of entertainment we had. I played all the time." Tom said.

"Sounds familiar. I could never really get into pinball, I always just dreamed of leaving, and moving to a big city. I went out into the toolies with friends and drank and got high to enjoy myself."

"I did that sometimes too. I gather you are from a small town?"

"Yea, I hated it so much. When I was eighteen, I moved here. I just had to leave that little town."

"How old are you now?" Tom looked puzzled.

"How old do you think?"

"Early twenties." He said cautiously.

"Thanks, I'm twenty-eight."

"You are kidding! I will be twenty-eight in October!"

"Really? How weird. So when did you move here?"

"About a year ago. My dad owns a bakery back home and I worked for him for a long time, but I couldn't handle it anymore. One gay bar and that was only on Friday and Saturday nights, it was a drag."

"All small towns must be alike. Same thing here." I sighed.

"I guess. Where are you from, here in the state?"

"Yea, western part. You probably never heard of it, Orchard."

"Like hell I haven't. I come from Orchard!" Tom said excitedly.

"You are kidding! There are only two high schools, which one did you go to?"

"Orchard and you?"

"Central. That's where I've seen you before, at football games!" I said.

"You played?" Tom asked.

"No, but you did. I remember I used to have a crush on you, I thought you were so cute, but I always figured you being a jock, must be straight as an arrow."

"You and all the cheer leaders! I played it straight until I was out of high school." Tom explained.

"Me too. I didn't think there were any other gays in the city except me!" Tom was the man I used to drool over, I was so amazed!

"You just didn't hang out in the right places. If you had stayed around a little longer after you graduated, you would have found there were a few of us. Enough to fill a bar every Friday and Saturday night. Unfortunately, most of them married and were weekend fags! I wanted more, and finally decided the only way I was going to find it was to move to a larger city."

"So, have you found a lover here?" I asked.

"No, not yet but, I have had fun trying!" Tom laughed again. He had a deep loud laugh.

"Want another drink?" I asked.

"Sure, thanks."

"What are you drinking?"

"Bourbon and Coke." Tom replied.

"I'll be right back." I couldn't believe it. Now if I had ever imagined someone as hot as Tom was gay when I lived at home, I might have stayed put! I just couldn't believe I moved to the big city, and then met someone from my hometown, not to mention my age! I got the drinks, walked back over to Tom, and handed him his drink.

"Thanks Marshall. Another game?"

"Why not."

"So Marshall, you have a lover?"

"I did. I met someone after I moved here and we just broke up recently. It lasted nine years off and on. It is definitely over now!"

"That's a long time. Why did you break up?"

"Oh, lots of reasons. We couldn't agree on our sex life, and he was nine years older than me. He wanted a one on one relationship, and I didn't. I wanted to experience all the men I could."

"Must have been hard to break up."

"It was, but it was for the best. We still talk to each other, sometimes."

"I've only had a relationship last for nine months. That was the longest, and he was married and had kids. It was basically a weeknight thing. It was still hard to leave him. That's kind of why I moved up here. I was tired of one night stands, and weeknight romances."

"I guess. I got tired of the day-to-day living in the same house having to report home bullshit. I guess there are pros and cons." I said.

"Did you ever tell your family you were gay?" Tom asked.

"No. I think they suspect, after all I lived with a man for nine years, but no, I have kept that part of my life to myself." I answered. "And you, does your family know?"

"Yep, they sure do, and that is pretty much what got me moved here," Tom responded.

"How's that?" I asked.

"My parents told me they would rather I was dead than gay. They couldn't handle it. They didn't want anyone to know. So, I just decided I would leave and go somewhere that no one knew my business." Tom explained.

"I totally understand," I replied. We continued comparing notes on Orchard and people we both knew, things we both had done. I still couldn't believe he came from my hometown!

"That was last call. Want another drink?" Tom asked.

"Ok. Might as well, I haven't got any other plans."

"Well, we could go back to my place and have a drink there." Tom suggested.

I was taken back by that proposition. I hadn't really planned on talking to anyone, let alone going home with anyone. What the hell, what else did I have to do? So many men so little time I thought. "Why not, you sure?"

"I'm sure. I'd really like to get to know you better." He grinned.

We finished our drinks in silence. I wondered if this was a good idea, and then again, why not. It was great to talk to someone about my own hometown.

"Ok, let's go." I said as Tom put his empty glass back on the table. I followed him out of the bar and we stopped in the parking lot.

"Where are you parked?" He asked.

"Over there, that white car. And you?"

"Right here, that motorcycle. Want to just follow me?" Tom said.

"Sure." Tom hugged and kissed me. I was shocked, but it was not a total surprise. He had a motorcycle. I had always wanted one, but cold weather made me hesitant to buy one.

"I'll drive slow, and keep an eye out for you. If I lose you I'll pull over and wait."

"Ok. Guess I'll see you at your place." He walked me to my car and kissed me again. I gave him a ride back to his cycle and he kissed me again and gave my crotch a squeeze. I was getting the picture very clearly. "See you at your place."

"Ok." He got on his cycle and drove off. I followed him out of the parking lot. He was really hot. I was bummed out about work. I wasn't even catching the come on. Now following him home I wondered if I should go to his place or not. I realized I had slowed down and almost lost Tom. I speed up and caught up to him.

I decided he was hot enough, and what the hell. I hadn't had sex in a long time, and he was nice. He was easy to talk to and I did like him. I wanted to bed as many men as I could, and he would certainly fulfill that desire. We pulled up in a parking lot behind an apartment building and stopped. I got out of the car and walked over to Tom.

"I was afraid you'd changed your mind there for a little while." He looked a little worried I still might.

"I thought about it. I wasn't really getting the idea at first. I had work on my mind but, I'm here."

"Yes, I see. Follow me." We walked into the building and up to the third floor. His place was small and rather messy. We walked into the living room and sat down. I really wanted to clean up some of the junk.

"Want another Manhattan Marshall?"

"Sure, that was the offer you made." He walked into the kitchen and mixed the drink. He came back out, handed me my drink, and sat right beside me.

"You know you are very sexy. I have wanted to take you home since the first night I saw you. You just seemed not to care if anyone found you hot or not." Tom explained.

"I really haven't cared recently, Tom. I guess I'm still getting into the single life style."

"Well, I'm glad you came back here." He stood up and took off his shirt, shoes, and socks. "It's hot in here don't you think?"

"It feels fine to me." What a line. He was built. And his chest was like a rug, with a slender line of hair all the way to his waist. He was very sexy and appeared to be hung. I took a good look at his body. He sat back down and in one movement unbuttoned every button on my shirt. He began to kiss me and rub his hands on my crotch. Before I knew it, my pants were unbuttoned and my underwear slid down, and his face was between my legs. He wasted no time, but it felt good, and I let him do to me as he pleased.

He stood up and took off his pants, and when he did, I realized that left him naked. He reached down pulled off my shoes, socks, grabbed my jeans, and they were off in seconds. The next thing I knew I was on the floor and Tom was on top of me sucking my chest and rubbing his body against mine. It had either been a long time since he had sex, or he enjoyed being rough. His body was hard against mine, his grip firm and tight. I found myself on my back and Tom on top of me, licking and sucking my skin. Tom reached over under the couch and pulled out rubbers.

"I'm HIV positive. I play it safe." He panted.

"Me too, we all are probably going to die of AIDS anyway, but might as well play safe." I said. He had me in so many different positions I couldn't remember them all, I just know we came to an exhausted, pleasant collapse on the floor. The next thing I remember was waking up with a dull pain in the middle of my back. I realized that my shoe was under me and Tom was still lying on top of me in the middle of a sound sleep. I looked up and realized how muscular and firm he was. His hair was almost black and that color went from his neck all the way down his legs, and yet his back was soft and hairless. The morning after he still looked cute. It wasn't that I had too much to drink and imagined he was cute. I tried carefully to roll him off me, but he woke up the minute I moved him.

"Am I smothering you?"

"No, but I have a shoe in the middle of my back." I groaned.

"Oh, sorry." He rolled off me, and I threw the shoe from under my back. Tom got up, went into the kitchen, and got a glass of water. "Do you drink coffee?"

"No, I don't."

"Can I get you anything?" Tom inquired.

"Milk if you have any, or a glass of water."

"One glass of milk coming up."

"What time is it?" I asked.

"About eight. Why, you need to go?" He walked back into the room and handed me a glass of milk.

"No, not if it is only eight. I don't have to be in today until two or so." I said.

"Oh, ok. I'm off today, so I don't have to worry. Did you sleep?" Tom asked.

"For the most part. I was so exhausted from work that I could have slept anywhere probably. So, did you enjoy yourself?"

"Yes, I did. And you?" Tom asked.

"A great deal. You have a great body, and some great moves." With that statement, I felt the need to go home and be alone. He was good looking, and he was good sexually, but I wasn't sure I wanted to stay any longer.

"I think I should get going. I have a cat that is going to wonder what happened to me. Why don't I give you my number and you can call me later?"

"Ok, if you need to go. I will give you a call."

I wrote down my number and handed it to him. "I'll expect to hear from you." I stood up to put on my clothes, Tom hugged me and began to kiss me and run his hands over my body. I found myself responding to his touch. He had a way of getting to me that I just found myself giving in. We ended up having sex again on the living room floor. After, Tom went into the bathroom, and while he was gone I got dressed. I really wanted to leave and collect my thoughts. When he came back out to the living room, he looked disappointed that I had dressed.

"Got dressed, huh? I thought you might want to take a shower first." Tom offered.

"No, I really need to get home. Give me a call, ok?"

"I will."

He walked me to the door, kissed me again, and hugged me. "Talk to you later Marshall."

"Later, Tom." As I walked to the car, I wondered where Tom was coming from. Was he just horny, or did he really want to see me again? Did I really want to see him again? I felt confused and uncertain. As I started home, I thought about work and the things I needed to do for the day. I dug an old joint out of the ashtray and smoked it. I at least felt a little more relaxed.

When I got home, I was relieved to see my own place. At least it was clean and neat. Geoff greeted me at the door meowing, actually bitching. "Hello Geoff. Yes, I know I was out all night! Come in here and I'll get you some milk." I poured Geoff milk and petted her.

I walked out to the living room and checked the recorder. The light was blinking, so I played back the messages. "Hello Marshall, its Tom. I just wanted to tell you I really enjoyed last night. I'll be at the Hole tonight if you want to drop by. Later." And that was the only message. I had just left his house! I was glad I hadn't given him my cell number. I felt somewhat boxed in already. Maybe I shouldn't have given him any number! At least I didn't give him the address.

I went upstairs to take a nap. Geoff joined me and started purring. When I got up, I showered, dressed and went in to work. Work was calm and relaxing for a change. It took my mind off Tom. He was coming on strong. At my break I got high and decided to call Darrin.

"Ins and Outs, Darrin here, how may I help you?"

"Hi dude. Its Marshall, I need to talk to you. You got a minute?"

"What's up, I'm kind of busy."

"I met this guy last night and he's coming on strong."

"So, tell him to get lost."

"I'm not sure I want to do that. He is really a hunk. He's hot in bed. I just think he's gonna want to move in really soon."

"Marshall, you don't have to let him. So, see him again and see what goes."

"I guess that's as good of a choice as any."

"Look, I've got a lot of customers right now. If you still want to talk why don't you call me this evening?"

"Ok Darrin. I'll let you go. Thanks for the advice."

I went back to work and let the thought of Tom slide. After work I felt like seeing what would happen a second time, so I went by the Hole. I walked into the bar and I didn't see Tom anywhere, so I sat and ordered a drink. As the bartender served me, a hand was on my back.

"So, you decided to drop by. I'm glad." It was Tom. He had a big smile on his face.

"Yea, I did. So how was your day?"

"Great. I just slept and got high. And yours?" Tom asked.

"Not bad. Work went fast today. So, you get high?" I replied.

"Yea. I was going to offer last night, but I wasn't sure you still did. I remember you said you did when you were younger."

"Oh, I still do. Want to go to my place and smoke a bowl?" I couldn't believe I heard myself saying that!

"Yea sure. I'm kind of tired of the bar scene any way."

"Well, ok, let's go. You can follow me this time."

"Ok, I think that will work." We walked out to the parking lot and drove to my place. When we got there, Tom pulled his motorcycle into the garage beside my car. I wasn't sure I liked that, but I knew he expected to spend the night from that maneuver. What had I done to myself.

"Come on in." I said.

"Nice place, you renting?"

"No, I just bought this place. I want to do some remodeling, get it back to the original look." I explained.

"And what look is that?" Tom asked.

"The look of the Victorian era. I want to put the woodwork back to wood stain, and just make it look like it would have when it was a new house."

"Sounds like a lot of work!"

"Oh, it will be. However, it will be worth it in the long run. Come on in and sit down. Let me go find my bong and bag." I walked upstairs and got the bong and baggy and went back down. Geoff woke up from a nap and followed me. As I filled the bowl, Tom played with my chest under my shirt. Geoff jumped up on the couch and stuck her tail in Tom's face.

"Well, hello there." Tom said.

"Tom this is Geoff, Geoff Tom. You can push her off the couch if you like. She can be obnoxious." I said. Tom pushed Geoff down on the cushion and continued to play with my body.

"Tom, I don't know how far I want this to go. I want to have sex with you tonight, but I don't know if I want to make it a daily thing. My motto at the moment is so many men so little time."

"Oh, Marshall, I wasn't thinking of anything permanent, I just go with the flow, and right now I want to spend time with you. I really think you are attractive."

"Ok, as long as it is understood, we are NOT becoming an everyday item."

"Understood," Tom replied.

I lit the bong, took a hit and handed it to Tom. He took a hit and gave it back. I took a hit and handed it to Tom. Talking as I held in the smoke, "Want a drink?"

"Yea, that sounds good." Tom said.

"You can turn on the tv if you want to."

"Anything in particular you want to watch, Marshall?"

"One of the movie channels is fine." I went to the kitchen and made a drink. Geoff came with me, so I put down a bowl of milk for her. I gathered up some chips, dip, and went back to the living room. "Here you go."

"You got the munchies, too?"

"Yeah, I guess I do." Tom scooped up the dip.

"I like this dip. What kind is it?" Tom asked.

"Oh, just a cucumber dip I threw together. Nothing special."

"It's great. You got a maid?" Tom said as he looked around the room.

"No, why?" I laughed at that one. Me afford a maid?

"Well, the place is so clean. I could never be this neat unless I had a maid."

"I just can't stand a messy place. I like things to be neat and not messy."

"I guess I'm just a little lazier. I don't like to take time to clean very often." Amen to that I thought.

"There is a late movie on I wanted to watch, some old classic. Want to try that?" I asked.

"I guess so." I turned the television to the channel and we started to watch the movie. Tom moved right next to me and his hands were under my shirt again, playing with my chest. He did make me feel good. I had to admit that. He was so pushy in a way, yet he had a childish like attitude that caused me to let him do whatever he wanted. Soon I felt the buttons being undone and then his lips on my chest and his hands on my crotch. Then my jeans were unbuttoned, and his hands were down my pants. I was too hot to ignore him, and started to unbutton his shirt and pants. It seemed like just seconds and we were in the middle of heated sex again. He somehow had a way of getting me into a sexual situation rapidly.

We barely had time to take a breath before Tom was on top of me again working on my chest with his lips and my crotch with his hands. This man was incredible. Either he was a sex machine, or he had gone without for a long time.

"You always this horny?" I asked.

"Usually. Sometimes I get real active and other times I could care less. Right now you make me never want to stop."

"Really. Well, you are making me very hot, but I would like to take a break before we start again."

"Well, then I will stop," he laughed. "But I guess we are even in mutual attraction part then." The break wasn't long before Tom had his way.

Somehow even though we had agreed that we would *not* become an every night item, we did. I found myself calling Tom and inviting him over when he didn't call me. And when he called me, I found myself saying yes. I was experiencing some different feelings and desires with Tom.

Pushy as he was, he was always kind. I wasn't sure where this was leading to, but I was definitely enjoying it.

I acquired the habit that when I invited Tom over to my house, I just met him in the nude. There wasn't much use being dressed, because he wouldn't be there but what seemed like five minutes and I would find myself naked anyway. It was kind of fun to sit around naked waiting for Tom to come over and see the expression on his face.

I was really enjoying getting to know Tom. Geoff on the other hand got so she left the room and went up stairs whenever Tom arrived at the house. She did sleep on the bed with us however, after Tom fell asleep.

One night after we had been seeing each other for a month I suppose, I panicked. We were in the middle of heated sex and Tom said I love you. I don't think he really realized he said it, and I said nothing. But, it hit me strange, and for the next couple of days I avoided him. I didn't return his calls, and I didn't go out. I wasn't sure I wanted him to love me, and I wasn't sure I wanted to talk about it. I was afraid he would leave my life if I said he couldn't have feelings for me.

I got to thinking about my motto of so many men and so little time, and was that what I wanted? On the third day of avoiding Tom, a deliveryman showed up at work. He handed me a bouquet of white daisies. When I opened the card, it said, "*Marshall-- Whatever I did, I am sorry. Please talk to me! I'm desperate, Tom.*" He knew how to get to me. I thought about him all afternoon, and that evening, I did call.

"Hello."

"Tom, this is Marshall."

"Marshall. Gee, do I know a Marshall?"

"Ok. I deserve that. I am sorry, something just happened the other night that freaked me out."

"What?"

"Well, can we meet and talk in person?"

"Yes. Your place or my place or do you want to meet on neutral grounds?"

"Here or your place is fine."

"Which one!" Tom insisted.

"Tom, why don't you come over here?"

"Ok. I'll be right over." While I waited for him, I had the automatic urge to strip. I surprised myself. I hoped we could talk this out without ending seeing each other. The doorbell rang and I went to answer the door.

"Hello Tom, come in."

"Hi Marshall." He walked quietly into the house. We sat on the couch.

"I just will get straight to the point. The other night I guess I just felt strange. While we were having sex, you said 'I love you Marshall' and it freaked me out."

"Why? I guess I probably did, I don't remember for sure."

"Well, I guess because I'm not sure I want you to love me. I thought we had agreed we would just go with the flow. I told you when we met my motto was so many men, so little time."

"Yes, I know, we did. But the flow can't end up with being in love? I didn't say I was moving in. I do care about you though." Tom looked irritated.

"I know you didn't say you were moving in. I'm just not sure I love you or want to love you. I don't want to hurt you, but I don't want to stop seeing you either."

"Great. Then what do you want Marshall? Don't relationships usually end up growing into something? I mean if we are just friends, would we continue to have sex? Or am I just a friend with benefits?"

"Yes, relationships change. I don't know if I'd call you a friend with benefits. I don't think that term fits," I said in frustration. "I was tied down to a relationship for nine years, and I was nineteen when I started that relationship, I just am not ready to be tied down again."

"Well, then, what are you saying?"

"I don't know! I am saying I don't know how I feel about you exactly. I don't want to stop seeing you. I guess part of the problem is that you had never said anything about loving me until we were having sex. And saying it then had a big impact on me. It was like dropping an ice cube on my back while I was asleep. It just took me off guard."

"So, Marshall, what do you want to do about it?"

"Well, for one thing, I would like to start doing something else besides have sex every time I see you. I don't mean we can't have sex anymore, but do you realize in the month we have been seeing each other all we do is spend our time in bed, either fucking or sleeping? Can't we go out to a movie, or drinking or whatever else you like to do and see life from another side? See if we can do anything enjoyable together besides sex! I might be in love with you too. I can't tell when our entire relationship is one continual state of sexual encounters and nothing else!" I was shouting.

"Yes, we can do something else! You never seemed to mind that we weren't, though." Tom yelled.

"Well, the reality just hit me recently!" I shouted in defense.

"Ok, then, let's do it. Like right now. We could go to the Hole, or to a movie, or a ride on my bike. It's a warm summer night!" Tom shouted back.

"Ok!" I yelled. Tom walked over and hugged me and I pushed away. He pulled tighter and I gave in. I hugged him back. He just had a knack of getting to me.

"You know, you jackass, I almost met you at the door naked as usual. I am so confused about you!" I confessed in a much softer voice.

"Well, you creep, I wouldn't have minded if you had met me at the door naked. I would have liked that. But, let's go for a ride on the bike. Change the pace a little, ok?" Tom said softly.

"I think that is a good idea. I guess I am beginning to feel trapped, and that your only real interest in me is sex."

"Marshall, I am interested in more than that. It is just that the sight of your brown eyes that perfectly combed hair and little moustache turn me on. It makes me want to jump your bones constantly."

"Yea, like right now I can feel your excitement. Let's go before you won't leave."

"Ok." Tom sighed.

"Any special place you like to ride your bike?" I said calmly as we walked out the door.

"Well, there are a few places I get off the road and just relax. Want to see one of those places?"

"Yes. It would be nice to get away from the city for a while." We got on his bike and drove off. We headed north of the city and got on the highway. At first the ride was a little scary, and I held tight to Tom. Then as I got the feel for the bike, I began to move my body with the bike instead of squeezing Tom so tight. We pulled off onto a little dirt road and headed toward some rock formation. It was a good feeling to be out in the summer heat at dusk, riding on a bike. Tom slowed and pulled off the road.

"Well, here is one of my special places. If we walk back up to that rock formation, I can show you a little secluded place I like."

"Ok I'm game."

"Let me get my backpack off the bike. I always carry it." He walked over to his bike and got a backpack out of one of the saddlebags. He walked back over to me and hugged me.

"So, Tom, where to?"

"Just follow me." We walked up a path next to the rock formation. It wound around behind the rocks and ended up above where we parked. Then we walked down another trail that went into an open space that was surrounded on all sides by rocks. The only way in was the path. It was almost like a cave that lacked a roof.

"Like it?" Tom asked eagerly.

"Yea, it is really different."

"Sit down. I like to sit up here and relax. I come here when I am uptight. I was here last night in fact. Want to get high?"

"You have to ask?" I teased.

He pulled out a joint and lit it. We sat there and smoked in silence as I took at the surroundings. I found myself relaxing. It was a very calming place. Tom moved over next to me and put his arm around me.

"Know what I have always wanted to do up here?"

"Let me guess. Have sex?" I said sarcastically.

"You do know me well."

"It doesn't take much. That's all that is ever on your mind!" I snapped.

"Well, do you feel like it?"

"Just let nature take its course, ok? Let me sit here and enjoy the peace and quiet. Hold me and don't push me." I said sternly.

"Ok, I will." For once he did just hold me tight without grabbing me or taking my clothes off. We sat there and just stared at the sky and the clouds. It was calming, and I was feeling very relaxed. I felt Tom's body next to mine and for the first time since we had met, I started unbuttoning his shirt, I started the sexual encounter. He, for once, didn't react by grabbing me or, undressing me. He let me undo his shirt and take it off, and unbutton his pants and run my hands over his body before he interrupted me.

"Hold on for a minute." He got up and took a blanket out of his backpack. I wasn't surprised. He spread it out on the ground and laid down on it. I walked over and began to complete the unbuttoning of his pants. For once he let me take the lead and didn't take over. I undressed myself, lay on top of him and began kissing him.

I guess he could last only so long, he turned me over and we had sex in his usual pushy take control manner. But, I did enjoy at least the small change we made. We just laid

43

there for a while and didn't talk. The sky was beautiful as the sun went down. It felt so erotic to be naked in the outdoors.

"You look relaxed. Did you enjoy sex in the great outdoors?"

"Yes, I did. I am relaxed. It has been a long time since I did it out in nature. I had forgotten what a turn-on it is."

"Marshall, I'm glad we are talking and are together again. The past couple of days I've been very uptight and unhappy. I feel so much happier when I'm with you." Tom sighed.

"Well, I feel better too. You just have an effect on me I am not sure I like. It is like I lose control of myself, and you take control of me. I don't like that feeling, and yet I really do enjoy being with you. In some ways I would say I do have feelings for you. You just scare the hell out of me most of the time."

"I don't mean to take control. I just have strong desires around you, desires I have never felt before. I can't stop myself from acting on them."

"Oh, I believe you, I feel that in you. I think that is why I feel like I loose control of myself around you. If we could just have more nights like this one, nights where we at least tried to do something besides just having sex I would be calmer. More nights that when we did have sex, I had a chance to take charge, I might feel better about losing control."

"I liked sex tonight. I think I can give a little. We will start doing things during the evening. Not just have sex first. We'll save it for last, or maybe first, and then do other things." Tom nervously rambled.

"Oh god! I don't know about you. I'm willing to try. I'm still not sure you are getting what I am saying. I *am* willing to try!" I said in frustration.

"I'm glad. I'll try to listen and get the drift of what you are telling me." We laid there for a long time in silence. Then the wind started to blow, and it got a little cool. I sat up and looked at the sky.

"Want to get dressed?" Tom asked.

"Yea, it is a little cool. Wonder what time it is?"

"I'll look." He leaned over, got his watch, and looked at it. "It's almost eleven. I guess we should head back. I have to be up early tomorrow."

"Yea, let's dress and leave." I think Tom wanted to have another romp in nature. I guess he realized it wasn't the night to push me. We did get dressed and drove back to my place. We, of course, had the romp in bed anyway.

For the most part, we did do things other than just have sex for the rest of the summer. I started to explain to him in great detail all the changes I wanted to make in each room of the house. We went to movies, went to the Hole, we even rode the motorcycle a lot. Sex didn't change. Any place, any time Tom could persuade me, we did. However, we were doing other things and even getting along.

I was sad when fall came and it began to be too cold to go riding on the motorcycle off-road. It was early winter really, not fall at all, though it was officially fall. We found ourselves being confined to home again. I wasn't dealing with it well at all. In my mind I was thinking about the relationship I had left, nine years of my life, my youth, gone. I had wanted to just get laid by a different man every night. Was I making a mistake?

Fortunately, Tom's birthday took over my thoughts. It was coming up in October. I thought about what I wanted to do for him. That took my mind off the fact we were beginning to be back into the pattern of doing little else than having sex. I wanted to do something he would like, but something that didn't allude to sex in any way. It was difficult to come up with something he wouldn't turn into being sexual. I gave it a great deal of thought, and still couldn't come up with any ideas. I decided to call Derrek.

"Hello."

"Hello, Derrek, this is Marshall."

"Hello Marshall. How are you doing?"

"Oh fine, and you?"

"Just fine. What is up?"

"Are you busy?"

"No, uh, not really, is something wrong?"

"No, Derrek, nothing is wrong. I just need a suggestion. Remember earlier I told you I was seeing Tom?"

"Yeah, uh huh."

"Well, I still am, and his birthday is coming up soon. I need a suggestion of what to do. Specifically I need a suggestion for an activity that has NO sexual overtones at all."

"Why is that Marshall?"

"Well, because Tom can turn a sneeze into sex. I want to do something with him that isn't remotely sexual."

"Nothing with sexual overtones, huh, let me think."

"You know I thought about dinner at home, but he always eats in the nude. I thought of a movie, but he'd find the dark stimulating. I thought of a party, but he'd just take me to the bathroom and have sex with me with our guests right there in the house."

"Lord, he's that bad?"

"Yes!"

"Take him bowling," Derrek laughed, "no, seriously, how is this, take him shopping for his birthday gift. Then take him to dinner at a restaurant that is a mom, dad, kids, you know, a family style place. Then after go get ice cream. At least part of the evening he will be off the idea anyway."

"That's not a bad idea. I can at least have him busy for a while. I know what the end of the evening will be anyway. Thanks Derrek. I won't keep you."

"Yea, uh huh you are welcome Marshall. I hope it works!"

"Me too, I'll let you know. Talk at you later."

"Take care. Talk to you later. Bye."

"Bye." Well, at least I had an idea. It might work.

The day of Tom's birthday he had to work, and so did I. We agreed to meet at my place after work. I told him we were going out for the evening, and he said ok. All I could think about at work was the evening. Trying to find pit falls in my plan, and come up with any possible problems I might encounter and change plans accordingly.

When I got home I quickly showered and changed, so that when Tom got there I would be ready. Then there would be no possible chance for sex. I had just gotten dressed when the doorbell rang. I knew it must be Tom, hoping to catch me in the shower.

I ran down to answer the door. "Hello Tom, come in."

"Oh, I see you are ready to go."

"Yes, I am. Happy birthday. I hope you will enjoy what I have planned." I gave him a hug.

"Oh, I am sure I will. We aren't going to sit down for a minute?"

"No, I really want to get going."

"Ok, let's go." We walked out the back door to the garage. We got in MY car and left.

"So, where are you taking me?"

"First of all to the mall to let you pick out your own gift. I couldn't decide what to buy, so, I decided to take you shopping."

"Oh, that's neat. I don't think anyone has ever let me choose a gift before. I like that. Thank you." He leaned over and kissed me, and grabbed my leg. At least we were in the car going to the mall. I took him to one of the men's department stores.

"Look around Tom. Buy whatever, new shirts, pants, or a jacket anything that you need or want."

"Does it have to be a shirt, pants, or jacket?"

"Well, no. If you don't want clothes, we can go somewhere else."

"No, this store is fine. I just wondered if I had to buy one of those three things you mentioned."

"Not at all, I said anything you want." I was thinking I had hit my first pitfall. Tom walked over to the underwear and began looking. I should have known! He was pulling packs off the shelf, putting them back, and motioned me to come over.

"Look, what do you think of this?" He held them up for me to see.

"Underwear? That's what you really want?"

"Yes, look at these. I can't wait to try them on to show you how they fit!" He said excitedly.

"I think I can imagine. There isn't much to them. They will cover very little, Tom. I have a good picture in my mind."

"This is what I want. I'll get several colors, one for every night of the week! One style for every week of the month!"

"If that is what you want." We took them to the salesclerk and made the purchase.

"Anything else you would like?"

"Well, not really. Let me look around." He walked around the store, not really looking at much. Then he came back over to me and stood.

"Well?" I quizzed.

"No, I don't see anything else I really want. This will do fine. I like the underwear selection. It's all different, and I have a pair for every day of the month."

"Ok, then we can go to dinner." We left the store, went to the car and headed for the restaurant. Tom tore open one package of underwear and held them up.

"Look Marshall. I like these."

"I'm glad. They're different. Are you sure that's what you really wanted, thirty pairs of underwear?"

"Yea, it is. I hate to spend money on underwear. I would never buy these for myself. Thank you!"

"You are welcome."

"So, where are we going for dinner?"

"I thought we'd go to one of those pizza places that have all those games, Tom. I've never been to one, and you like to play the games in the bars. I thought it might be fun."

"I do too. Thanks. I'm so excited about this birthday!"

"I'm glad. I just wanted to be out of the house, and do something different to celebrate."

"Well, thanks." We drove to the pizza parlor, and smoked a joint in celebration of Tom's birthday as we drove. He opened every single package of underwear. Then he held them up looking at the colors and styles he had bought. I could just imagine his thoughts, which pair to model first. After that it would be raw sex. We got to the restaurant parked, and walked in. We sat at a table and looked at the menu board. It was certainly different from the Fez. And, Derrek was right, this place was great, full of families with lots of kids and games.

"So, what kind of pizza did you want, Tom?"

"One with everything on it, I guess that is the one called the Suicide?"

"Ok, I'll go order. Medium or large?"

"I'm hungry, a large you think?" He asked.

"Yea, I'm hungry. A large." I walked up to the counter to order. Surely in here he wouldn't find anything to trip his sexual trigger.

"May I take your order, sir?" Asked the waiter.

"Yes, I'd like a large Suicide and a pitcher of draft beer."

"Will that be all?"

"Yes."

"If you'll pay at the end of the counter, your number will be called when your order is ready." He handed me a number, and I walked down to pay for the meal. As I paid, I looked at the various games. It was time to get Tom playing a game. I walked back to the table and sat.

"This place is just full of games Marshall. Want to go play one of the games?"

"Sure. It sounds fun to me." We walked over to one of the games where there was no one playing. It was some kind of a seek and destroy type game. As with pinball, Tom played and played, and I thought I was never going to get a turn. Finally his turn ended and I got to try. In seconds it was over, and Tom was at the controls again. While he played the second round our number was called I went and got the pizza and beer. I took it to the table, and went back over to Tom. He beat some kind of record, and got a token to play a free game.

"Good game. You topped the highest score!"

"I know. You need to finish your turn."

"Ok, then we need to eat. I got our order." I played again, and again, my turn was over rapidly. I wasn't really concentrating, though.

"Sorry you didn't do better." Tom consoled.

"Oh, that's ok. After we eat, I'll try again."

"Maybe you'll do better after you eat."

"Maybe." We sat and ate dinner. The pizza wasn't bad. I could have done better. I could certainly see where the name came from! It was better to eat mediocre pizza, drink beer, and be out doing something, than it was to stay home and have good food and liquor and fight off the sexual advances while trying to celebrate.

After we finished dinner, we went back to the games. We both really got into playing and played for a long time. It *was* possible to get Tom's mind off sex for a while. You just had to get him out of the house, and in public. I was feeling good about that. We tried out every game in the place.

Finally, Tom walked up to me and sighed. "I think I'm about played out. I'm ready to go home."

"Ok. We can go. Did you have fun?"

"Yes, I did." We walked out to the car, and got in. Tom picked up his packages and flipped through the selection of underwear he had bought again. When we got home, he took his packages and ran upstairs to the bedroom. As he ran up, Geoff ran down. I could guess what he was doing.

While he was gone, I got out the card I bought, and the cake I baked. I put them on the dining room table, and went to the kitchen to get plates and silverware. Tom appeared in the dining room as I returned, standing there in a pair of his new skimpy underwear.

"Well, what do you think?" He said turning in a circle so I would get full three hundred sixty-degree view of him modeling his new tiny little bright red and black striped undies.

"They look better than I thought they would. Don't cover much, though."

"I really like them. They make me feel sensuous. Thank you." He noticed the birthday cake. "For me? Did you bake this?"

"Of course I did. I wasn't sure what your favorite flavor was, so I baked a layer of chocolate, lemon, vanilla, and cherry."

"Thanks! It says '*Happy 28th Birthday!*' That's nice. I like chocolate, but the combination sounds good. Why don't you strip down to your underwear, and we'll have birthday cake sitting in under shorts?"

"Ok." After all, I thought, it was his birthday and we had spent most of the evening out. I undressed, and we ate cake. While we ate, he looked at his card.

"This card have a special meaning? *'Sex . . . . Now that I have your attention, I just wanted to say Happy Birthday. Hope it's a good one, Marshall.'* I like it."

"Well, I thought it was you. When I saw it, I looked no further." I felt his bare foot between my legs. I guess he'll never change. He could use his toes just like his hands! He could be impossible!

"The cake is really great. It's been a nice evening."

"I am glad you enjoyed it. I have one more surprise, but you need to wait down here for a few minutes. You can fix drinks while you wait."

"Why? What kind of surprise?" Tom asked eagerly.

"Don't ask questions. Fix us a drink, and I'll yell at you when you can come upstairs."

"Ok. You have my curiosity piqued."

"Good. Do not come upstairs until I call you!" I realized we would have to have sex, so I got bubble bath as a last gift. I thought I would take control, run a tub of hot water and bubble bath and be sitting in it for Tom. You can't avoid the inevitable. I ran the water, put in the bubble bath, took off my underwear, and slid into the tub. I saw Geoff fly by the bathroom. I sensed Tom was, at the very least, standing on the staircase.

"Tom, you can come up here now." I yelled. In seconds he entered the bathroom naked with drinks in hand.

"Oh, a bubble bath. May I join you?"

"That's why I'm in here, for you to join me." He slipped into the bubble bath and handed me my drink. We sipped our drinks. We let the bubbles and warm water play with our skin. As soon as our drinks were finished, I was attacked and sex began. This time was a little more exciting. I did enjoy sex in a bubble bath. It reminded me of the massages Craig and I used to do. Perhaps I should do that to Tom. The experience was worth the trouble. We got out of the tub and dried one another.

"Marshall that was fun. I haven't taken a bubble bath for a long time!"

"I haven't either." We walked to the bedroom and climbed into bed. "Happy birthday Tom. I hope you enjoyed it."

"I did. Thanks."

I tried to fall asleep before I was attacked again, but I wasn't fast enough. However, this time, I felt like I was feeling real emotions for Tom. He confused me so much. I could never really tell if I wanted to have sex with him or not. He never let me have a chance to see if I wanted to. He was so forceful most of the time, and yet, I did enjoy it. I never really tried to stop him. His desire, that excitement to have sex with me, his little boy charm, it always melted me into a pool of sensual desire.

The following night I did give Tom a body massage, which of course turned to sex. In the next few days we returned to being at home and sex machines again.

I decided to buy him a late birthday present, and get a game box to hook up to the television. I had hopes it would be something we could do together, to avoid his always thinking about sex. I bought it, came home, and hooked it up before Tom came over. I wanted to surprise him. And I knew I'd better have it ready to play, or we would never get it hooked up. When Tom arrived I took him in to see what I bought.

"Here you go Tom. This is the reason I wanted you to come here tonight. It's a late birthday gift."

"A game box for the tv!"

"Yea, you had so much fun on your birthday I thought this would be fun to have at home."

"Let's test it out." We put in one of the games I bought with the box and started playing. It made some strange noises, and Geoff came to investigate. She noticed motion on the television screen and tried to catch what she saw with her paw. In frustration she finally left. Tom and I sat and laughed for a long while.

We did have fun playing games. We got into quite a heavy competition with each other. Tom conquered more of the games levels than I did. By the time the evening was over, I had begun to get very good at one of the games myself. We went to bed, the usual, finally went to sleep. Sometime in there Geoff got on the bed.

Over the course of the next few weeks we played the new games quite frequently, but I began to miss going out and doing other things. I tried to talk to Tom about it, but whenever I suggested something, he had one excuse after another. I got so frustrated I began to be angry. I needed to talk to someone! I called Colt. He told me he had the next day off because of conferences, so he came over to my place and I fixed him lunch. When Colt arrived Geoff met him at the door.

"Hi Colt." I said as Geoff rubbed up against him.

"Hi Marshall, Geoff." Colt hugged me and then petted Geoff.

"Come on in" I said and picked up Geoff and put her in the living room.

"I'm glad you called Marshall. We haven't talked in a long time. You sounded angry over the phone."

"I guess I am Colt. I called you because you go back to Craig and me, and I need to talk."

"Why, has Craig asked you to give it another try?"

"No, so far as I know, he left the state. It's Tom. He confuses me. You know how Craig and I fought over monogamy and how I always wanted many partners?"

"Yes, I remember, so many men, so little time, and Tom feels the same way as Craig?"

"Hell, I don't even know for sure. It's just we fight over sex. The problem is I am tired of sex nightly on his terms."

"Are you sick? You, tired of sex? That's what you and Craig ever fought about constantly. What happened?" Colt gasped.

"It's Tom! That is all he ever thinks about is sex. I mean we don't even go out any more. I go to his place, or he comes here. Wherever we are, he rips off my clothes and fucks me. Before I can catch my breath, he's at it again."

"So, what's your problem?"

"You don't know what it's like. I don't even know if I really care about him."

"Marshall, I think you must. I have never known you to let any man push you into seeing him a lot unless you cared about him."

"But, that's the problem. I enjoy Tom, and I even enjoy the sex. But, he just never lets up. When I want to do other things, he seduces me, and we end up staying at home. I get angry with him and we argue. Then I find I miss him and we are right back where we were. Then I am angry with myself."

"And you have talked about the sex and your feelings with Tom?"

"Well, sort of. One fight we had was over him telling me he loved me. And one fight was over doing nothing else but having sex like bunnies."

"And, do you love him?"

"I don't know. We haven't discussed that for a long time. I need time away, and yet I don't want to loose him either."

"That statement right there sounds like you care about him a great deal, Marshall."

"Maybe, I think I care. I need a space to see him and not to see him."

"Have you tried seeing each other maybe four or five nights a week, and take two or three nights apart?"

"No, I hadn't even thought about that."

"Well, it's worth a try, isn't it?" Colt asked.

"It couldn't hurt I guess. You want a drink with lunch?" I asked.

"Yea, sure, it's my day off."

"Still scotch and water?"

"Yea that's fine." Colt said. "Lunch smells good."

"Nothing special. Just some fresh bread, soup, and salad."

"Sounds good to me." Colt and I ate lunch and talked about his class. We reminisced about when we had met and worked together in a bar. I felt better talking about the past. And I felt like at least I now had an idea in mind of how to see if I cared about Tom or not. A couple of nights a week apart would be a good way to see how we felt.

"Thanks for lunch, Marshall. It was great. Give me a call later on. Let me know how things go with Tom."

"Yea, I will. Thanks for talking to me." We walked to the front door. "Goodbye Colt. Talk to you later."

"Later Marshall. Good luck." Colt said as he hugged me goodbye "I hope this all works out for you."

The rest of the afternoon I spent cleaning house, petting Geoff and thinking about how to put this to Tom. I felt it was at least a logical way to see how I felt. I fixed dinner for Tom and sat the table. I was hoping we could have a nice dinner and talk this out during dinner.

He didn't even really know what was about to hit. He wasn't aware that I was as upset as I was. But, if we didn't talk about it now, I would blow up in an explosive manner that would not be the best way to handle it. I heard his motorcycle pull up and went to the door.

"Hello Tom." I said as he came in.

"Hi Marshall. Heard me pull up, hey?"

"Yea, I did." He hugged and kissed me. We walked into the living room. "So, how was your day?"

"Fine. Work was even kind of fun today. And your day?" Tom replied.

"Oh, fine. I had Colt over for lunch. I hadn't seen him in a while."

"So, how is he?"

"Oh, fine. He had the day off too."

"That's good. Something smells really good. You cooking something fancy?"

"No, not really, just a roast."

"With you, Marshall, even hamburgers aren't simple!"

"Is that a criticism or a compliment?"

"What do you think?" Tom replied, looking confused.

"It had better be a compliment. Want a drink before dinner?" I said tersely.

"Sure. Want to smoke a bowl?" Tom asked.

"Yes. You know where it is. I'll fix the drinks. You load the bowl."

"Ok." We sat on the couch, took a hit and a drink. Geoff jumped up beside me and purred.

"Tom, I have to talk to you about something that is bothering me. I have been feeling like I need to express myself more openly." I began.

"Ok, so what's up? You kicking me out of your life?"

"No, I am not. But it is about you and me."

"So, Marshall, just blurt it out and get it over with."

"Tom, how would you feel about cutting down the time we spend together?" I began.

"Oh, you have found somebody new?"

"No, let me finish. I don't really know how I feel about you for sure. I enjoy your company, but we see each other so often, I haven't been able to really tell how I feel. All I am suggesting is that we see each other five nights and days a week. Have two apart for a while. This is not forever." Geoff leaped off the couch and ran upstairs.

"And the purpose of this five on and two off?" Tom responded in a huff.

"I need to see how I feel being alone, doing things alone. You came into my life right on the heels of Craig. I have never been alone. I'd liked to see how I feel with other men, if I miss you. I just want to get a space to sort my life out."

"You have met someone, haven't you?"

"No, I have not! When would I have a chance?" I felt my voice get louder.

"Don't shout at me. I've got feelings, too!"

"I'm sorry. I know you do. Are you so certain about how you feel about me?"

"Yes, Marshall, I am!" Tom said emphatically.

"Tom, perhaps you are. I just know when I first moved up here I started dating Craig, and ended up living with him. All we did was fight. I really think most of the problem was that I got involved too soon after moving from a small town and being so young. Besides, it has only been just barely a year since I broke up with Craig."

"Oh, so he has called you and wants to get back with you!"

"No, he has not. You are missing my point."

"No, I am not. You want to gradually get rid of me." Tom sighed.

"No, I don't! I just want to have a few days to myself to see what I feel inside."

"Are you sure?" Tom asked.

"Yes, Tom, I am. I just want some time alone, sometime together. I said only two days apart. I'm fucking HIV positive, I don't know how long I will live!"

"Well, hell, I am too, and I don't know how long I will live either! Oh, I suppose we can try it. I just think either you love me or you don't. We get along don't we? Or have I missed something else?"

"Yes, for the most part we get along," I tried to emphasize, "but, sexually you never let up. I'd like to JUST sleep together occasionally."

"Oh, so now sex is a problem too!"

"I didn't say that! Maybe we should table this discussion for now." I suggested.

"No way. You brought it up. We need to come to a decision now." Tom demanded.

"Well, then, what do you think of five days on, two off?" I asked again.

"Like I said, we can try, I guess. I'd rather do that than loose you completely."

"Ok, then let's try it. Okay Tom?"

"Alright. Can I kiss you, or is that too sexual?"

"God! You just don't get it. Yes, you can kiss me." And he did. We sat in silence for a while, and I remembered dinner.

"Are you hungry?"

"I was. I guess I still am."

"Well, dinner should be ready. Smile, we'll have sex tonight, ok?"

"I guess. Let's eat. Anything I can do?"

"Come help me put the food on the table." I sighed. He did it again. I promised sex. Why did I do that!

"Marshall, for how long are we doing this?"

"I don't know, for a while."

"Well, two weeks, a month, a year?"

"Push, push, push! Do I have to set an exact time limit?" I felt angry again.

"I think you do. I need to know how long before you make a decision." Tom pleaded.

"A month then. I need a month. It is the near the end of October. Give me until Thanksgiving."

"Ok, until Thanksgiving."

We ate dinner in silence, except for asking to pass something. Geoff rubbed against my legs while we ate.

After dinner we cleaned up quietly, and went to the living room. I walked over and hugged Tom. He looked like a rejected puppy dog.

"Want to play a game?" I asked.

"That's fine. Want another drink?" He replied.

"Sure. I'll fix it. Load another bowl, please."

"Ok. Which game?"

"Pick one, I don't care." I said in frustration.

"How about Auto Theft?"

"That's fine." I walked back out to the living room and handed Tom his drink. We played games, smoked a few bowls, and drank a number of drinks. We were very competitive, due mostly to the heated discussion we had. As we drank more we began to loose interest in playing and decided to stop.

We lay on the floor beside each other. I looked into Tom's eyes and he looked hurt. I almost said forget the deal. But then I thought, damn it I have a right to say what I want. I don't want another nine years of constant arguments. He reached over and put his arm around me. I knew it was time to keep my promise, but I resented it. We had sex and I was not very responsive to Tom. He did notice.

"You were kind of cool. Angry?" He quizzed.

"Not angry, as much as frustrated. You don't somehow understand how I feel."

"And I'm not sure you understand how I feel." Tom said firmly. "And does this new arrangement include sex with other men?"

"Well, yes, I want to see how that makes me feel. I want to have some time to see what it would be like to see someone else. I have told you, I just feel there are so many men and there is so little time."

"Well, you can do what you want, but I am not having sex with anyone else on the two days apart," Tom said.

"And I plan to do just that," I said.

"I just don't understand what is wrong with the way we are," Tom said in frustration, "I don't think you understand how it makes me feel."

"Perhaps I don't. I don't think it will do any good to continue this discussion tonight. Can we just go to bed?"

"Yes, I guess. I don't really feel like talking about it any more either." He sighed.

We went up to bed. For once went to sleep, no sex. It felt nice. I didn't sleep very well, and kept waking up. I felt guilty about Tom in some ways. Yet I felt I needed the space. I was so tired that when the alarm went off I could have sworn we had just gone to bed. I rolled over to see Tom was awake, and said as cheerfully as possible, "Mornin."

"Mornin. You sleep?" Tom asked.

"No, not really. You?"

"Not much." Tom said.

"Want some breakfast?"

"No, not today. So when does the five on, two off start?" Tom asked.

"Next week?" I said meekly.

"Ok. What nights apart?"

"I don't know. I'd like one weekend night to myself." I said.

"Which one?"

"Either one. Which one do you think?"

"Depends if the two nights are back to back." Tom's voice was a little shaky.

"I'd prefer they were. That's my whole point." I explained.

"Well, then how about Thursday and Friday apart?"

"Sounds fair." I said.

"Ok. Next week then. Want to take a shower with me?" He smiled that boyish smile of his.

"Sure. I didn't say I was stopping anything we usually do." We got up, showered together, and Tom left for work. I sat and smoked a bowl before I went to work. Geoff sat beside me for a while and I petted her. She seemed to know I was feeling down.

At work I thought about Tom constantly. I wasn't sure this was the right move. Now that it was settled, I didn't want to back out. I just felt so much pressure from him I needed to see how I felt away from him.

The rest of the week we did do things outside the house. Tom was making a real effort to prove to me we could do other things. We spent time with friends, at movies, out dancing, playing games, and even riding his bike. He was making my decision hard to follow through on, I had to stand my ground, and I wanted to see other men. Wednesday night he made a big deal of not seeing me again until Saturday. How lonely he would be, and what a boring time he was going to have. I stuck to my guns. I told him he needed to go out and do something different, that was my plan.

Thursday night I was lonely, and stayed home. I just felt the need to be in my house alone. It did seem strange without Tom, but I did weird things I hadn't done in a long time. I moved the stove and refrigerator out and cleaned the floor. I spent the evening cleaning, rearranging dresser drawers. Things that just hadn't been done for a while. Friday night I decided to go out. I went to the Twenty-one instead of the Hole, so I wouldn't run into Tom. Several men hit on me, but I got rid of them. I had forgotten it was Halloween weekend. I got really drunk at the end of the evening. Some guy talked me into taking him home. His softness in bed was such a shock I wasn't very stimulated. Sex was so dull he got up and went home. I did miss Tom in bed!

The next couple of weeks Tom kept the bargain and we did have time apart. I went out, saw other men, had sex with other men, and began to enjoy my time away. Tom on the other hand did nothing. He stayed home, watched television, and waited to see me. That wasn't what I had in mind.

I enjoyed the arrangement we had. Five nights and days of Tom were doable. Two nights to myself was fun. I was enjoying the experience of being with different men, seeing what they were like, I guess recapturing the youth I lost with Craig. Unfortunately, the month of time was already ending. My mind was absolutely set on extending this new style of our relationship longer. I didn't want to go back to seven days a week with Tom quite yet. As Thanksgiving rolled around, I was sure of my decision.

The hard part was I had to tell Tom my answer. I had a feeling we were going to have one hell of a heated discussion. Tom had never gone out on our two nights apart. He wanted to prove some kind of love and loyalty to me. I wasn't ready to back off yet! For our discussion night, I fixed dinner, and asked Tom to come over to my place. He had agreed, and I had not hinted at my decision. When he got to the house, I had dinner ready, and the table set. I was determined to make my point clear. I heard him pull into the drive.

"How was work?" I asked as he walked in.

"Oh, fine. And you? How was work?"

"Good. I added a new salad to the menu today. I was really pleased the management agreed to my idea."

"Congratulations. Smells good, I'm hungry."

"Well, dinner is ready if you want to eat."

"Ok. I'm ready." He hugged and kissed me. "I almost forgot to do that."

"Why don't you go sit down Tom? I'll serve dinner."

"Alright. So, what's your decision?" Tom asked.

"Let's eat dinner first, and talk after dinner."

"Sounds like you are buying time."

"I would just like to eat first." I snapped.

"Oh, alright, let's eat first."

We sat and began eating dinner. Tom's foot was on my leg and he had that grin on his face. I could see he was certain he had convinced me to say that I wanted to end the arrangement we had. He was going to be disappointed.

"Good dinner. You are a creative cook."

"Thanks. It is my profession. I have to be." I said trying to down play the compliment.

"Well, I think you are a good chef."

We finished dinner and Tom helped clean up. After we got the mess cleaned, we walked to the living room and smoked a bowl. I took a deep breath and turned to Tom.

"Listen to me before you react."

"I don't like the way this conversation is starting."

"Just listen, please." I pleaded.

"Ok, I will. But, I think I can already guess the answer."

"I'm just beginning to feel comfortable with you and not threatened. It feels nice to see you and then be away for a couple of days. If you would let me continue this for a little while longer, I think our relationship could work out."

"I knew it! Marshall, I can't take it any more. You want to see me, and you don't want to see me. Well, I have given this a lot of thought too. I cannot be a five-day lover, and a two-day free agent. I may regret this, but it's over. Unless we start seeing each other again daily, and start working at a definite relationship, I don't want to see you at all!"

"Tom you are just upset. I just can't go back to the daily thing yet. Just let me have a little more time!"

"No Marshall, I won't. If that is your final decision, then mine is we are through!"

"I can compromise, how about if two nights a week, we have a stranger join us for sex. We pick up a third person. We can experiment, see where it goes?" I coaxed.

"Why would I want to share you with another man? The whole point of this arrangement was to give you time to decide, not add new rules," Tom shouted.

"Tom, just think about it over night."

"I don't have to Marshall. I've thought about it for the last month. I love you! Either I am your lover and we work on our problems, or I am not your lover. I'm not a part time fling any more. I don't want to share you, I don't want strangers to share our bed with us, I just want you."

"I'm not ready to commit to that yet . . ."

"Fine. Have a good life Marshall. I can't take it any more." He got up and walked to the door, put on his jacket and left. I got up and ran behind him.

"Tom, sleep on it!" He didn't stop, or answer. He got on his motorcycle and rode off. I hadn't expected quite that reaction. I was stunned. I went back into the living room and sat. He'd call. He'd cool off and call. I smoked a bowl and waited for Tom to call. He never did. I got Geoff and I went to bed expecting to wake to a phone call and awoke to the alarm. Then the Fez was calling to tell me they needed me to come in for the Thanksgiving special. A cook hadn't come to work. Tom didn't call. At work I expected a call but, never got one.

I began to work on my house. I thought Tom would call soon. Mean while I could take some time to start stripping the woodwork and start fixing up some areas of the house. I really got into working on the house and by Christmas I had it all torn up. I realized then that it had been almost a month since I had last seen Tom. I rationalized to myself what was meant to be, was meant to be. Maybe I was being stubborn, but I refused to call Tom.

I continued stripping the woodwork and trim, and remodeling the house. I called the gang for help and they all agreed to help. I don't think it was the number one priority on any of their lists, but they agreed. The first night they all showed up in old clothes to help. I was impressed. We worked all evening on removing layers of wallpaper and began stripping the staircase of layers of paint. I fixed them dinner for all their efforts and served them drinks at the end of the evening.

For the next few weeks they came by regularly. Sometimes all four of them, sometimes one or two, other times three, they all put their time in and they did come and lend a hand. Some projects were too difficult for us to undertake, so we left them alone. Slowly the house began to be completely ripped apart.

Christmas Eve I had to work. Christmas Day Colt, Derrek, and Sampson had all invited me to spend time with them. Even Darrin offered not to go to his parents and have me over to his place, but I just wanted to stay home. I fixed Geoff and me dinner and we had our own little Christmas. New Years Eve I did have the gang over, and New Years day I spent alone working on the house.

The head chef walked off the job after the first of the year. His position was offered to me and I took it. Between getting used to the new job, and refinishing the house I was busy. I had so many things I needed to replace in order to get the house back into the original state.

At the end of February my birthday came along. I sort of thought Tom might call for a birthday wish, but he didn't. I was sitting thinking about turning another year older, my gift to myself, when my doorbell rang. I got up and answered the door.

"Well hello Colt. What are you doing here?"

"Well, I know you don't like unannounced guests, but happy birthday. Here's a gift for you." Colt gave me a hug.

"Come on in. Thanks. You have been helping me with the house with no complaints. I'm glad you stopped by." I said.

"You don't have any plans do you?" Colt inquired.

"No, not really, why?"

"Well, I sort of invited a couple of other people to stop by." Colt said hesitantly.

"Like who?" I asked.

"Well, Darrin, Derrek, and Sampson."

"Oh, no. I have very little booze. There are dishes in the sink, I am a mess. I can't entertain." I grumbled.

"Don't worry. They will bring their own booze. None of us are worried about dirty dishes or messy hair. Aren't you even going to open your gift?"

"Yes, I am. You just got me side tracked." I replied. I opened the package Colt had brought to find a recipe book of Victorian menus. "Thanks Colt, this is neat. I can cook authentic meals from the era the house was built in. Thanks."

"You're welcome. I have a bottle of bourbon in the truck. I'll run out and get it."

"I'll pick up a little while you go to your truck." Colt left, and I began to frantically tidy up to make the place look more presentable. I washed my face, combed my hair. When he came back in, he had Derrek with him.

"Hello Marshall, happy birthday." Derrek greeted me. "This is for you." He hugged me as he handed me a gift.

"Well thank you Derrek. You didn't have to get me anything." I opened his gift to find a bottle of JD. "Thanks Derrek. Would you like a JD and Coke?"

"Sure Marshall. Thanks." Derrek replied.

As I went to the kitchen to get some glasses, the doorbell rang. "Would one of you get that please?"

"Sure." Colt replied. I heard Darrin's voice from the front door asking what Colt was doing answering the door. I returned to the living room to see Darrin also had a package.

"Happy birthday guy." Darrin said as he handed me a package, with a hug.

"Thanks Darrin. That was nice of you to get me something." I opened Darrin's box to find what Darrin always called a skin flick. "Think I need some stimulation?" I asked.

"Well, you haven't been going out lately. We've all been here working on your house. I just thought you might need a reminder of what sex was." Darrin said teasing.

"I think I can remember, but thanks anyway." The doorbell rang again and Geoff appeared to see what was going on.

"Hello Marshall. How are you?" Sampson greeted me. He gave me a hug and pat on the back.

"Oh, ok. And you?"

"Doin' pretty good. Here, happy birthday." He said

"Well, thank you Sampson." I opened the box to find a set of crystal wine goblets. "Thanks Sampson. These are really nice." I hugged him.

"I tried to find something that would go with the Victorian era you are trying to create in here." Sampson explained.

"I think they'll do well. I don't have anything to drink except bourbon. I know that suits Darrin fine. What about you Sampson?"

"Oh, for one night bourbon and Coke is fine." He replied. "How about getting high Marshall?"

"Man that sounds good. Sure." Sampson pulled out a joint and he and I smoked it. I was very touched with the fact all of them had shown up as a surprise. Sometimes friends are better than lovers. They all had been here working on their free time for the past month and a half. It was nice to just sit and enjoy their company without working on the house.

"Dude, you are lucky I even showed up tonight," Darrin said, "considering how much time I have spent here working recently!"

"I'm glad you came over. I appreciate all the work all of you have done. It's nice to see all of you for some reason other than working on the house."

"Are you ever going to get this place back together?" Derrek teased.

"Eventually. I think some of this I'll hire out. You boys need to come to the garage with me. See what I did on a break I took from working on the house earlier this week," I kind of grinned.

As we walked to the garage Derrek offered, "Marshall, if you are serious about hiring some work out, let me give you a bid on it."

"Ok Derrek, I'd appreciate that."

"Why to the garage," Darrin asked, "are you remodeling the garage too?"

"Don't give him any ideas!" Sampson said.

"I want to see what is up," Derrek said.

"Follow me boys," I added. I took them to the garage and turned on the light.

"Lord, a Jaguar!" Colt announced.

"Are you sure?" Derrek asked.

"When did you get this?" Darrin asked.

"Pretty uptown if you ask me," Sampson added.

"I picked it up yesterday. I decided I was going to have to buy myself my own birthday present, so I did." I explained.

"Some present. Can we go for a ride?" Colt added.

"Sure, come on," I said proudly. We all piled into the Jag and went for a spin around the block.

"I just love the smell of new cars," Derrek said.

"Rides nice," Sampson said.

"Seems to have enough get up and go," Darrin pointed out.

"I really like it," Colt responded.

"I like it too. I've always wanted one. Finally my career affords me one!" I said. We got back to the house and went in.

"You shouldn't have broken up with Tom until after your birthday you fool. Maybe he would have bought the Jag." Sampson laughed.

"Or at least some trinket to go with it!" Derrek teased.

"Well, I guess I goofed up. At least this has turned into a celebration any way." I replied, thinking about Tom.

"Your friends felt you needed to have a celebration of some kind to break up your working and remodeling schedule. You know real life?" Derrek said.

"Besides, we needed a break from remodeling!" Colt replied.

"I do appreciate it." I replied. We all sat around, drank, and played games. It was a nice way to celebrate my birthday and it was a surprise. It made the day extraordinary. They all left at the same time. It had been a good birthday.

Over the next few months I worked on the house, letting Derrek and some of his subcontractors do the tough stuff. As the weather got warm, I turned to the yard, and left the inside of the house for the contractors to complete. I spent most of the summer putting the yard together like I wanted it to be. I started to cruise the bars again and pick up men. At first it was really exciting. Someone new every night. Sometimes two or three men in my bed all at once, it was something I had never done, always wanted to try.

Fall arrived and I was so frustrated with this project still being under way. Some weeks there were workers all over the house. Some weeks there was no one. I had to wait for supplies to be ordered and arrive. It seemed like this project was beginning to take forever. The holidays came and went and I was still having work done.

My birthday rolled around again and the house finally took shape. It had been a long slow project, but I was pleased to see the wood stained, and to have the house look as it had when it was built. It just felt as authentic as I could get it.

Now I had all this free time. I wasn't sure what to do with it after spending months waiting for workers or parts to show up! I thought about what I had done before the relationship with Tom had entered my life. I began to go out again.

At first I avoided the Hole. I didn't want to run into Tom. But, I really found I didn't like the other bars when I was out cruising men, so I started going to the Hole again. To my surprise I didn't see Tom. I had really thought, even hoped, I would run into him, but I didn't.

The rest of the winter I spent as I had once in my life, going out, seeing friends, having fun, sleeping with strange men. For a few weeks I dated a guy, but he was so into himself I let that end. One night while I was at the Hole playing pinball, I heard a familiar voice from behind me.

"Mind if I play a game of pinball with you?"

I turned around and it was Tom. "Well, hello Tom. How are you?"

"Fine and you?"

"Fine. I am surprised you are even speaking."

"I don't hold grudges Marshall. Bygones are bygones."

"I'm glad to hear you say that. Sure, let's play a game of pinball." Even after eighteen months, Tom still could beat me. It was nice to see him. It felt comfortable even. We chatted as we played.

"Tom, it is so nice to see you. It's been awhile."

"Yes, it has. How's work?"

"Great. I'm head chef now."

"Congratulations. It doesn't surprise me. You are such a creative person with food."

"Thanks and your job?" I asked.

"Oh, I changed jobs. Right now I've just started with a restaurant supply business. I'm one of their sales representatives."

"Oh, how wild. Is the Fez one of your accounts?"

"Yes, it is. I was looking for you to tell the truth. I have been assigned the Fez and wanted to see you before I showed up at the restaurant."

"I'll be damned."

"I was afraid you'd be pissed." Tom stated.

"No, not at all. You should see my house. I have completely redone it."

"I'd like to see it sometime." Tom said earnestly.

"Why not now?"

"Is that such a good idea?"

"Why not Tom, what happened, happened and is in the past. Besides, you are one of the few people who would understand what I have done. I talked your ear off about what I wanted to do."

"Well, if you are sure. I wouldn't mind going to see your place."

"Ok, then, let's go."

"I'll follow you Marshall." We walked out to the parking lot and I looked for Tom's bike. I didn't see it.

"Where's your bike?"

"At home. With this new job, I have to travel with many supplies, so I bought a car. It's that sedan."

"Oh, really. I can't imagine you in a car! Is it new?"

"It's this year's model, but it is a demo. Where's your car?"

"I traded it in on that Jaguar over there."

"Nice set of wheels. Aren't you uptown?"

"Not really. I got a good deal, I think. I have had many problems with the electrical system though."

"Hope that isn't a continuous problem. I guess I'll follow you, even though I know the way."

"Ok. I'll see you at the house." The words sounded normal. We drove to the house. As I parked in the garage, Tom parked out front. He walked to the front door, as I hurried in the back. I ran through the house and let him in.

"Gees. You really did change this place around! It doesn't look like the same house. I feel like I stepped into the past!"

"That was my intent." I said. Geoff came up to Tom and rubbed up on his legs.

"I didn't think Geoff ever liked me." Tom said.

"Perhaps she has changed her mind." I replied.

"Did you sell your tv?"

"Oh no, watch this." I walked over to the wall and opened the sliding doors. "Ta da. I just hid the tv. It's a fake wall."

"Looks great."

"That's only the beginning Tom. Come look in the dining room and the kitchen." I excitedly drug Tom through the entire house pointing out each feature I had added or changed. He was very impressed. We ended up in the upstairs bath.

"God Marshall, you even have one of those old time toilets with the water tank up by the ceiling and a pull chain. You thought of everything! It looks so different. You've even replaced a lot of furniture!"

"Yea, I have. But, I told you a long time ago, I wanted this place to look as it did new." I said.

"You have accomplished your goal." Tom observed. We went back downstairs.

"Want a drink?" I asked.

"Ok. You still smoke?" He asked.

"Of course." I said.

"You want to get high?" Tom asked.

"Yes, of course." Now that was new, asking what I wanted to. I brought Tom his drink and we sat and I loaded the bowl and we took a hit. "Feels good to have you here to see the changes Tom."

"It's nice to be here to see them. After we first stopped seeing each other, I decided I'd never see you again. I hurt. I dated and tried to forget you. I even went with a guy for a couple of months, but it didn't work. Partly because I still missed and loved you. Partly because he wanted me to be someone I wasn't."

"I dated for a while, too. At first I spent most all my time with the house. But, I did date. I even slept with as many men as I could for a while there, two, three a day. One guy I hooked up with for a month or so, was so into only himself I just ended it."

"I know the feeling." We smoked a little more and finished our drinks.

"Want another drink?"

"I guess. I haven't been drinking in a while." Tom said cautiously. "I may get drunk fast."

"You'll be fine." I walked to fix the drinks and Tom followed me. He was looking around the kitchen.

"I can't believe all that you have done. This doesn't look like the same place!"

"It is good to hear that I accomplished my goal."

"Know one of the things I miss about you, Marshall?"

"No, what Tom?"

"Your knack with food. I remember eating all your test recipes. All the dips and chips we used to eat at night. I miss that."

"I have a new dip I'm experimenting with if you want to try it."

"Sure, I'd like that. Let me carry the glasses."

"Ok. I'll get chips and dip." This wasn't quite the Tom I remembered. We walked to the living room together. He sat the glasses on the sofa table. I put the dip and chips on the coffee table. As he turned to sit, I hugged him.

"Whoa, what are you doing Marshall?"

"What came naturally. I felt the urge to hold you."

"Felt good." He hugged me and I kissed him. I didn't feel any hands grabbing at me or buttons being unbuttoned, just a nice pleasant hug and kiss. Geoff jumped up by Tom. He petted her and she purred.

"Tom, I have to tell you something."

"You want me to leave?" he sighed.

"No, not at all. I finally did realize I love you. But it had been such a battle between us. I decided to let it go. I'm glad you are here to hear that."

"I felt much the same way Marshall. I still love you. No, I am still *in love* with you."

"And I am sill in love with you. I would like you to spend the night."

"If you really mean that, I will."

"I really mean that."

"Ok, I will."

"Music or tv?" I asked.

"I miss your old movies, tv." I turned on the television and found an old movie. We ate chips, dip, and began to watch the movie.

"Interesting taste. I kind of like it, Marshall. It's bittersweet."

"I haven't perfected it yet, but thanks." I put my arm around him and he slid up close to me. We leaned against each other and just hugged. He seemed more settled and not so aggressive. He was so very attractive. I felt an overwhelming emotion right now. I guess it had always been there. "Tom, for the first time while I'm with you, I feel a strong emotion. I'd call it love."

"Marshall, are you sure it isn't just loneliness?"

"Yes, I am sure. And if it is, I still would like to see where it goes."

"Are you talking about dating again?"

"Yea, I guess I am."

"Let's let tonight be tonight, and see where we are in the morning." Tom cautioned.

"You have a deal, Tom." I leaned over and kissed him. He kissed me back, still no moves. I took his hand and put it on my crotch. He left it there, but he didn't try anything either. Geoff jumped off the couch and ran off.

"A new Marshall? I think you scared Geoff."

"She will get over it. I see a new Tom?" We sat, kissed, and hugged for a while. I stood up and stretched. I took off my shirt, shoes and socks.

"Hot in here don't you think?" I grinned.

"I think I have heard that line somewhere before."

"Want to go upstairs and see if we can still make love?" I said.

"Not have sex?"

"No, not have sex. This time, make love." I took off my pants. I was now naked.

"You are stealing my moves Marshall." Tom said. We walked upstairs and Tom undressed. We crawled into bed and began to kiss and hold each other. Again Geoff appeared from nowhere, got on the bed, and purred.

"What's with Geoff? She is by me, and leaves and then comes back." Tom asked.

"I guess she senses a change between the two of us, she seems to feel comfortable with you now." This time I felt I wanted Tom to put his moves on my body. He was still aggressive, but not as overbearing. I felt like we were making love, not having sex. We rolled up next to each other and fell asleep, not having a second go at sex. It was nice, comfortable. In the morning I woke up and looked over at

Tom. Geoff was beside his back. I leaned over and petted her. It felt very comfortable. I kissed him and that woke him up.

"You kiss me just now?" He asked rubbing his face.

"I did. Why?"

"I thought maybe I was dreaming."

"Want to take a shower together?" I asked.

"Wasn't that supposed to be my line?" Tom teased, "Yes I would."

"Used to be your line. Not today anyway." We took a shower together that was just a shower, got dressed and went to the kitchen and ate breakfast. No grabbing, no pushing for sex. It was different.

"Tom, I want to see you again, tonight."

"I would like to see you, too. Let's take this one day at a time for now."

"Good idea." We finished breakfast and Tom left for work. We made a date to meet here for dinner. I was excited. Perhaps we had both changed. I didn't have to go to work and I decided to get an opinion on the situation, so I called Sampson.

"Hello."

"Hello, Sampson, this is Marshall."

"Well, hi Marshall, how are you?"

"Oh, fine. So what's new?"

"I'm working on another novel. And you?"

"Well, that's what I called for. Could you do a Tarot card reading for me sometime today?"

"Sure, Marshall, later this afternoon I can. Why, you meet some hunk last night?"

"Well, in a way. I'm not saying anything else. I want you to read it first."

"Ok, then, why don't you come over about two?"

"That's fine. See you then." I said.

"See you then, bye."

"Until two, bye." Until two I wasn't sure what I was going to do to occupy the time. I needed some groceries and had to plan dinner, so I decided to let that fill the time. I looked through cookbooks and recipes I had, to plan dinner. I decided to use the cookbook Colt gave me and make a Victorian style dinner in my Victorian house.

I made a grocery list and went to the store. I came home and put the groceries away and started part of dinner. I watched television and hoped two o'clock would hurry and get here. I went to check on bread that I was letting rise and put it in the oven to bake. I put together a salad while the bread was baking. When those two projects were done it was time to go to Sampson's. I rolled a joint and left.

Driving to Sampson's I was really curious if he would be able to tell me anything about Tom. I got to his place and parked. I was lucky enough to find a place right out front. Walking up to his building, I noticed how nicely it was landscaped. My yard had come out just as good and I did it myself. I rang his bell and he let me in.

"Hello Marshall, come in."

"Hi, Sampson. How are you?"

"Fine. So, you have a man you want me to read in your cards, huh?"

"I don't want to say anything. You just do the reading and I will tell you after."

"That's fine. Don't trust me hey." We walked into his dining room and sat. He handed me the cards and I pulled out the joint I had brought.

"Shuffle the cards until you feel comfortable. If you have a specific question, think about that while you shuffle."

"I will. Want to smoke this?"

"Sure. You are one of the few friends I have that actually brings anything to share." We lit the joint and smoked it while I shuffled the cards. I concentrated on Tom, where he and I were going. I felt "comfortable" and handed the cards to Sampson.

He took the cards and laid them out on the table. He pondered them and looked at me and then he studied them again. "Well, Marshall, you have met someone, or I should say have connected with a man you already know. Someone you already have feelings for. Craig back?"

"No, but I've been asked that before."

"Hum. You care about this man, but he has changed. So have you. You want to know if it will work, right."

"Maybe." I wasn't giving out any information yet.

"It could. He still cares about you, but for one reason or another, he is afraid to let himself go with you. If you can show him you really care, he will let down his defenses. I also see a long distance move. Are you planning on moving?"

"No, I just barely got the house finished! It's not in my plans right now."

"I'd say with the situation with this man, you are going to have to sit and do some heavy explaining about your feelings. There is something he really needs to hear from you."

"Ok. Anything else?"

"You must have really concentrated on this man. That's all that is up. Communication, love, marriage cards, and a move, a big move."

"Thanks that helped."

"Oh, that's all you're going to tell me? You need a reading, it's about a man, and marriage comes up, a big move comes up and you say that helps and that's all!"

"Ok, ok. I saw Tom again and I am going to see him again tonight. He seems different. I have realized that I really do love him. I just wanted one of your uncanny readings to see if I was crazy, or perhaps, on track with what I felt."

"Tom, the sex maniac, Tom?"

"That Tom. I tell you he's different. I'm different. I feel like I do love him, something I wouldn't admit before."

"Well, from the cards, I guess you are on the right track!"

"I hope so Sampson. I hope so. I feel different this time. He doesn't seem as pushy or as aggressive. We'll see what happens."

"I wish you luck, Marshall. So how is being head chef going?"

"I really have gotten into a system and work is going fine." We talked about his book and comedy routines and just life in general. I was caught up in the reading and was fairly preoccupied with that. Finally I realized I needed to get home to finish dinner. I really wanted this to be one nice dinner.

"Well, Sampson, I hate to run, but I need to go. I've got dinner started and need to get back to it. Thanks for the reading."

"You're welcome. Let me know how things go. I hope it works."

"Me too. I'll keep you posted." He walked me to the door and gave me a hug.

"That's for luck. See you later."

"Later Sampson." I walked to the car and drove home. I could smell the bread I baked as I walked into the kitchen. It made the whole house smell good. I began the next part of dinner and kept busy with preparations until almost time for Tom to arrive. I pulled out the candlestick holders and the candles, one of my fancy table clothes, the good china, and the crystal. Made the table look *elegant*, as one of my uncles would always say. As I finished with the table the doorbell rang. I went to the door and it was Tom.

"Come in. Good to see you."

"Good to see you too, Marshall."

"How was your day?" I gave him a hug and a kiss.

"Oh fine. That felt good." He hugged me. "And your day? Smells like you spent it baking."

"My day was great. I did spend most of it baking. I wanted to fix you something special. An entirely home made meal from scratch."

"I haven't had one of those since the last one you fixed me!"

"You should enjoy it then. This one is special. It is from a Victorian Meal cookbook. Come in the living room and sit." We walked to the couch and sat. I looked Tom deeply in the eyes and hugged him again.

I whispered in his ear, "I do love you. I guess I always did."

He whispered back, "I always have loved you. I never stopped." We both sighed and held each other. We sat there for a while enjoying the moment. I was enjoying the peaceful feeling, in particular. Always before I felt threatened or pushed. Now I didn't.

"Tom, I don't know what is different, but I feel at ease. I never used to." I said.

"I know. I feel like I don't have to push you to get a hug, a kiss, or, well . . ."

"Or to get me to make love to you." I added.

"I was going to say sex."

"To me it used to be sex. Last night wasn't. It was different. I'm even looking forward to making love again tonight." I said.

"Really? I'm glad. I am looking forward to trying again too."

"How about before dinner?" I requested.

"Marshall, this is the second time you have stolen my line." Tom grinned.

"I guess it is."

"I'm ready if you are." Tom still had that boyish grin, that hadn't changed.

"Follow me upstairs then." We walked upstairs and sat on the bed. Tom made no moves. He let me slowly undress him, kiss him, and caress his body. He then slowly undressed me and caressed my body.

"You know, I don't think I ever noticed how hairy your stomach is. You have a smooth hairless chest but a hairy stomach." Tom commented as he played with the hair on my stomach.

"Perhaps that is because you are actually looking at me instead of worrying about trying to climax." I replied. We did make love. It was amazing. We laid there for a while and said nothing.

"You used to really like to eat in the nude. Tonight I am willing to do that because I want to, not because you insist we have to. Want to?" I said.

"Third time, my line! Yes, I'd like to. But I would like it if you wore your jockstrap." I put on my jock. We walked to the kitchen and ate. The evening went smoothly and calmly. We hugged, kissed, watched some television, played games and talked. This was different. When we went to bed Tom was almost asleep when I put the moves on him. For the third time we made love. For the third time I felt warm and happy. This was beginning to look good.

From the time he had arrived, making love, the candle lit dinner for two, television, games, and then in bed was romantic. I don't think I'd ever felt romantic with Tom before. In the morning when I awoke, Tom was in the shower. I got out of bed and joined him to his surprise.

"God," Tom shrieked, "you scared me, Marshall."

"Sorry, I didn't mean to. I just wanted to surprise you."

"You did." Tom said.

"Why didn't you get me up?"

"We used to argue about that. I didn't want to spoil the memory I had of last night. I'm afraid it will all blow up again."

"I have those fears Tom. But, if we work at it like we have for the past twenty-four hours, I believe we will be fine."

"I really do too. I just needed to hear you say that."

The next few weeks Tom just kept astounding me. We went out drinking, dancing, to movies. We rode his bike into the hills and he even invited friends over. We were really enjoying one good time after another. I started meeting him naked at the door again. It was really great.

We decided to go back to Orchard together to celebrate a month of the new relationship. We did many of the things we had done as teenagers, having as much fun now as we did then. In August we took another vacation out of state and had a great time. It was just a quick little trip across over into the unique scenery of our neighbor state. Talking in an open and direct manner about things that bothered us became natural. We learned to use statements that were fact and not an attack on the other person. Things really were going terrific.

Tom's lease was up at the end of the month, so we decided he'd move here and we would see how we did living together. We worked at our relationship. We had some fights. They weren't over sex, they were over things like keeping the house clean, squeezing the toothpaste tube in the middle. We were like a normal couple. We managed to work on our differences and begin to live life as a couple. I got urges now and again to be with a stranger, and now and again Tom was able to deal with someone being in our bed. For the most part, I guess things were pretty good.

Our relationship just seemed to continue to blossom and four years seemed to just fly by. Now we had a new situation to deal with. In the last week Tom came home and looked really upset. He announced to me that he was being transferred to California in October. He would turn down the offer if I wouldn't go with him. After many hours of discussion and thought, I had decided to go with him. Living on the coast, changing our life style sounded exciting.

I knew that the corporation that owned the Fez owned a couple places in California. I found that I could transfer out and have a job. The idea of living on the coast appealed to me. Perhaps that was what our relationship needed now, a change. A little shift in our lives, a little something different to keep things moving along in a new and different way. Soon we would be off to new city, a new home, and new plans to make, a major change in our life. We were both very excited about this move.

Zee Partee

"Speaking of houses Derrek, since you and Jason finished with the remodeling of the house, how do you like it?" Darrin asked.

"We like it fine. It was something I wanted to do anyway. It was more of a redecorating job really." Derrek replied.

You know talking about houses and moving, makes me think about how we all met." Marshall said.

"We all met basically through Colt didn't we?" Derrek responded.

"Yea, you did," I replied, "I met Marshall first."

"God, Colt, we met years ago. We were both a lot younger and just starting out. We worked in the same bar part time to earn extra money. We got to know each other and just started hanging out together." Marshall recalled.

"Admit it gentlemen, you both worked in a bar to meet men, not to earn money," Sampson teased.

"Partially," I said, "we used to stay after hours and tell stories about some of the weird patrons we had, and we had several weird ones."

"I met the two of you at the same time," Darrin interjected, "one night at the store. Colt and Marshall came into the store one night. I gave them static for being browsers and not paying customers."

"And as I recall we bought many things we weren't going to buy, because of your harassment." I responded.

"Oh, come on Colt, you loved it and you know it." Darrin said defensively.

"Sure we did Darrin. We did have fun talking to you. We even went to the Circle for a cocktail with you. That was the beginning of our friendship." Marshall recalled.

"I met Colt when we lived in the same apartment complex." Derrek said. "We ran into one another walking our dogs, and started to talk. We got to know each other, and started going out for drinks. We even let Clem baby sit Max when he was a puppy."

"And I, like Darrin, met two at once. Colt and Derrek were out bar hopping with a friend of Derrek's, who also happened to be a friend of mine." Sampson added, "We got introduced in the bar and became friends. Colt took me one night to dinner at the Fez to taste one of Marshall's latest dinners and I met Marshall then. And one day when I stopped by Colt's, Darrin you were there, and I met you."

"That's right Sampson," Darrin responded, "and I met Derrek at one of Colt's Halloween parties."

"Yeah, uh huh, I believe I met Marshall the same night." Derrek said.

"Yea, you did." Marshall said.

"Then we all ended up seeing each other at parties we each had and got to know one another. That was the beginning of our gang." I added.

"Then we started to harass one another for favors." Darrin said.

"Yea uh huh and ended up with this yearly party to keep track of each other." Derrek added.

"So, Derrek, what are you and Jason up to these days? I saw more of Jason in the bar before you two got together, than I have recently." Sampson inquired.

"Well, we are thinking about taking a cruise next month. We sent for some information." Derrek answered.

"That would be fun!" Darrin said.

"I don't know about anyone else, but I need a drink!" Marshall stated.

"I agree." Darrin added.

"Mine needs freshened." Sampson added.

"Might as well." Derrek joined in.

"Coming right up." I responded.

Derrek and Jason

A cruise, that was not a though I had ever had before. A year ago I was single and buried in my work. Now I was going on a cruise with a lover. I was happy with my life then, I thought. But I met Jason. Colt had called on a Sunday and asked me to go out. I had not really planned on going out, I was even reluctant to go, but I did. When we walked into the Twenty-one Nightclub, we went back to the dance floor and I noticed a tall guy standing there. He was with someone else, but he kept smiling and looking in my direction. I smiled back, but did not do much else. Then he and the man he was with left the bar, and I was disappointed. I even asked Colt if he did not think the guy was smiling at me, and he agreed.

Then he came back into the bar alone. I decided to go ask him to dance no matter what song played. I did not want to miss a chance to talk to him. We danced and talked most of the night, and I found out that he was there with his best friend, as I was. We exchanged phone numbers and that week I asked him over for dinner. I asked Colt to come over and help me on dinner so I would have company to keep me from getting nervous and someone to help me fix a simple dinner.

"Colt I really appreciate you comin' over to help on this."

"No problem Derrek. I like to cook, and if I can help anyone else, I am glad to."

"Well, I really do appreciate it. You know I have spent all day trying to remember what Jason looks like, exactly. It is really bugging me."

"Well, I guess you'll find out soon enough. What time is he coming by? I want to be sure I am gone before he arrives." Colt replied.

"Oh, I'm not sure. I think I said about six."

"I can't believe you are so nervous!" Colt teased.

"I AM NOT. It's just your imagination!"

"Right, that's why you can't remember what Jason looks like, or what time you told him to come by," Colt said. "I wouldn't be surprised if you remember the day wrong."

"Now, tell me again Colt, how do I fix this salad?"

Colt and I spent the afternoon putting together dinner for the evening and I kept asking Colt to repeat directions over and over. After what seemed like an eternity, we had dinner together. Darrin would say that is because I am blond.

"Well, Derrek, I think I am going to head for home. Remember to put the rolls in the oven before you serve dinner so they will be warm. And don't forget to take them out!"

"Ok, yea uh huh, I will remember. I am not sure I want you to go right now. Stay for a few minutes longer and talk me through dinner again, okay?"

"Ok, but I think you know what to do. Stop being so nervous. Do you want me to take Clem and keep him tonight?"

"No, I want Jason and Clem to get acquainted, thanks anyway." I explained. "You are right, I am just nervous. I just hope I do not mess up anything Colt." I was getting butterflies in my stomach.

"Well, Derrek, I think I should be going. You have everything pretty much organized."

"Thanks Colt for coming over and helping me on this. I do appreciate it. Be careful driving home, ok?"

"I will." I walked Colt to the door and gave him a hug. As I shut the door, I felt really nervous. I found myself walking to the window and constantly looking out, checking the time, pacing the floor and hoping things would go well. Finally I saw Jason pull up. I was relieved, and anxious, at his arrival. I turned to walk to the door to open it as he rang the bell, and Clem followed me to the door. As I opened the door, Clem began to bark at the arrival of a stranger.

"Hello Jason, how are you?" I turned to Clem, "Stop that, this is a friend of mine Clem, Jason, this is Clem, Clem this is Jason. Now be quiet!"

"Hello Clem, nice to meet you."

"Please hold your hand out so he can sniff you and give you his stamp of approval. He will quiet down in a minute here. Come on in."

"Nice place Derrek." Jason said as he let Clem sniff his hand.

"It is home. Did you have any trouble finding it?"

"No, not really. It was pretty easy."

"Would you like something to drink, water, pop, beer, hard liquor?"

"Sure, Derrek, I'll take a Coke if you have that."

"Yea, uh huh sure, follow me to the kitchen." We walked back to the kitchen and I got glasses out and fixed us both a Coke. As I was putting the ice in the glasses, I looked at Jason's face and made a point of memorizing every feature so I would not forget again. "Here you go." As I handed him his Coke I reached over and kissed him. He was a little taller than I had in fact remembered.

"Thanks," Jason sipped his Coke and replied, "This hits the spot."

"Good. You can sit here at the bar. I need to go into the kitchen and check on dinner. I will be right back, ok?"

"Sure, I'm fine. I'll get acquainted with Clem."

I turned and walked into the kitchen and checked dinner. Everything looked done to me. I guessed it was time to serve dinner and hope it was ok. I walked back to the bar to tell Jason he could take a seat.

"Well, dinner looks ready, if you want to take a seat at the table, I will bring dinner out."

"Where would you like me to sit?"

"Either place is fine."

"Sure smells good. I'm looking forward to a home cooked meal."

"I hope it is good. I have a little confession to make. I did not do this all by myself. I had Colt come over this afternoon to help on it."

"That's ok. It still smells good. Have I met Colt?"

"Yeah, uh huh, he was the guy that was with me the other night when I met you in the club."

"Oh ok, your friend," Jason responded.

"I will be right back." I walked into the kitchen, got dinner out of the microwave, oven, and refrigerator. I began carrying it to the table."

"Need any help with that stuff?" Jason offered.

"No, I have got it." I yelled to Jason. I walked back to the dining room. "Damn, those rolls!" I said under my breath.

"Something wrong?" Jason asked.

"No, I just need to go back into the kitchen and do something I forgot." I walked back into the kitchen and put the rolls into the oven. I walked back out into the dining room and joined Jason.

"Sure looks good."

"Let's eat. Here, go ahead and serve yourself." We filled our plates and began to eat dinner. To my relief, dinner tasted great. I was surprised and impressed with the meal. We ate silently.

"Tastes great Derrek, help or no help."

"Thanks Jason."

"Derrek, is there something burning in the kitchen?"

"Oh lord, the rolls!" I leaped up from the table, sprinted into the kitchen, and discovered the rolls, burned. I took them out, sat them on the counter, and walked back to the dining room. I knew I should not have invited Jason to a home cooked meal! Oh well, at least everything else was ok. If Darrin were here, he would say it was another blond moment.

"Sorry, Jason, we will not be having rolls with dinner. They are a little over done."

"Looks like there is plenty to eat anyway."

"I hope so. So how was your day off? Do anything special?"

"It was fine. I did some shopping and relaxed. How was your day?"

"Oh fine. I ran around this morning to some of my accounts and checked out some new leads." We both turned back to eating dinner. It was that nervous moment in time when you have met someone new and the conversation lags. It seemed like dinner lasted for hours. Jason finally pushed his plate back and leaned back in his chair. I realized I was full, and in a nervous response, I began to clear the table. Jason got up and began to help.

"Oh, just leave that Jason. I just want to put the dishes and silverware in the kitchen. I will clean up later. Want another Coke?"

"Actually, I'll take Gin and Tonic if you have it. But let me help you carry this stuff to the kitchen first."

"Yea, uh huh, fine. I will fix your drink." I stopped and let Jason walk up by me and leaned up and kissed him again. We cleared off the table and went into the living room.

"Oops, I forgot your drink. I will go get it Jason."

"Are you having one Derrek?"

"Yeah, uh huh, I will get a beer, why?"

"If you weren't going to have one, I wasn't either." Jason explained.

"Oh no, that is fine. I am having one." I walked to the bar, mixed his drink, got my beer and took them to the living room.

"Here you go."

"Thanks Derrek."

"So, what did you want to do? Watch tv, listen to music, go to a movie?" I asked.

"I think I'd just like to sit here and listen to music."

"Ok. I will put on some background music." I picked up the remote and turned to some soft music. "That music all right?"

"It's fine."

I leaned back on the couch next to Jason and put my arm around his back on the couch.

"This is a nice place. I do like it."

"Would you like to see the rest?" I asked.

"Sure."

"Okay, this here is the living room, over here we have a hallway." I took Jason through the entire house leaving my bedroom for last. "And here we have the master bedroom, for the master, right Clem?"

"It is a nice place, big rambling ranch house Derrek. This four poster bed an antique?"

"Yeah, uh huh, it belonged to my grandmother." I walked over to the bed, sat, and kicked off my tennis shoes.

"It's nice looking. Mind if I sit on it?" Jason inquired.

"No, not at all!" Jason sat on the bed right next to me and also kicked off his shoes. I leaned over and put my arms around him. "I am glad you came over tonight. Sorry about the rolls."

"Dinner was good without the rolls. I'm glad I came over too." Our lips seemed to meet and I kissed Jason and held him close. As we kissed, I began to unbutton his shirt. As I did, he unbuttoned mine, and in moments, we found ourselves naked and in a passionate embrace.

From the glimpses I had caught of his body as we undressed, he was more muscular than I had thought. He had hair on his chest but not his stomach. As I kissed him, I began slowly moving down his body to his chest and continued to travel slowly downward. His body felt solid and hard under me, and he seemed to be enjoying the moment as much as I was.

My nervousness changed to excitement as we kissed and played with each other. In one quick motion, I was turned over, pulled up, and found Jason working his way from my neck down my body with his hands and lips. The sensation of his body on top of mine was very exciting.

"You are a solid mass of hair head to foot aren't you?" Jason said as he caressed my chest. I did not answer. I just enjoyed the sensations I was feeling. I was getting too excited to let this go any further.

"I don't want to ruin the moment, but I use condoms." I said hesitantly.

"I do too. I was about to ask if you had any condoms." Jason said. We changed positions several times and finally collapsed in a satisfied sigh.

We fell asleep next to one another. Sometime in the night, Clem jumped up on the bed to join us. The next morning when I woke up, I felt a little strange to have someone next to me in bed, and yet it felt good. It had been awhile since I had shared my bed with anyone else. It just felt a little odd to see someone there. I got up quietly and went into the bathroom to get my bearings. I guess it was more of a reality check to see if I was dreaming or really awake.

When I looked in the mirror, I realized that this was reality, my hair was a mess! I walked back into the bedroom and realized Jason was looking at me. I was a little embarrassed at first. It had been awhile since I had stood naked in front of someone. But the smile on Jason's face made me feel more comfortable. I quickly crawled back into bed.

"I see you woke up." I managed to say.

"Yes, I did. I still cannot believe how hairy you are, especially for a blonde-haired person. Such dark hair. It's quite sexy."

"You sleep ok," I said avoiding the comment about my hairy body.

"Yeah, it felt a little strange not to be in my own bed, and to wake up next to someone this morning. And you?"

"Yea, uh huh, I slept fine. Did Clem bother you?"

"Only once. I woke up and he was on my pillow. It was a little different sleeping here. The dog being here and I am used to a waterbed. This bed is a little more solid." Jason replied.

"I know. I used to have a waterbed. Lord, my hair is a mess. I am embarrassed!"

"Don't be. You look cute that way."

"Well, thank you for saying so. Sorry about Clem. He likes to sleep on pillows, huh?" Clem crawled up next to me, and I leaned over and kissed Jason. Looking at him now that I had adjusted to the fact he was here in my bed had aroused me. We embraced, and Clem jumped off the bed. Once again we were having sex. This time I felt more at ease and really enjoyed Jason's body. I was able to let go and enjoy. I just collapsed on top of Jason. We laid there silently for a few minutes.

"Would you like to take a shower?" I asked finally.

"Yes, I would."

"The towels on the rack are clean, and there are more under the sink if you need them."

"Ok, thanks." Jason quickly got out of bed and hurried to the shower. I sensed he was as sensitive about me seeing him walk around naked as I was about him seeing me. I decided to go to the kitchen and make a pot of coffee and let him have the bedroom to himself. Clem needed to be let out anyway, so I pulled on a pair of my jogging shorts, put on my ball cap and went to the back door to let Clem out. I got in the morning paper, made coffee, and sat to read. As I got up to pour a cup of coffee, Jason came into the kitchen.

"Hello." He said.

"Would you like a cup of coffee?"

"Sure, sounds good."

"Here you go. Cream or sugar?"

"Sugar please."

"Uh huh, here you go. Would you like some breakfast?"

"No, I don't think so."

"You should, breakfast is the most important meal of the day." I said.

"No, thanks. My job involves serving breakfast to lots of people. It makes me not want to make anyone else have to serve breakfast to me."

"Suit yourself." I looked at Jason again. He was a very attractive man. I was still feeling odd at having someone in my house. It was nice, just so different. I guess my state of uncomfortable ness showed just a little to Jason.

"Derrek, I have some things I need to do today. I should go and get started. I'll give you a call later on today if you are going to be home."

"Yea, uh huh, I should be home this afternoon, but even if I am not I have my calls transferred to my cell phone so I get them anyway."

"Okay, then I'll call you later this afternoon and maybe we can get together."

"Sounds good." I stood up, walked over to Jason, and gave him a hug and a kiss. I had to reach up to kiss him on the lips. He hugged me back and I walked him to the door. We hugged and kissed again.

"Talk to you later today." He said as he left.

"Okay, enjoy your day off." I went back to my office to look over the things I had on my calendar for the day. I heard Clem barking and remembered he was still in the yard. I went to get him and we went for our jog. While we were out running, I began to feel excited that Jason was going to call me later in the day.

When I got back into the house, I took a shower and imagined Jason taking a shower in my bathroom. I stopped briefly and looked into the mirror. I had love handles I needed to get rid of. It was time to go back to running every morning, and exercising again. I needed to look better than I did now. I got dressed went out to check on some accounts and make calls on my clients. I was so busy I had almost forgotten that Jason was going to call. When the phone rang, I remembered he said he would call.

"Hello."

"Hello, Derrek?"

"'Tis me, Jason?"

"Yeah this is Jason. I am back home and thought if you wanted to drop by later you could."

"Yeah, uh huh, that sounds fine. What time would be good for you?"

"Anytime from now on. What's good for you?"

"Well, to tell the truth, I am probably going to be busy until around three or so. Is that all right?" I asked.

"Yeah, that's fine. I'll be here." Jason responded.

"Tell ya what. I will give you a call when I am on my way, will that work for ya?" I suggested.

"Sure, that's fine." He gave me directions and hung up. I got busy with files on my desk, returned some calls. I ran out and checked some sights, checked on supplies and talked to a prospective client. I was caught up in work and the time flew by pretty fast. I finished up a little earlier than I had expected. This way I could go home take a shower and be fresh when I stopped by.

When I got home, I let Clem out while I got ready. I called Jason to let him know I was on my way. On the drive over, I began to get a little nervous again, but when I got to his place, I felt fine. I walked up to the door and rang the bell. Jason answered it rapidly and buzzed me into the building.

"Hi Derrek, come on in. How was the rest of your afternoon?"

"Busy, and yours?"

"Relaxing. I just kind of hung out and enjoyed being off work." He did look relaxed and casual. He had on jogging sweats, a sweat jacket, and a painter's cap. He was so cute. His jacket was unzipped to the waist and I noticed the hair on his chest again. He had me so embarrassed about being hairy head to toe I had not actually noticed how slightly hairy he was. He was cute dressed like that. I followed him into the living room and gave him a hug and kiss.

"You look cute." I said.

"Thanks. Want to see the apartment?"

"Yea, uh huh, why not." We walked through his place and seemed to end in his bedroom last, as we had ended up in mine the night before. I commented on his waterbed, and we sat on it. The sequence of events repeated the night before. This time I felt much more comfortable. His touch did not make me nervous this time.

"You ok?" I asked.

"Yes, you?"

"Yeah uh huh. I was a little nervous coming over, but I am glad I did."

"Why were you nervous?" Jason asked.

"Wweeelllll, I wanted to do what we just did, but I was not sure you would want to."

"Why wouldn't I?" Jason asked.

"Oh, I do not know. Mind if we just lay here?" We both seemed relieved and glad to be with each other. We laid there hugging.

"You hungry?" I asked.

"I guess. Did you want me to fix something?"

"No, I thought we could go out if you wanted to."

"No, I'd rather fix something here." Jason offered.

"Yea, uh huh, fine. I need to ask you a favor. Would you mind terribly if Clem came over with me sometimes?"

"No, he could come with you. You miss him that much?"

"Well, it is not that I miss him so much, it is just that if I were to spend the night, I could not leave him alone for that long is all."

"Oh, I hadn't thought about that. Yeah, he can come with you if you are spending the night. Are you hinting for an invitation tonight?"

"Sort of I guess. I mean I would not mind if . . ." I fumbled for words.

"Well, I wouldn't mind either. You are welcome to stay if you want."

"Yea, uh huh, I would like to. Tell ya what then, I will run home and get Clem while you fix dinner."

"That's fine."

"And, since you are going to fix dinner alone, how does this sound? I will clean up dinner when we are done. How is that? Fair?"

"Fair. It's a deal Derrek." We got up and I quickly grabbed my jeans and pulled them on, and then quickly grabbed my shirt to finish getting dressed. I did not want him to see my love handles. I guess Jason noticed.

"Are you ashamed of your body or something?" Jason asked.

"Well uh, well, I uh am a little heavier than usual. I have not been keeping up with my jogging and workouts recently. It is kind of embarrassing." I replied.

"Well, I guess all that hair covers it up I think you look very fit." Jason smiled.

"Thank you for saying so, I appreciate that comment," I stammered as I turned bright red. "I think I will go get Clem now." So I ran home to get Clem. I stopped on the way to get some caramel corn to munch on and a movie to watch, as a surprise. When I got back to Jason's place, he had dinner fixed. We sat to eat and Clem sniffed around Jason's apartment.

"He's not going to do anything in here is he?" Jason asked nervously.

"No, he just needs to get his bearings by sniffing around your place." I assured him. I ate dinner and watched Clem to be certain he did not do anything.

"That was a good dinner. Thanks. I brought a movie and munchies if you would like to do that. Or if you have another suggestion, we could do something else." I said.

"A movie sounds fine. I need to go to bed early any way. I have to be up early to be to work in the morning."

"Yea, uh huh, I am an early riser anyway, so that works out great." Jason got up from the table and began to clear the dishes off.

"Sit down, relax I said I would clean up after dinner and I will."

"Yes, you did say you'd clean. It's just an automatic habit." Jason replied.

I got up, cleaned up the dishes and pans, and put things away, asking many questions about where things were and where things went. We walked into the living room to sit.

"Let me run out to the car and get the movie. I will take Clem with me so he can relieve himself."

"I'll be right here." Jason replied.

I ran out to the car and got the movie and caramel corn. Clem did his sniffing and running around to find the spot to relieve himself. I went back to the apartment with Clem right behind me.

"Here is the movie. Want to watch it now?" I asked, and felt myself grin.

"Sure." After Jason started the movie, we sat on the couch next to one another. I kicked off my shoes and snuggled up beside Jason. We watched the movie and munched on the caramel corn. When the movie was over, we talked about my business and Jason's job and got to know a little more about each other.

"Derrek, I don't mean to end the evening early, but I need to go to bed. I have to be up by four."

"Uh huh, that is fine. I usually go to bed early anyway. I will take Clem out for a walk and exploration of the neighborhood. I will be right back."

"I'll get ready for bed while you do that."

Clem and I went for a brief walk, he was so curious about being in a new place I had a difficult time getting him to do his duties. It seemed like it took him forever to complete his job. When we came back in Jason was getting into bed. I walked into his bedroom and he was waiting for me.

"I just thought I'd save some time and get into bed. Hope you don't mind."

"No, not at all. That is fine. I have a question for you though. Clem is used to sleeping with me, as you know, but would it be ok if he slept on your bed?"

"Guess so. If that is what he is used to, it will be hard to stop him anyway."

"Thanks. I know Clem will appreciate that, won't ya?" I looked for the light switch and turned off the lights. I was still a little uneasy undressing in front of Jason. I crawled into bed and snuggled up next to Jason. I reached over, put my arm around him, leaned up, and kissed him. He kissed me back. I rolled over on top of him and kissed him a little more passionately. His reaction was very positive and we began to rub our hands over each other, exploring and playing.

"Ah, here, I feel some of that excess weight you are so worried about." Jason teased.

"I know, it is embarrassing, I really need to get back into shape." I replied. With that Jason gave me a passionate kiss. We again made love, this time I really did feel very comfortable. I let myself really enjoy his motions and actions. Jason felt warm and fuzzy next to me. We lay next to each other and cuddled. Clem jumped on the bed and the three of us fell asleep.

Next morning I woke to Clem pawing my face. I guess he was a little nervous being in a strange place. I looked over and Jason was still asleep, it was before four. I did not want to wake him, so I tried to quietly get out of bed and take Clem out for a walk. As I was pulling on my jeans, Jason woke up.

"Something wrong?" He said groggily.

"No huh uh not at all. I am sorry I did not mean to wake you. Clem needs to go out."

"Oh, I forgot about him. What time is it?"

"About three-thirty."

"Oh well, I need to get up anyway."

"I am sorry we woke you. I will take Clem out." I grabbed my hat and shirt. While Clem and I were out walking, I took notice of the neighborhood again. It was going to be a beautiful fall day. We went back to the apartment to find Jason showered and dressed.

"Clem do his thing?"

"Morning. Yea uh huh, he did. Sorry we woke you." I apologized again.

"That's ok. It was not that much earlier than I needed to be up anyway. Did you want some breakfast, since it is an important meal?"

"Only if you are eating. A cup of coffee is fine."

"Like I said, I seldom eat breakfast. I have already started some coffee. Did you want to take a shower?"

"No, huh uh, that is ok. I will wait until I get home. Usually I go for a run before I shower."

"Run? You some kind of jock?" Jason asked.

"Yea uh huh, I was in high school. Since then I have discovered if I do not exercise I get pretty heavy pretty fast,"

I explained, "I have to keep on it, like I said I am heavier than I like right now."

"You have a pretty stocky build, you'd have to gain a lot of weight to notice it," Jason commented.

"No, huh uh, unfortunately it shows right away," I said. We sat, poured a cup of coffee, we did not say much. We just kind of looked at each other quietly.

"Butuful morning is it not?" I said cheerfully.

"I guess. I haven't really looked yet."

"When do you get off today?" I asked eagerly.

"Oh, around three probably, maybe earlier."

"Want to get together this afternoon and do something?" I asked.

"Guess we could. Why don't I give you a call when I get home Derrek?"

"Yea, uh huh, sounds good." We got up and Jason got ready to leave. We walked to the door together. I stopped and gave him a hug and a big kiss. "Talk to you this afternoon."

"Ok. I'll give you a call." Jason replied.

"I will be looking forward to hearing from you." We walked out the door, got into our cars, and drove off. Clem jumped in my lap. When I got home Clem and I went for our usual run around the neighborhood. We came back in and I read the paper and drank another cup of coffee.

I was not able to concentrate on the paper. I was thinking about Jason. I thought about what things we could do that would be fun. I got up and got ready to go to some of my accounts. I spent the morning going to the appointments I had made and making calls on a few new accounts to check progress. At lunch I checked the movies currently playing, and tried to think of some place to go out to dinner that would be nice. I had some ideas in mind for when Jason called so we could decide what we wanted to do. I went back to my office to complete some paperwork.

When Jason called, we decided to meet at a restaurant that was in-between our two places, and go from there. During dinner we decided to drive back out to my place and watch television. The next few days we went back and forth between our places. We spent time with each other going out to dinner, to Bobs, Jason's favorite bar, or the Twenty-one for drinks on the weekend and just staying home watching television on the weeknights. We came to an agreement in that time that we would spend one night at his place and one night at my place. We also came to the agreement that whoever fixed dinner, the other cleaned up. At the end of the first week I realize that I was beginning to have feelings for Jason.

One night we had been out and he was supposed to stay at my house, but he had forgotten his contact lens solution. I offered to go buy some, but Jason went home instead. We did not spend the night together, I felt a little hurt and realized that I indeed did miss being with him for the night. The next day Jason called, and I did not answer the phone.

I felt angry and hurt, and did not talk to him that day at all. The following day he came out to the house to leave me a card. I saw him arrive, went to the door, and asked him to come in. We talked and I explained to him I had felt a little hurt and angry. That I thought I was beginning to fall in love with him. He said he had felt scared and that was why he did not stay the night, because of the feelings he felt he had. We decided to spend that night apart and do some thinking about how we each felt.

Being home alone felt awkward! I thought a lot about Jason. Some of my anger was because I had feelings and my own concern that developing feelings so soon was a bad idea. But it was something I wanted to continue to see where it was going.

When we talked the next day we both decided we were beginning to have feelings for one another and that we wanted to continue to see each other. We made plans to meet at his place that evening and talk more.

Our conversation ended with us making love. From that day we spent every night together. Over the next couple of weeks I surprised Jason twice. Once I stopped in at the restaurant he worked at and had lunch. The other I stopped by his place unannounced in the middle of the afternoon, on his day off. I was between appointments and decided to surprise him. It was worth it. We ended up making love spontaneously.

Over the next few weeks as we were together driving places, I pointed out where I had gone to school, where my parents lived, accounts I had, and places I had lived. We drove into the hills a couple of times to be away from the city, and took walks along the canal by my house. It seemed like no time had passed when we realized it had been a month. I wanted a celebration, so I bought a card and one red rose to take to Jason's house.

"Lord, Clem, I told Jason I would be at his place by six! I am running behind schedule again!" I got ready to leave, gathered up Clem, the rose, the card, and left the house. I got in my car and drove as fast as I thought I could get away with to make up time. When I arrived at Jason's place, I hurried to the door with Clem.

"Hello Derrek. Come in."

"Hi honey. Sorry I am late."

"That's ok. I was late getting home from work and it gave me a few minutes to relax."

"That is good." We walked in the door, Jason petted Clem and we went into the living room. I hugged Jason and gave him a kiss. I handed him the card and rose, "Happy first month, I love you."

"I love you too." He read the card and gave me a kiss and a hug. "I like this saying '*I wasn't looking when I found you . . . but I'm glad I did. Love, Derrek*'. And a rose how nice."

"I thought one month, one rose." I smiled.

"That was nice of you. So where is it we are going?"

"Well, I thought I would take you out to dinner at that little cafe downtown, will that work for ya?"

"That's fine." He walked into the kitchen, put the rose in a vase, and came back out to the living room with an envelope in his hand. "Here, this is for you."

I opened the envelope and read the card. I was feeling happy that he had got me a card. "Thanks honey. It is a nice card. Nice saying *'I wasn't looking when I found you . . . but I'm glad I did. Love Jason.'*" I gave him a kiss and a hug, and he lifted me off the ground. "Well, ready to go?"

"Yea sure I'm ready." Jason said. We hugged and kissed again and went out to my car.

"You know Derrek," Jason said when we got into the car, "I was thinking today, my lease is up soon and I really don't want to renew it. I am getting tired of traveling the distance back and forth between our places. Maybe I should look into renting a place closer to yours."

I was hoping this was a hint to see if I would ask him just to move in with me! "To tell you the truth I was wondering how you would feel about just moving in with me when your lease is up. I have fallen in love with you."

"And I love you. I have thought about living with you, but it is your place."

"I would like it if you would. Tell you what, I was thinking of redecorating my place, and I would like you to be a part of helping me on that. We could redecorate it before your lease is up so that when you moved in it would be a place we decorated together, it would feel less like my place, and more like our place." I looked over to see the reaction on his face. He was smiling.

"I really like the idea. It would make me feel more comfortable living there."

"Does his mean you will move in with me?"

"Let's talk about it some more. The idea sounds good." Jason smiled.

"Yeah, uh huh, we can talk more. I am willing to compromise on it." We arrived at the cafe and went in. We were seated and looked over the menu. I was trying to decide what to order.

"Derrek, would you be willing to put your house up for sale?"

"To tell you the truth, no I would not. I had that place custom built so that my office was attached to the house, but had a separate entrance so clients that came to the house would not have to enter the house. I was thinking at the time I had it built that if ever I had a lover I would want the office space separate from the house for his sake as well as mine. I do not think we could even find anything comparable that would be worth the money we would spend."

"I suppose that is true. Your office is separate from the rest of the house for the most part, just that one door off the hall."

"Yea, uh huh, and I have a private walk that goes to the office and not to the house, too."

"I know. I guess I just feel it would always be your place."

"Tell ya what, that second bedroom is furnished as a guest room, but I have never really used it. We could make that your room to do with as you want."

"That would be fine. But, what if we ever had guests?"

"We could turn one of the other bedrooms into a guest room. The basement is finished. A guest room could be down there. That could be part of the redecorating." The waiter walked up and asked if we were ready to order. "Could we have a few more minutes?"

"Certainly sir." And the waiter walked off.

"Well, Derrek, let's order and let me think about this during dinner."

"Yea, uh huh, that is fine. What sounds good to you?"

"Uh, I'm not sure. Let me look at the menu a little more."

"I think I will have the New York steak," I said, "sounds good to me."

"I think I'll try the prime rib." The waiter walked back and we ordered. We just stared at each other while we waited, both in deep thought. This was not exactly the way I had imagined the evening's conversation, but it was exciting to think that we were talking about living together. After dinner we walked to the car and started for Jason's.

"Thanks for dinner. Could we pick up Clem and go back out to your place?" Jason asked.

"Yeah, uh huh why is that?"

"I need to see your place in person to picture in my mind how we could change it around and what it would look like."

"Sure. I really think with some redecorating it would look entirely different. If we made the plans together, it would almost be like getting a place of our own."

"That's why I want to go back out to your place, so I can look at exactly what is there and think about what we could do." Jason explained.

"Yea, uh huh, we will get Clem and go back out to my place." I was wondering what kind of changes Jason wanted to make. I had been thinking of carpet, paint, window coverings, maybe new furniture. I wondered what he was thinking of, but I did not want to ask, I would let him tell me. We stopped to pick up Clem. Jason got is car and drove out to my place. We pulled into the garage about the same time.

"Imagine meeting you here." I said.

"Imagine that."

"Here we are. So what kind of ideas did you have honey?"

"I don't exactly know. Let me look around and think." Jason looked around the room.

"You want something to drink, cup of coffee, water, pop, something stronger?"

"Glass of Coke is fine." He turned and started to look at the living room. I walked back to the kitchen to get us both a glass of Coke. When I went back to the living room Jason was not there. I sat on the couch and waited for him to come back. In a few minutes he returned.

"I could put my bedroom set in that second bedroom. I think it would look fine in there, and we could sleep in there sometimes. I do like my waterbed better than your mattress. My couch and love seat could go in here. I think they are a little newer than yours."

"Yea uh huh, what else?"

"How would you feel about re-carpeting the living room and the hall? Maybe even repaint and change the color?" He said hesitantly.

"That is basically what I planned on doing. Anything else?"

"Let me think." Jason sighed. I was relieved that we seemed to be on the same track for the most part.

"Did you look at the basement again?"

"No, I haven't yet. I was still thinking about the main floor." He walked over to me and put his arms around me. He gave me a kiss and a hug. "This is a nice first month gift. Not one I expected, but one I am happy with."

"Me too. Look around some more and then we can talk about the changes you want to make and the changes I was thinking of making and go from there. Okay?"

"Ok Derrek. I think I'll wonder around again, look and think."

"Yea uh huh, I will sit here and let you think." We spent the rest of the evening discussing making changes in the house and talked about what each of us thought would be best. We decided to think about it over night and talk again later. Jason wondered off again, I went and let Clem out again while I waited for his return.

"Derrek, would you come in here?"

"In where?"

"The master bedroom."

"Yeah, uh huh. Let me get Clem in first." I walked to get Clem and then back to the bedroom. I was expecting

Jason to have something he wanted to change in there and instead I found him naked on the bed waiting for me.

"Why don't you join me?"

"Yea, uh huh." I turned out the lights, undressed and climbed into bed with Jason.

"I think it will work. I guess putting my things in here, and changing things around a little it would feel like ours."

"I think so too. Does this mean you have decided to move in with me?"

"Yes, I guess it does."

"Well, this is a nice first month's gift for me!" I gave him a hug and kiss. "I love you honey."

"I love you too." We cuddled up to each other exhausted and slept. The next morning when the alarm went off I lay in bed daydreaming while Jason took a shower. I got up when I heard the shower water turn off and went to the kitchen to make a pot of coffee. I even scrambled some eggs for Jason. As I set the table, Jason came into the kitchen.

"I wondered where you were."

"I thought I would fix you a little breakfast today."

"Oh, thanks. I usually don't do breakfast, but for you I will." We sat at the table to eat. "I do think I will feel better if we change the house around. I'm glad you offered that."

"Yea uh huh, I think you will feel fine. I am excited about living together."

"Derrek, what is with that ball cap? Every morning you have that on. Why?"

"It covers my messy hair. That way no one can tell if I have showered or not."

"I think your messy hair is sexy. You don't need the hat around me anyway." We ate breakfast and had another cup of coffee.

"I need to get going Derrek."

"Yea, uh huh call me later and let me know how your day is going."

"I will." Jason got up from the table and got ready to leave. I walked him to the garage door, and hugged him good-bye. "Talk to you later. Have a good day."

"Talk to you later. You have a nice day."

As Jason drove off I went back into the house. Clem greeted me with a bark and I put him out. I poured myself another cup of coffee and read the paper. I was excited about Jason moving in. We needed to get started on this project soon. I felt tired, so I got Clem in and went back to bed for a while.

Over the next couple of days we came to some final decisions about what changes to make. I scheduled the remodel through my business and arranged for the work to be done. Most of the changes were simple. It would just take timing and patience to get everything completed.

I also began to change some of my usual habits. I was not taking an afternoon nap anymore, instead I was going back to bed for a while after Jason went to work. I went back to running every morning and doing aerobics. The house was in various states of mess and uproar as the workers put in a half wall in the dining room, painted, carpeted, installed vertical blinds and whatever else they had to do.

Thanksgiving the house was almost finished. We had plans to go to dinner at some of Jason's friends. I had a terrible cold and we had to cancel our plans. Jason was disappointed, but he came by with a take out dinner late in the morning. We were both exhausted having been so engrossed with the house remodel and work. We relaxed, both having a day off together for once. We spent the afternoon watching television while lying in bed. Jason played nurse and brought me aspirins and cough drops throughout the day. Late in the afternoon he decided I needed a sponge bath and that turned into the most fun I we had had for a while.

Middle of December the house was completed. Since Jason was moving in, I decided to go out with Colt one last time *single*. Colt fixed dinner at his house. As we ate dinner I talked about the house and plans Jason and I had. We ended up not going out, but staying home instead and talking. It was a nice evening, but I did miss Jason. He had gone out with his best friend too. Colt and I caught up on life, and I explained all the changes to the house and he talked about school.

Moving Jason's things into the house was a chore. We had talked about having everything moved by a moving company, but then decided that perhaps we should do it ourselves. Since neither one of us had a truck, I decided to call Colt and see if he would be so kind as to lend us his pickup.

"Hello."

"Hello Colt, this is Derrek."

"Hi Derrek. What's up?"

"Wwweeellll, I have a favor to ask you."

"Soooooo, fire grisly."

"You know the house was being redecorated so that when Jason moved in it would be more ours and less mine."

"Yes I remember, so what's the favor?"

"You are my best friend in the whole world Colt."

"Yea, I know that line, what do you want?"

"Well, we were wondering," I paused dramatically.

"Get to the point Derrek!"

"Could we borrow your truck tomorrow to move Jason's things in?"

"After all that I don't know. Seems like a really big favor." Colt teased.

"Ah, come on Colt, I will fill it up with gas, and take it to a car wash and make sure it is returned spotless." I pleaded.

"Just teasing, sure you can but, one of you will have to take me to school, or pick the truck up at school." Colt responded.

"Actually, I thought if you would not mind, I would come and get the truck tonight, and give you my car to drive tomorrow."

"That's fine. Are you sure you trust me with your expensive car?"

"Yea, uh huh do you trust me with your truck?"

"Yes, I do. You've borrowed it before."

"And you have driven my car before."

"I know. Just not to school. Do you want some help moving?"

"I will see. When you get home from work tomorrow, we will see how far with moving things we are. If we are not done, I would appreciate that help on that."

"Ok. That's fine. What time did you want to get the truck?"

"I would like to come right now. Will that work for ya?"

"Sure. You want me to keep Clem tonight and tomorrow?"

"Yea, uh huh, if you would not mind."

"I wouldn't. Guess I'll see you in a little while then."

"Very shortly."

"Tell Jason hi. Bye."

"I will, bye." I hung up, told Jason hi for Colt, got Clem and went to get the truck. Colt was in his garage taking the tonneau cover off the bed of his truck when we arrived. I got the truck, said bye to Clem, and went back home. Jason and I spent the evening putting things in boxes and moving small things first.

The next morning we got up early and started to move the remaining things to the house. We had not made quite enough room for everything he had. As we brought more stuff over, we found we had to make more room by rearranging the furniture. That slowed us down. We were still moving when Colt pulled up. He had Clem, Max, and dinner. We took a break and ate.

He helped me finish moving Jason's furniture over while Jason began to put assorted items away at the house. It was a relief to have help! It made the move much easier. That first night of Jason being "permanently" there we were so tired we just went to bed. For the next few days we really did not get to enjoy the house. We were busy unpacking, rearranging, and putting the house in "order".

Getting Jason's stuff placed in the house took some time. We arranged and re-arranged until we were both comfortable. After we got his stuff settled I thought I should do some kind of a moving in party. So I decided to make our anniversary of two months be the time we celebrated the move as well as the two months.

I had one idea when I was clearing out drawers in the bedroom to make room for Jason's things. I ran across a cloth fig leaf Colt had given me as an April Fool's gift one year. It gave me an idea for a surprise for Jason. We went out to dinner that evening, Jason's treat to me, and came home to enjoy the redecorated house.

"Thanks for dinner honey, I really enjoyed it."

"You're welcome." Jason replied.

"House looks good, huh." I observed.

"Yes, it does."

"I bought some fire wood today, would you mind starting a fire? I will be right back." I said.

"Sure, that sounds good. It is cool in here."

While Jason started a fire, I slipped into the bedroom, stripped, and tied the fig leaf on. Picked up the two roses and the card I had hidden, and walked back to the living room. Jason was sitting on the love seat in front of the fire and did not notice me. I walked up behind him and stood there a minute.

"Uh hum." I cleared my throat to get his attention. He turned around and looked startled. I handed him the roses and the card.

"Thank you." He opened the envelope and read the card, staring at me out of the corner of his eye. "Nice card. You have anything on under whatever that is?"

"It's a fig leaf. Why don't you look for yourself?" Jason turned and slowly lifted the fig leaf.

"Guess not. Interesting get up. Where did you get that?"

"Oh, as an April Fool's joke, Colt gave it to me one year."

"Somehow that doesn't surprise me."

"Yea, uh huh, I thought you might like it." With the warmth of the fire and being next to naked, I was getting excited. I guess Jason noticed, because he certainly reacted positively to the situation. He stripped, then untied the fig leave from my waist, and tied it to his waist.

"Well, what do you think?" he said to me as he shook his hips back and forth.

"Does look a little odd seeing it on someone else." I commented. We made passionate love on the floor in front of the fire and then watched the fire burn.

"Happy second month honey." I said.

"Happy second month to you too. I can't believe you wore that!"

"I thought it would be different."

"I'm not sure I like it, but it does leave little to the imagination." Jason commented.

"Yea, uh huh, I guess. Not to change subject, but this place sure does look different. I think this is the first time in the week it has been finished, and that you have lived here, I have really stopped and noticed." I said to Jason.

"It does look nice. I guess this is the first time I have really stopped and looked myself. I do feel like it is ours and not yours. The changes did help a lot."

"I am glad. I bought a bottle of wine, would you like some?" I asked.

"Sure, a celebration bottle of wine?"

"Yeah, uh huh." I retied the fig leaf on, and went to the kitchen to get glasses and the wine.

"While you are up, would you mind getting a vase with water for the roses?"

"Yea, uh huh, sure." I carried the wine, two glasses and vase to the living room and sat next to Jason. I poured him a glass of wine, and one for myself, and put the roses in the water.

"To two months of life together." I toasted.

"Two months. Cheers." We took a sip of the wine Jason reached over and lifted the fig leaf once again. "Interesting idea."

"Yea, uh huh, I think so. I really am happy you are living here now. It feels less hectic knowing we do not have to travel back and forth."

"I'm glad I'm here too. It is less hectic than traveling back and forth!" We embraced and smiled at each other. I pulled the comforter off the couch and we snuggled on the floor in front of the fire to watch it burn.

"Another glass of wine?"

"Please." I sat up and leaned over to get the bottle of wine. Jason sat up and I poured his glass and then mine.

"I love you Jason."

"I love you, too, Derrek." Jason put another couple of logs on the fire reached over and again lifted the fig leaf and smiled. We kissed. The idea of having him living here, and sitting in the living room in front of a cozy fire stirred me up again. I found myself making love to Jason again. I had gotten over being nervous and embarrassed! It was difficult to believe that just one month ago we were discussing the possibility of his moving in, and now it was a done deal. The celebration was a little more romantic than last month.

I stood up to put another log on the fire and saw through the window it was snowing. "Look honey, it is snowing."

"The perfect night for a fire, it is comfortable and warm inside, blowing snow and cold outside."

I let Clem out in the yard to play in the snow. He ran and ran and got covered in snow. When I let him in the house, he shook off and sat by the fire. The three of us sat and watched it snow and enjoyed the fire.

With Jason living with me a topic kept crossing my mind that I had not really brought up previously. I wanted to know if Jason had been tested for HIV recently. I decided I had to ask. It was close to the holidays and I wanted to discuss it before the holiday season really began. One night after dinner I just burst out with my concern.

"Jason, I have a question for you."

"Yes, what is it Derrek?"

"How long has it been since you were tested for HIV?"

"Awhile, why?" Jason asked.

"Because I think, it is important to know."

"When was the last time you were tested?" Jason asked.

"Just before we met. I want to go back in again soon. Why don't you go with me?"

"Derrek, I'd rather not know."

"Jason, that is not a very good attitude."

"Maybe not. I just don't feel sick, and I don't see the point."

"Feeling sick is not a reason to be tested. It is for your own good. There are some preventive things they can do now if you test positive." I explained.

"I don't want to go."

"Uh huh, but I want you to. I would like to know."

"It's my life, not yours."

"It could very well be my life."

"How Derrek? We practice safe sex."

"So, condoms break, things could happen. Do you see my point?"

"I guess. I just don't want to know is all." Jason said.

"Yeah uh huh, but if we test negative for a years time and stay together we could have unprotected sex. Wouldn't you like to get to a point we could do that?"

"I suppose. I could go with you."

Later in the week we did go in. The wait to find out the results was a killer. The wait always seemed longer than it really was. But the day finally arrived when we found out.

"Well, what were your results Derrek?"

"Negative again. And yours?"

"Negative! I am relieved."

"Now, Jason, was it not worth it to find out?"

"Yes, I guess it was Derrek. Let's celebrate."

"Good idea. What would you like to do?"

"How about getting a bottle of champagne?"

"Yea uh huh, sounds like a good idea." We did go home and have a good evening. It was a relief to know we were both negative. We had a chance to have a normal sex life in the future.

Our life of living together began to flow. We established some routines and the idea of being a couple became normal. One morning when Jason did not have to work, and I had to leave early, he decided to sleep in later. I went out to the living room and removed all the light bulbs from the lamps. I then went into the kitchen and removed all the light bulbs from the light fixtures and appliances.

I knew Jason would get up shortly after I left to have a cup of coffee and then go back to bed. I put garlic salt in the coffee pot and hid the coffee can. In its place I left a little coded note to help find where I had hidden the coffee. I left for work and wondered what Jason would say when I got home. I loved pulling practical jokes on friends and family.

My early morning was busy. I had to drive to several different sites to solve problems. On my way from one account to another the phone rang, it was still dark out.

"Hello Derrek here."

"Damn you Derrek! You jackass!" Jason shouted in an angry voice.

"And a good morning to you too dear." I said lovingly.

"Don't you good morning me! You and your damned practical jokes!"

"What jokes sweetie dearest? I don't know what you are talking about."

"You know damn well what I mean. The garlic coffee, no lights in the living room, the kitchen, or the fridge. Hidden coffee. Cute Derrek, cute. Now where in the hell are the lights? And where is the coffee. This coded map and message makes no sense to me, I am not in the mood to try and decipher it holding a flash light." Jason continued to shout angrily.

"Aren't we a little cranky this morning?"

"Yes, we are! Very damned cranky! You didn't help much with my mood."

"The lights are in the hall closet. The coffee is in the laundry room. I did not mean to make you angry. I was just playing a little joke."

"Pay back is a bitch darling. You wait." He said coldly.

"Now is that any way to talk? It sounds like you are threatening me."

"Oh it's no threat, it's a goddamned promise. You just wait."

"I'm sorry Jason. Calm down. I have to go right now, but I will be home in about an hour. I am sorry my joke didn't make you laugh."

"Perhaps I'll see the humor in it later. I'll let you go."

"Talk to you later. Bye."

"Good bye."

The next couple of days I kept expecting something to happen. I was just sure Jason was going to pull a joke on me right away. He kept telling me to watch it. With the holiday season upon us Jason began to work long hours. He helped with a catering service for a while. One night he had to do a party that was late at night for executives. I knew he was going to be late, so I decided to go to bed to take a nap and get up when he got home.

I was sound asleep when a loud noise woke me up. I sat up in bed to see the lights were on, the television on and so was the radio! I could not think. I knew I had shut the television off before I fell asleep. I had not had the radio on at all. As I woke up a little more I began to realize I had been paid back. Getting up I found a timer hooked up to the television, lights, and radio. A note was attached, "*Pay back is a bitch aint it hon?*"

I turned off the television, radio, lights and went back to sleep. When Jason got home I was still asleep. He came in and woke me up, obviously wondering if his gag had worked.

"Sleep ok dear?"

"Yea uh huh, just fine. Why do you ask?"

"Oh no reason just wondering." As he got undressed, he tried to casually look and see if the timer was still in position. I had left it in place.

"So, how was the party?" I asked.

"It was ok. A bunch of loud noisy people drinking, celebrating the Christmas season. You sure you slept ok?"

"Yeah, uh huh, fine. Why do you keep asking?"

"Oh, no reason. I just wondered."

"It's killing you is it not? Not knowing if your little joke worked or not?"

"What little joke?" He blushed and grinned.

"Oh, the tv, radio, and the lights."

"Oh, something wrong with the tv, radio and lights?" Jason said as his face turned brighter red.

"No huh uh, not at all. Pay back can be a bitch though hon."

"Oh, so you did find the note?"

"Yea uh huh, I did. Cute dear, cute. I would say we were even." I said to boost his ego.

"I'm not so sure about that Derrek, but at least I did pull a joke on you. Being even, I don't think so."

"Yea uh huh, you did. And for that we are even"

For the time being that was the end of the jokes on one another. As the hostility over my little joke faded away, Christmas came creeping up on us. Colt and I decided to go buy Christmas trees together while Jason was at work. We went to pick out one for his place and one for Jason and me. I helped him decorate his, and then came home, and Jason and I decorated ours.

We got out his boxes and my boxes of ornaments. We began to hang them on our tree. Jason was concentrating so seriously on where to put some of his ornaments I could not resist myself, I quietly stripped, and hung some of my ornaments from my body hair. I wrapped a strand of lights around my waist and let them dangle between my legs. I plugged the lights in and began to sing, "Oh Christmas Tree, Oh Christmas Tree," and Jason turned around to see what I was doing.

"You had better unplug those lights before you burn something very near and dear to your heart." Jason said. "You make quite the unusual tree."

"Well, I was hoping to get a rise out of you." I said.

"Well I would say you gave yourself a rise." Jason said looking at me. The obvious break happened in the middle of decorating the tree. Eventually we got the tree trimmed and sat back and admired our work.

Jason had car trouble several times that week. After taking his car to a mechanic, he decided he needed to buy a new car. One afternoon he just came home with a new car. I was kind of surprised he just bought a car without me, but I knew he was frustrated with the problems he was having. He wanted an economy car, but one not too small. He ended up with more of a midsized sedan, but he was quite pleased with his purchase.

We began to discuss gifts. We decided not to buy one another many gifts, and instead have a Jacuzzi bathtub put into the master bathroom as our gift to one another. We went to Colt's for Christmas Eve dinner. Sampson and Ron were also there and the five of us went downtown to see the lights. As a surprise for Jason, Ron, and Colt, Sampson and I had rented a horse-drawn carriage to ride around in downtown. We all had a great time riding in the carriage. Jason, Colt and Ron were surprised.

Christmas day we spent alone together. We just enjoyed having time off from work and relaxed. Jason cooked a dinner and we watched television and built a fire. New Year's Eve we had Sampson, Ron, Colt, and Leo, Jason's best friend, over. We all played games and drank into the night. Everyone spent the night, including everyone's dog. New Year's Day we again stayed home, just watched football games, and built a fire.

"That is quite the roaring fire you have going there." Jason said.

"Yea, uh huh, certainly is. Makes this room very warm huh?" I replied. "You know speaking of hot we need to schedule getting that Jacuzzi tub installed."

"Yea, we certainly do. I am so looking forward to having that in the house." Jason said.

"I will call tomorrow and get that set up."

The next morning I did call, and discovered that installation would not be for several weeks. I was disappointed, but what can you do but wait. Our third month together was soon. I was hoping perhaps we could get the tub installed by that date. In the mean time we decided to rent a room at a lodge that had mineral springs. I managed to get an appointment set up to have the tub installed the weekend we were gone. That would be a surprise to Jason when we got back.

For our trip, we both took some time off work so we would have 4 days to relax and drove up to the lodge to get away. The drive was beautiful, lots of snow on the ground, beautiful scenery. Jason and I seemed to be in our own worlds as we drove. I was looking forward to time away alone with Jason.

"Derrek this is a nice place. Have you ever been here before?"

"No, I haven't. Colt is the one who suggested this place."

"It seems nice. What were you telling me about private rooms?"

"Colt said if we didn't want to go into the public caves that you can rent private rooms and sit in the mineral water in private."

"I'd like to do that I think."

"Yea uh huh, I would prefer a private room as opposed to the public caves. I do not really want to sit around naked with a bunch of straight men."

"Oh, come now, it could be interesting." Jason teased.

"And embarrassing." I added.

"Let's check this place out."

"Yea uh huh, sure, ok." We walked around the lodge and around the grounds. It was a pleasant area. Quiet, secluded a peaceful place to get away from the city. We stopped by the front desk and reserved a private room to sit in. It was a nice to be alone with Jason away from our day-to-day experience. We got towels and headed for the private room.

I was shocked at how warm the room was. Now I could understand why the desk clerk said there was an hour time limit on the rooms. You would not be able to handle the heat and steam much longer than that.

"It's hot in here Derrek. I can see why your time is limited to an hour."

"Yea uh huh so can I. The water does feel good. It is good for your skin you know."

"So I've heard. It does feel good."

"And it is so relaxing." Looking at Jason through the steamy air, he looked so cute, so sexy. I began to rub my foot along his leg and up to his thigh. He reciprocated by playing with my leg and moving closer to me. We kissed, and embraced. It was steamy and hot, but we managed to make love anyway. It was an exhilarating experience. We went back to our room and took a nap.

When we woke up, we were hungry. We went down to the lodge restaurant and had dinner. After dinner we went for another walk. As hot as the private steam room had been, it was equally as cold outside. That was just unbelievable to us.

"This is a nice way to celebrate our third month." Jason reflected.

"Yea, uh huh, it is. It is very relaxing here. I am enjoying myself."

"Me too. I noticed a pool in the lodge. Want to go swimming?"

"Sure, why not." We went back to our room, got our trunks, towels, and went for a swim. The pool was almost empty. It was almost like a private pool just for the two of us. I told Jason I needed to go back to the room to get another towel and I would be right back. I actually went back to put three roses on the bed, and the card I had brought along. I almost forgot to take a towel back with me. After we finished swimming, we went back to the room. Jason went into the bedroom ahead of me.

"Roses again. You never forget. I appreciate it."

"I just am so glad we met. I like to do something to show that feeling each month."

"Well, I have something for you. Wait." He walked over to his suitcase and pulled out a box. He handed it to me. I tore it open, and inside was a miniature recorder. I had been complaining lately that I wished I had a small recorder to keep in the car to record reminders and ideas on. So I would not forget them later.

"Thank you honey. This is nice. It's exactly what I wanted."

"You are welcome."

"I'll have to test it out." I played with the recorder for a few minutes. It was difficult to hear my voice. I would have to get used to that. We spent the rest of the weekend relaxing and enjoying the steam room and the pool again. It was hard to leave when the weekend was over. It had been a nice break from the day-to-day routine. I was certainly hoping the tub had been installed while we were gone. I had left Darrin in charge of that project. He had never called my cell, so I figured no news was good news.

When we got home from our trip Clem greeted us at the door. I did a quick inspection of the house to see if all was in order. Jason sat down on the couch to stretch out after the drive and I checked the bathroom. I was so happy to see the Jacuzzi tub had been installed and looked great. I decided we should test out the tub, but I still wanted to surprise Jason. I walked back out to the living room and walked up to Jason.

"Honey, I am kind of sweaty from the car, I think I am going to take a shower."

"Ok, I think I am just doing to stretch out on the couch and relax while you do that." Jason replied.

I walked back to the bathroom and ran water into the tub. As the tub filled, I undressed and slid into the tub to see how it felt. I wanted to turn on the jets, but not until I got Jason in the room. "Jason, could you come find me a bar of soap please?" I yelled out.

"Can't you just get one yourself?" He yelled back.

"Pretty please can you get me a bar of soap?" I yelled back. I could hear footsteps in the hallway, and Jason appeared in the bathroom.

"When did that get installed!" he gasped as he entered the room.

"While we were gone I replied. Come on get in here with me so I can test out the jets!" Jason stripped and slid into the tub with me.

"Wow you have the water hot."

"I know, just trying to repeat the heat from the steam baths at the lodge." I said. We both just sat in the tub and let the streams of water massage our bodies. It was so refreshing to just sit back and let the water move around our bodies. It was worth the wait. We sat staring at one another in the warm water massage.

"Derrek, you have lost some serious weight." Jason mused. "Sitting here looking at you in the tub reminded me of that first night we spent together and you were so shy about being naked. I just realized you have really lost weight."

"Well thank you for saying so. I have been running religiously every morning, and exercising four or five days a week. Just want to look my best for you honey." I said grinning. We got back to the daily routine. Life was going good. Valentine's Day, and our fourth month anniversary were close together, so we decided to celebrate them as one. I decided to go to Ins & Outs and let Darrin help me find something different for Jason.

"Well, will you look who blew into the store?" Darrin commented as I walked in.

"Yea, uh huh, I need something for Jason, for Valentine's Day. I knew you would have many things I could choose from."

"I just got a new item in. Here, come look at this." We walked to a counter and Darrin showed me silk roses in a vase.

"Since when do you carry something as simple as silk roses?" I asked.

"That's what they look like, but they aren't. Watch and learn." Darrin took one of the roses and unfolded it. It was underwear!

"Underwear! I cannot believe it. Yea, that will do great."

"How many boxes can I sell you guy, five, six?"

"No, huh uh, just one Darrin."

"Cheap skate. Ok then, one. They are four packs, do you want assorted colors, or all one color?"

"Assorted I think."

"And here you go sir. Hope Jason likes them! Don't you think you need a bottle of scented massage oil to go with that? Or perhaps you would prefer to purchase a set of flavored condoms?"

"No thank you, Darrin. Just the roses will do nicely." I said.

"Now how is a guy supposed to make a living if his friends can't even splurge a little when they come into the store?" Darrin badgered.

"I reckon a guy will have to do his number on a total stranger instead." I responded.

"Oh, alright, let me ring that up. I hope Jason enjoys the gift." Darrin grumbled.

"Thanks. Enjoy your Valentine's Day."

"I will, thanks for coming in the store."

Jason and I had a romantic candle light dinner at home that he had prepared as a surprise for me. I was anxious for him to see the roses. I bet he would think the same thing I had.

"Good dinner. Now I have something for you." I left and got the box, returned and handed it to him, and he pondered it.

"What is this Derrek?" Jason looked puzzled.

"Open it up and find out!" I was anxious to see his reaction to the gift. He carefully opened the package saving the wrapping paper, and pulled out his surprise.

"Silk roses, four of them, how different." He looked disappointed.

"They are not silk roses exactly. Look at them carefully honey," I suggested.

"Oh my lord! They are underwear!" Jason exclaimed. "How unusual!"

"Yea uh huh I thought they were. Model them for me please?"

"I hate to unwrap them. I want to save them for a while," Jason sighed.

"Well, I guess you don't have to unfold them now. I was just anxious to see what they looked like."

"I could unwrap one of them I guess. Let's see, which one?" Jason chose one of the roses and carefully unwound it. He held them up for me to see. "Very intricate folding to get these to look like a rose." Jason said.

"Yea uh huh I bet it took a lot of work to get the original folding done. Now I bet the person who thought up this idea is rich."

"Probably so, it is an interesting idea."

"So, aren't you going to model them for me?" I asked.

"Guess I could. You have seen me in underwear before though. What's the difference?" Jason questioned.

"For one, because they are silk. For two, because they are the sexiest pair I think you have." I explained.

"Ok, ok, I get the idea." Jason walked off to the bedroom. I played with the other three "roses" while he was changing. It was a very intricate wrap. I wondered how someone ever figured out how to fold them like that.

"Derrek, if you want to see these, come into the bedroom now."

"Yea, uh huh I will be right there." I walked into the bedroom and there Jason was, standing by the bed, in his rose. He seemed to fill them out a little more than he filled his other shorts. I walked over to him and gave him a hug. "You seem to fill these out a little more than any of your other shorts."

"The silk feels good on my skin. I think that caused me to fill them out a little more."

"Oh, I didn't realize that. They look great."

"I think they look hot." Jason looked in the mirror.

"May I touch your rose pedals?" I laughed.

"If you are very careful." Jason giggled.

"Yea uh huh, I will be very careful on that." I reached over and ran my hand down Jason's backside. The silk was exciting to the touch. We turned Valentine's Day into the romantic occasion it has always been thought to be. We did have a great evening. A simple evening home, talking.

We both got very busy with our careers, and enjoyed our free time together in a number of ways. Windy March came, and so did Jason's birthday. On the morning of Jason's birthday I took Jason out to breakfast. I was not able to decide what to buy him, so I took him shopping for a gift. He was somewhat disappointed at first. When we went out to stores, he enjoyed being able to pick out something he wanted.

We spent the day together. I took him to lunch, and we just enjoyed the day we took off to celebrate his quarter of a century mark. In the afternoon Jason went to meet Leo for a drink, and I stayed home to prepare some surprises for him. He was not sure how to take me staying home, but he did not say much.

While he was gone, I picked up the cake I ordered and I cooked dinner for him. I found a banner in the card shop for his birthday, and I put it up in dining room. I got tickets to a St. Patrick's Day party at the Twenty-one that I put inside the birthday card. When he got home, the table was set, the banner in place, and dinner was ready.

"So, this is why you wanted to stay home," Jason said as he walked in.

"Yeah, uh huh. Surprised?"

"Well, not totally. I figured you were up to something. Where did you find a banner saying *'Happy Quarter of a Century'*?" Jason asked.

"Oh, at one of the card shops. You hungry?" I asked.

"Yes, I am. Something smells good in there. Thanks for the banner." He walked over to the table and gave me a kiss. He noticed the card on the table and picked it up. He opened it up and pulled out the tickets. "No wonder you told me not to buy those St. Patrick's tickets. I was almost mad at you that day."

"Yea uh huh I would not say almost. I knew you were mad. I did not know how we could use two sets of tickets. Happy birthday." I hugged him. "Did you enjoy this afternoon?"

"I did. It was fun to be out with a friend for a while."

"That's good. I have dinner ready if you want to eat."

"I'm ready. What did you fix?"

"The same dinner I fixed the first night we spent together. Only this time I got microwave rolls!" I laughed.

Jason was laughing with me. "I'm glad. It was funny that night though smoke coming out of the kitchen and you sprinting to the oven."

"Well, I was embarrassed!" We sat down to dinner, and ate by candle light. I hoped everything turned out ok.

"This is a very good meal. I can tell by the look on your face you are dying to know if I like it or not."

"Yea uh huh, I was. I thought I would take you to a movie after dinner. And then perhaps go for a nightcap."

"Sounds good. What movie?" Jason smiled.

"It's your birthday, you choose." We finished dinner, and while I cleaned, Jason looked at the movies playing.

"I think this comedy is what I want to see. Several people at work have said it is good."

"Yea uh huh what time does it start?" I asked.

"The nearest theater starts at eight. We could make that one."

"Yea uh huh, it is okay by me. I will let Clem out while I finish the dishes. Are you going to change?"

"No, I don't think so, are you?" Jason asked.

"Yea uh huh, I think I will." I got Clem in, changed, and we left. The movie was a good comedy. As we left the theater we compared the parts of the movie we each found most amusing. We talked about how it was left wide open for a sequel.

"It was a good movie. There were so many funny lines I wanted to remember, but can't!" Jason commented as we walked to the car.

"I thought the same thing. Did you want to go for a nightcap, or do something else?"

"A nightcap sounds fun. Let's go to the Twenty-one."

"It's your birthday, wherever you want to go."

We had a couple of drinks and danced. This was the bar we had met at, so it was a special place to finish the celebration. We left before closing and went back home. Jason went to the bedroom to put on his sweats. I went to the kitchen to get the cake.

"Surprise!" I yelled as Jason came into the kitchen. "A birthday cake for the birthday boy."

"It looks good. *Happy 25th* on the cake as well I see. Let's cut the cake and eat."

"Yea uh huh. So you want me to cut you a piece of it now?"

"Sometimes Derrek, your constant teasing! Yes, that is what I just said, let's eat."

"Uh huh, honey, should I cut the cake now?"

"Yes, cut the cake, please!"

We ate cake. I cleaned up the dishes, put the cake away and let Clem out. Jason sat and relaxed. We decided to go to bed. It had been a long day. We got Clem and went to the bedroom.

"Anything else you want to do?" I asked.

"Well, maybe one thing." Jason smiled, and got into bed. I joined him. I knew what he wanted. That was an easy wish to figure out.

A week later he got to use his St. Patty's day party tickets. That was a loud celebration. Lots of green beer, green hats, green food. We had a good time.

April came and went quietly. For month six we bought each other the same gift, six roses and a card. We went out dancing. The rest of the month was work and getting into spring. May brought with it my birthday. Our seventh month anniversary was the day after my birthday. The two celebrations got intertwined. Jason took me to breakfast. We both worked, and after work we went to a movie. He bought a little music player, a shirt and shorts for summer. He fixed dinner, and asked me to join him for a drive.

"Where are we going?" I asked.

"You'll have to wait and see."

We ended up headed for downtown. I had an idea where we were going. But I was not sure exactly. I waited a few more minutes, and found I was correct.

"Sampson's? Why are we at Sampson's place?"

"Just go with the flow."

"Yea uh huh, whatever." I said.

We walked into Sampson's place. In the living room was the gang to celebrate my birthday. We all talked, I opened presents, and we had a few drinks. I was surprised. I had not planned on seeing the gang. When we got home, I made the same request of Jason he had made of me on his birthday.

The yard was beginning to grow, flowers were beginning to bloom. It was summer. It was so beautiful we decided to have a little get together to share our house with our friends. We invited the gang over, Jason's friends and had a barbecue. Everyone had a great time, and we made plans to have a Fourth of July party.

On the fourth we all got together again, set off fire works, and enjoyed the day. Clem and Max hid from the explosions. There were fireworks flying through the air and exploding all over the yard. We had quite a celebration. I wanted to go away and have a little summer vacation. We had been together ten months almost, so that was my excuse to get away. We agreed to check out a resort area for our trip.

Many resort areas were running specials for their off-season, so we rented a condo, and left the city for the weekend. Driving to the resort we got lost looking for the condos. We discovered we had driven by them once, when we finally found them.

"This place is nicer than what I expected." Jason commented when we arrived. Walking through the condo we were impressed with the layout. I had not realized these were rented out in the off-season. We walked up to the loft and looked out the glass doors.

"Yea uh huh, it is set up really nice. I like the idea of a loft bedroom. There is quite a view from the balcony."

"There is even a microwave in the kitchen. All the modern conveniences, including cable tv. I think I can handle two nights here." Jason said.

"Yea uh huh I can, too." We unpacked and went for a walk. It was a beautiful area. We went to buy groceries, came back, and fixed dinner. We had planned to eat out, but the kitchen was so well equipped we ate at the condo. After dinner we went to the village. One of the bars had a live band, so we went in to listen and have a few drinks. It was good to be away from home. It was even kind of enjoyable to be away from the responsibility of Clem.

The next morning we got up early and walked around the village. We stopped and had coffee at a little cafe. The view from the cafe was breathtaking. We spent the morning looking around shops in the village. We had lunch at one of the sidewalk restaurants.

After lunch we walked up a hiking trail and took in the scenery. We came across a little stream in the forest. It was surrounded by so many trees you could only see a few feet away. Jason walked back into the woods to look at the vegetation and I played in the water. I saw a reflection in the water that looked like a naked man. When I looked up, I was correct, it was Jason. He motioned me to follow him, and I did. We walked behind a grove of trees. I took off my clothes as well, and we made love in the dirt.

The weekend seemed to pass by so rapidly. We talked about staying another day, but we really had to go home. On the drive home we made plans to go away for our year anniversary. We decided we wanted to take one of those romantic ocean cruises. A cruise that lasted for two weeks on the open sea, I just hoped I would not get seasick. It was something neither one of us had ever done before.

I sent away for information about one of the gay ocean cruises in the Caribbean or Alaska or Hawaii. We both thought that would be more fun to go on. Now we had to determine which cruise to take. It was hard to believe we were about to celebrate being together for a year on a romantic ocean cruise. It was so exciting.

Interlude I Zee Partee

"You know, talking about how we all met, I am totally dumbfounded we all ever became friends," I said.

"How is that?" Derrek asked.

"Well, you all go to different bars," I responded, "and we have different ideas about how a relationship should be and how life should be in general."

"That's very true," Sampson said.

"Yea, Sampson, speaking of bars, I've always wondered what your fascination with Bobs is!" Darrin asked seriously.

"Well, I'll tell ya Darrin, it's really rather simple. Bobs is indeed a country western bar, with lots of cowboy hats and cowboy boots. I know, but . . . ."

"He can dance next to the man he is with," I interrupted.

"Thank you Colt, but that is only part of it."

"So, what is the other part of it?" asked Derrek.

"If I could finish without being interrupted" Sampson gave me a glare, "the men there are friendlier and aren't plastic like the other bars in this town."

"I disagree with that," Marshall said, "the men at the Hole are not plastic!"

"Uh huh, a little rough and ready maybe?" Derrek joked.

"Now, listen for a minute Marshall and let me finish," Sampson tried to continue, "When I first moved up here, I came from a small town that played only country music. I swore I would never listen to it again. And I did go to the other bars, for a while, to listen to popular music, piano music, or live bands."

"Dude I didn't know that. I find that hard to believe," Darrin questioned.

"Well, it's true. But, I ended up going to Bobs because I liked the atmosphere, and yes, because I can dance next to the man I'm with," Sampson scowled at me again.

"You can do that with popular music, too," Marshall pointed out.

"How often do you hear a slow song Marshall? Once in every ten, fifteen songs maybe?" Sampson pointed out.

"That's true I guess," Marshall agreed.

"Besides, I feel the men at Bobs are more interested in who you are. Not what job you have or what car you drive or how well you are endowed. They are just friendly and genuine."

"Yea, uh huh I guess that is true enough Sampson. I prefer the Twenty-one," Derrek said.

"Why is that?" Marshall asked.

"To tell you the truth Marshall, it is also, I guess, because of the atmosphere. I enjoy the more popular music, and that is what the Twenty-one plays. I have friends that I made from the Twenty-one, and we spend time together outside the bar."

"Yes, but how many men speak to you in a night Derrek? Just the men you made friends with at the bar? Or the ones that are trying to pick up the cute little blond jock?" Sampson interjected.

"I don't think that is true Sampson." Derrek protested.

"You didn't answer my question Derrek. How many men just speak to you to be friendly?" Sampson insisted, "With no intentions of having sex?"

"Lots," Derrek said, "men always speak to me. They are just as friendly as the men at Bobs."

Sampson continued, "But, how many are really just trying to get into the blond jock's pants?"

"I don't think that many. I have Jason, I'm not cruising."

"You are avoiding my point Derrek. Before Jason came along then. Most of the men who spoke to you were really trying to pick you up, right?" Sampson replied.

"I do not think so." Derrek said. "I think the men are just as friendly and genuine as at Bobs."

"And what about the Hole Marshall?" I said to change the conversation.

"Well, Colt, you've been there with me before. I just like the bar. I guess I like the fact it is more of a motorcycle crowd."

"Yea, sure, you just can't stay away from those burly men and their Harley's, that's all." Sampson added.

"That's not totally true Sampson. I moved here from a little town, too. The bars there played questionable music, at best. I still find the Hole the place I like best. Some of the music they play is popular now, and some of the music is from when I first moved here. I like that." Marshall explained. "Mainly I just feel more comfortable there."

"What about the men, are they friendly, plastic, genuine?" I said sarcastically.

"Those men are not plastic, sadistic perhaps!" Derrek teased.

"Wait a minute! The men are friendly. And before you say it Sampson, yes most of them who speak to me are trying to get down my pants. But I like that."

"That's my point Marshall. How many men are truly just interested in you as a friend, a person, a human being and not a piece of meat for the night?" Sampson added.

"I know. However, I do have friends. They are not interested in me sexually." Marshall replied.

"Then there's Colt. He just goes to them all, doesn't matter." Darrin replied.

"What do you expect of a bar fly, an old man hoping to get lucky?" Sampson teased.

"But really you go to them all just because that is where we meet at times." Derrek asked quickly.

"Yes, Derrek, I go to all the bars with each of you. I get to see Sampson's genuine men, Marshall's biker boys, Derrek's GQ crowd and Darrin's leather men."

"Not my leather men. Perhaps men in leather, but not specifically mine!" Darrin threw in laughing.

"Speaking of which Darrin, you only go there in hopes of seeing a naked ass hanging out of leather chaps, admit it," Sampson laughed.

"Oh, you're on to me! I love to see a hairy naked ass!" Darrin replied. "The Circle is a place where leather men go exclusively. And yes, I do like that. We don't get the average fag in the Circle. I frankly like that. Some men are afraid to come into the bar, and those men are best not in the bar."

"Yea, they heard you were in there, and were afraid of being raped, or talked to death," I said.

"Oh right Colt. Worthless queen, some friend you are. I'm over it." Darrin replied.

"What is the average fag Darrin? A man with at least two pierces in his ears, two and a half pets, and thirty to forty house plants he moves around with him like a little family?" Sampson jested.

"Doing your comedy routine Sampson? Cute line," Darrin said.

"I wasn't, but maybe I should and see where I can take it," Sampson mused.

"Darrin, you met Mat at the Circle didn't you?" Marshall asked.

"You know I did!" Darrin replied.

"And where else would he meet someone?" I responded.

"In a dark alley," Derrek teased.

"I tell you guys, I'm over it. Don't call me for any favors again guys," Darrin said sarcastically.

"You know I was just teasing you," Derrek said.

"Yea, I know," Darrin replied, "but, I have made some changes since I met Mat. I've come to the place I'm happy being at home with Mat, and doing things with him and not going to bars at all."

"I have to admit, I do see a change. For once, I'd agree that you are truly in love with someone," Marshall added.

"You even appear to treat him nice. Must be love?" Sampson added.

"Or old age," Marshall added.

"I tell you guys. I'm over it get off my case." Darrin laughed.

"Another round gentlemen?" I asked.

"Oh, why not," Darrin said, "I think everyone's about finished their cocktail. Let me help you fix them so they can find something else to talk about.

Darrin and Matt

In a dark alley! I certainly did not meet Mat in a dark alley. Talked to him in one maybe. That was one night about four years ago. I walked into the Circle, went back to play pinball and check out the video games. Marc and I had just had a huge fight. I was out on the prowl. I saw this hunk standing by the video games. I was instantly in awe with this dude. He was so hot in his leather vest, chaps, and hat. I damn near creamed my jeans, there on the spot.

In a way, he was somewhat heavy, but in his leather he looked hot. He also had one of those really bushy moustaches, and with his dark brown hair, it stood out like a spotlight along with his hairy chest. I was mad at Marc and decided to talk to this dude. I invited him to play pinball, and he agreed to play.

"My name is Darrin, and yours?"

"Mat. Good to meet you. Which game do you want to play?"

179

"I like Shuttle myself. It is more interesting." I said. Mat had a deep husky kind of voice.

"Okay, then let's play Shuttle." Mat said. We put coins in the machine and played. I chose Shuttle because I usually got my highest score on that particular machine. As we played I could see my skills were with me. I matched the highest score before I lost the ball. When Mat took his turn, he played and barely got a third of my score. My following turns I continued to play equally as well. I ended up making a particularly high score.

"Mat, you want to try again?"

"Yea, maybe I can beat you this game." Mat smiled.

We played again, but again I beat Mat. My skills were at their best. I was ready to go again.

"Dude another game?" I asked.

"No, I can see Darrin you are good at this game. How about a game of pool?"

"Sure, I enjoy pool. Want another cocktail?"

"Yes. I'm drinking JD and Coke." He said.

"Me too, only thing to drink, I'll be back shortly guy. Why don't you go get a pool table, if you can?"

"Sure. Meet you at the tables."

I went to the bar, ordered cocktails and watched Mat walk to the pool tables. He was hot. Since Marc thought I was screwing around, hell I might as well. Mat fit my fantasy man. I might as well take advantage of it while I could. I walked back to the pool tables and handed Mat his cocktail.

"Here you are guy, one JD and Coke."

"Thanks Darrin. There's a wait for the pool tables, so I signed our names."

"Ok, that's as good as you can do dude," I said.

"We might have to play as partners, is that agreeable?"

"Guess so dude. Listen, I have to be up front with you. I have a lover, but we are, and have been, fighting lately. I'm out on the prowl, cruising, and you are my target. I don't want to scare you off, but, I have to be honest."

"That does answer one question in my mind. I'm out on the prowl, as you say, as well." Mat said factually.

"I have been accused of having an affair so often, I am going to go home with you, and do what I'm already accused of doing."

"I have no problem with that. There is a definite attraction on my side. I guess there is one on yours!" Mat smiled again.

"Another up front statement. I'm HIV positive. If that bothers you, tell me now."

"I admire your honesty. It doesn't bother me. I'm negative, but I am still game Darrin."

"Good, then that's done. I want to play a couple games of pool, play another couple games of pinball. Get cocktailed and go fuck your brains out guy."

"Well, that about covers it all I think. I find your proposition unusual, but, acceptable." Mat looked almost relieved.

"I am glad that is settled. Let's play pool." We did play several games of pool, pinball, and got cocktailed. I felt like I had worked out my anger at Marc for the most part. I was ready to just enjoy myself. I was getting anxious to see what the rest of Mat looked like anyway.

"Good game Darrin. You must play pinball a lot!" Mat commented.

"Yea, I'm here four or five times a week. I enjoy the games."

"You want to play another game?" Mat asked.

"Naw, not really. I'd just as soon leave, you?"

"I'm ready any time you are."

"I'd say your place or mine, but, you know it has to be your place," I laughed.

"Let's go then." We walked to the door and to the street. We walked into the alley and looked at one another for a minute.

"Where you parked dude?"

"Over across the street, and you, Darrin?"

"Down the alley. Why don't we meet at the corner and I'll follow you?"

"See you at the corner." I walked to my car, got in and drove to the corner. I followed Mat down the street, thinking about Marc. I was certainly getting tired of fighting. Sick and tired of being accused of seeing another man. Now I was, at least one, once. I never have understood why Marc thought I was seeing someone else. We went out together, unless we were fighting. He's the one who drags men home to share our bed. "Three is so much more exciting than two." Anyone I talked to I'd been to bed with. If a friend called, I'd been to bed with him. It's wearing thin. Well, tonight I was just going to forget good ol' Marc existed. I parked behind Mat and got out of the car.

"This is it. My apartment is right here on the first floor." Mat pointed.

"Not much of a view guy. Your windows face the alley way between the buildings."

"No one can see in either."

"True, very true dude." We walked into the building and into his apartment. It was a small place. I guess I was used to the two-story duplex I lived in. I hadn't lived in an apartment in a long time. "Nice place. You like it here, Mat?"

"It's not bad. Someday I want to buy a house."

"Renting is like throwing money to the winds. I know I'm glad I bought a place."

"Someday. Come on I'll show you my bedroom." I followed Mat to his bedroom. It was so small his bed took up most of the room. Kind of wall-to-wall bed. Must be where the original idea for the name bedroom came from. I laughed.

"What's so funny?" Mat asked defensively.

"Nothing. I was thinking your room is wall to wall bed, hence the name bedroom."

"Oh, yea, it is a small room I guess. These old buildings weren't built with a king size bed in mind."

"No, they weren't. So, you still want to get it on guy?" I said.

"If you are concerned because of the HIV positive, it doesn't bother me. You aren't one for much romance are you?" Mat said.

"I can be. Like I told you earlier, I just want to be with another man tonight. That's what I've been accused of doing dude."

"Then, let's get to it. Stop talking and take your clothes off." We both stripped and got into bed. Mat wasn't as heavy looking out of his leather. He was built decently, just very stocky. He was hairy head to toe. Dark skin and decently proportioned. I slid on top of Mat. I started to kiss him and run my hands over his sides. He put his arms around my back and hugged me. We rolled around and let our bodies push against one another. I felt Mat reach for something on the floor. Before I realized what was going on a condom was in place and my hands were handcuffed behind my back. This man was quick. It felt good. Marc always fumbled around whenever we tried to do anything like this. Mat knew he had me under his control. I admired his assertiveness.

I felt him pull me up and turn me over. He lay on top of me. He was surprisingly domineering! He did a number of things to me that I struggled to push away, because of the sensation. With my hands handcuffed behind my back, I couldn't. I found it very exciting. He got me so excited I thought I was going to scream. Instead we both came to a physical explosion. The many cocktails took their toll and I dropped into a deep sleep.

In the morning I woke with my hands and forearms tingling with the sensation of no feeling. I still had on the handcuffs. I looked over to see that Mat was also awake.

"Want to take these off dude?" I demanded.

"Ask me politely." He commanded.

"Would you please take the cuffs off guy?"

"That's better. Sure." He got the key and released my wrists. As the feeling came back into my hands and arms, they began to throb with pain. It felt good last night. Right now, it was very tender and painful. I rubbed my wrists and forearms.

"You ok?" Mat asked.

"A little sore, but I'm ok. That was an interesting encounter we had. Some slick moves guy."

"There are many more I can do."

"I'll just bet," I sighed.

"If you are interested, sometime I'll show you. Want to take a shower?"

"No, I want to go home smelling like the morning after. I want to make a point to Marc."

"It's your life. Want some coffee, or juice?"

"Coffee sounds good."

"I'll go make a pot while you get dressed." He put on a robe and left the room. As I got dressed, I noticed he had a toy box full of all kinds of little sex aids. Things I sold at the store. I hadn't ever seen him before that I could recall. I walked into the kitchen and sat at the table.

"Quite a collection in there, hope you don't mind my snooping."

"No, they are out in the open. I told you I had lots more to offer." Mat walked over and sat down with the coffee. "Here you go."

"Thanks. Could I have some sugar guy?"

"Sure, I forgot to ask. I drink coffee black."

"Do you ever shop at Ins & Outs dude?"

"Yea, why do you ask?"

"The toys in your little toy box. I work at Ins & Outs." I said.

"I don't ever remember seeing you there. What days do you work?" Mat replied.

"Usually Sunday through Thursday."

"I guess I generally go there on Saturday. But not always."

"I work the late shift. I go in around four and work until eleven." I explained.

"I work a late shift, too. I have to do my running around before three in the afternoon."

"Guess that solves that mystery." I finished my cup of coffee and got up to leave.

"You leaving?" Mat asked.

"I need to go. Thanks for the evening. I enjoyed it. Maybe I'll see you again at the Circle dude."

"Perhaps. You never know. Good luck with your lover." Mat winked at me as he spoke.

Walking to the car, I thought that it had been an interesting evening. One of those men you bed once and never see again. Then I remembered Marc. He had grounds for his suspicions now. I was sure we would have a big fight. Especially since I did spend the night out. In all the times he had said I was seeing someone else, I was never out all night. I was now. Driving home I tried to think of how I wanted to handle Marc. Perhaps I would just let him wonder, not answer any of his questions.

When I arrived at the house I pulled into the garage expecting to see Marc's car, but it wasn't there. I went into the house Gent, my dog, greeted me barking and running to the door. No sign of Marc's presence.

"Hi ya boy. Where's Marc? You need out?" I let Gent out and went to our bedroom. The bed hadn't been slept in. I walked through the house. I couldn't find any place that looked like Marc had even been there since the fight last night. No notes, no sign of him sleeping on the couch, or taking a shower. He'd been gone all night, too. He wouldn't know I was gone! I checked the recorder for messages and there were none. If he had called, he hung up when the recorder kicked on.

So, I was screwing around. And what was he doing? I went to the bathroom and took a shower. I got dressed and went to the kitchen to make breakfast. I was getting angrier and angrier. No wonder he was always on my case. He was guilty about himself. So, he kept me off balance by throwing accusations at me! As I put my breakfast on the table, I heard Marc pull into the garage. He walked into the house and stopped at the table.

"You just get up?"

"Not too long ago. Where have you been?"

"After you left last night, I went over to my parents. I stayed there all night."

"And you couldn't call Marc?"

"I tried, but the recorder kept coming on. I figured you either weren't home, or didn't want to speak to me."

"Did you ever think, Marc, I might be avoiding calls in general? That I'd pick up the phone if I heard your voice?" I said hastily.

"No, I guess I didn't think about that."

"How are your mom and dad Marc?"

"Oh, they're fine."

"That's good. So, where do we stand today? You still on the binge I'm bedding someone else?" I felt my voice getting louder.

"I don't know. Let's not get into it again this morning." Marc said.

"All right, fine. You want breakfast? Or, did your mom already fix it?"

"No, she didn't. I can fix my own, thanks."

"What did you tell your folks Marc? You tell them we were fighting, again?"

"I told them we were both angry, that you left the house, and I wanted to be gone too. I didn't say anything else Darrin." Marc sighed.

"I'm going to the living room to watch tv." I snapped.

189

"Go ahead Darrin. I'm having breakfast."

I put my plate into the dishwasher and left the kitchen. At his parents! Huh. If I didn't feel guilty myself, I would have called him a liar. But, I don't want to have to answer any questions about last night either at this point. I'll let this one ride, my courage left me. I sat and turned on the television. I'd just have to catch him in a lie. Or better still, in the act. What a mess!

"So, Darrin, what did you do last night?" Marc said walking into the living room.

I jumped, Marc startled me. "God, you scared me. I didn't hear you come in."

"Sorry. I didn't mean to startle you. Did you go to the Circle?"

"Yes, Marc, I did. I picked up the man of my dreams and had wild and crazy sex with him." I said scornfully.

"Oh, so you watched one of your porn films again, huh." Marc laughed.

"Yea, I watched my skin flicks. Seemed realistic last night somehow though."

"I've got to get to work. We'll talk tonight."

"Sure, whatever Marc." He left the room, went and took a shower. He doesn't believe the truth when he hears it. When I say I've been to bed with someone else, he laughs it off. When I tell him I haven't he gets angry and we fight. It's not worth it, two years together or not. I heard him get out of the shower and go to the bedroom.

"I'm leaving for work. You'll be home around 11:30 right?" Marc questioned.

"Around then, I have to close tonight, and sometimes that takes longer. I'll be here as soon as I can."

"Ok, then, I'll see you tonight." He came into the living room. He leaned over and kissed me on the forehead. I didn't budge or try to kiss him. I just sat there. He turned and walked to the door.

"See you later on," he said as he left.

"Later tonight."

"I'm letting Gent in." He yelled.

"Fine!" I snapped. Gent came bounding into the room. He leaped on the couch beside me. "Hi ya boy. So you were home alone last night. Good thing you can't talk. You would blab all. Want to go for a walk?" From the barking and running up and down the living room, I could tell he did. When he was a pup he fit on the couch with me. Now, a full grown dog, he only fit on the couch alone. I got the leash and we went for a walk.

Marc was so loving when we first met. Then things had gone sour. I guess we just have too many differences. He is a "professional" bank hot shot who works days. I'm just a "salesperson" at a local "novelty shop" and work nights. He "helps people build their lives". I help people "live out their fantasies". Why we ever fell in love, I'll never know. I must admit, he did do a great deal to help me acquire the house, even if it was a foreclosure. That was how we met, at the bank.

"Havin' fun Gent? Sorry you seem to be caught in the crossfire. Dad will try to give you more attention." Poor dog he and I used to walk and play in the park all the time. Then when I met Marc, he was ignored. He was always there, even if Marc wasn't. I felt bad. He was left alone so much lately. We got back to the house and I decided to take a nap before I had to go to work. I felt tired, my arms and wrists still hurt.

Good thing Marc didn't notice the reddish color around my wrists. But, then, perhaps it would have been better if he had. Maybe it was time he moved back to his loft and we went separate ways. I hate living alone, but I hate these constant arguments! I went to bed. Gent went with me. He laid down right beside me and we curled up together. Guess he loved me, no matter what I did, or didn't do.

When I woke up, I realized I had slept most of the day. I had less than forty minutes to get to work. I ran and showered then drove to work. The place was empty and most of the afternoon it stayed that way. During the evening it got very busy. Right at closing time I had a customer with the biggest sale I had ever made. Of course, I talked him into buying extra things he really didn't want. A sale is a sale, and it would be good to show the boss. I was late leaving and getting home. I drove home in the same hurry I had driven to work so that Marc wouldn't be on the rag. I parked in the garage and ran into the house.

"So, where the hell have you been? It's after midnight!" Marc shouted.

"At work! I had a customer come in right at closing buying out the store. It was such a big sale I didn't close on time. I thought it was worth the effort."

"You expect me to believe that?"

"Well, Marc, it is the truth. Believe it or not, I don't care. I'm tired of your attitude problem, I'm over it." I snapped loudly.

"Oh, so it's me!"

"It takes two I guess, but all I did was go to work, do my job and hurry home to get yelled at. No, hello how are you, how was work, nice to see you, nothing like that. Instead I get where the hell have you been."

"You were with someone, admit it," Marc yelled.

"And when did I have time?"

"Well, Darrin, you close at eleven, and it's after twelve now. You tell me."

"Oh, right Marc. A five minute quickie. Yes, you are right, I stopped on the way home, had wild and crazy sex. Then I hurried home so I'd be here by twelve. If I were bedding someone else, I can guarantee you I wouldn't bother coming home at all!"

"Well, if you weren't doing something, what's with the dark marks on your wrists?"

Oh, shit! My wrist had turned black and blue. Dead meat in the water he had noticed. Oh, well, it's time to end this bizarre mess. I'm even thinking about trying to catch the man having an affair. It's not worth it.

"Well, answer me! What's with those marks?" Marc shouted louder.

"I told you. I picked up my fantasy man last night. And we had wild and crazy sex."

"You weren't kidding were you?" His voice faded.

"No, Marc, I wasn't," my voice softened, I felt relieved, "Marc, you have accused me for so long of being with someone else, I finally was. You honestly pushed me hard enough I finally did it."

"Then we are through. I knew you were! It's just you finally have admitted it!" Marc shouted.

"And what about you guy! You protest too much. You are so suspicious, just what the hell have you been doing? Why don't you just admit it Marc, you are the one who has found someone else! You are having the affair. You are just trying to find a way out of this relationship that makes me look like the culprit. You just can't admit you have fallen in love with someone else!" I shouted back.

"How long have you known?" Marc said quietly.

I almost collapsed. It was a stab in the dark, from my thoughts this morning. I really didn't believe what I had thought this morning. It was true. Damn, he was the one having an affair. I was stunned.

"Well, how long have you known?" Marc said louder.

"Not long. It's just been a suspicion, but now I know." My voice was crackling.

"So, what do you want to do about it?"

"Marc, I'd say split up is the best thing to do. If you love someone else, why stay with me?"

"Darrin I do love you. This just happened to me. You are always gone at night and I got lonely. I met this guy one night when I went out to kill time before you came home. I never wanted to hurt you."

"You have. You made it worse by trying to continue to live with me and then accusing me of seeing someone else. I'm numb, Marc. I just want to be alone to think. Why don't you just leave? Go to his place make arrangements to move in, or whatever!"

"No, Darrin, I don't want to leave you like this. Let me stay, let's talk civilly."

"Not now Marc, just leave! Go, leave me alone! I have to get through this by myself, get the hell out!" my voice began to rise again.

"I think I should stay Darrin."

"And I don't! Don't make it worse than it is. Just go. We can talk tomorrow. For now I want you to leave!" I was shouting now.

"Ok, I will. I'll stop by in the morning."

"Fine. Leave for now." He did leave and I went into the living room and threw myself on the couch. He was having an affair. I really hadn't noticed. He had me so wrapped up in trying to prove I wasn't doing anything I didn't even suspect him. I was hurt, but, he had to be out of my life.

At least for now, I couldn't live with him knowing he loved someone else! After being accused for months about screwing around while he was! I got out my mirror, supply kit, and did a line of coke. I got up and fixed myself one extra large shot of JD. I went back into the living room and turned on the television. I didn't want to think about this any more tonight. I wanted to get so trashed I wouldn't feel anything. I did another line of coke. Another shot of JD. I was not going to hurt any more. Not tonight.

Gent was licking me in the face. I opened my eyes and it was morning. Somewhere in there I passed out. I couldn't remember when, the television was still on. I got up and let Gent out. The argument of last night began to replay in my mind. Marc was coming by sometime this morning. I don't want him here anymore. I can manage without him. I'll get over the feelings, eventually. I heard the back door opening. It must be Marc.

"Morning Darrin."

"Hello Marc."

"How do you feel this morning?" Marc asked.

"Not too good."

"Darrin, I never intended to hurt you . . ."

"Don't start Marc. The point is that you did and have. That part is over and done. Now what we have to deal with is the next step. I want you out. I can't handle any more of this. Especially knowing you love someone else."

"Darrin, don't be so fast to jump to a decision. I thought I could stay away for a week and we could both think. Then we could talk."

"What good will that do Marc? Are you going to stop loving whoever he is in a week? Are you interested in changing our relationship?"

"No, I don't suppose I'll stop loving . . ."

"Don't say his name." I took a deep breath. " I don't want to know. If you really wanted to work out our relationship, you wouldn't have gotten involved with someone else. We've grown apart."

"Darrin, you are not being fair. I never set out intentionally to fall in love with someone else."

"But you did. Subconsciously you had a desire to be away from me emotionally. Or this could never have happened."

"You don't understand Darrin, I was alone, you weren't home and it just happened."

"Bullshit Marc. I wasn't home alone during the day? I wasn't here by myself? You think I never got lonely. Did I go out and find someone else to take your place?"

"I'm not so sure you didn't. What about the other night?"

"I'll probably never see that dude again in my life! He is THE only man I have ever seen in the two years we have been together. Even I am willing to admit, that by my action, I also must be subconsciously ready to be out of this relationship. It's over Marc. A week, a month, a year, isn't going to change anything. It's over. I'm over it."

"So, you are saying that you don't love me any more."

"Let's just say that the hurt I feel right now totally smothers the love I once felt. What about the love you feel for what's his name? You can't have us both! Is he willing to live as a part time lover?"

"I do love him. Different from you. I don't know that he wants to be a part time lover. He knows about you though."

"Look Marc, go to him. Decide what you two are going to do. I've made my decision, right or wrong. I want you out. I would rather be alone than try to juggle you and him in my thoughts. I won't do it."

"So, that's your final decision?" Marc replied.

"Do I have to spell it out? What have I been saying? Yes, Marc, that is my final decision!"

"What about my stuff?"

"Take what is yours. Move as much as you can now and get the rest when I'm at work. Leave the key on the counter in the kitchen when you finish."

"Fine! I will!" He stormed off and banged drawers, slammed doors, and gathered his personal things. He came back to the living room and stopped.

"I'll load this stuff in the car. I'll get the rest tonight when you are at work. Is that all right?"

"That's fine."

"I want to call you in a week and talk. Will you talk to me?"

"I can't say right now. Call me and see!"

"I guess this is goodbye then?" Marc glared.

"Looks that way. Goodbye," I said as casually as possible.

"Darrin I . . ."

"Don't say it, please don't say it. Just leave."

He turned picked up the things he'd gathered up and left. I sat there not believing what had just happened. How can something that takes so long to get started, end so fast? It took us months to get together. It took 24 hours to break up. Unreal. I felt empty, abused, and alone. What next? I got up and walked through the house to see what Marc had taken. I couldn't even concentrate on what was missing. I decided to take a nap. I hadn't gotten much sleep the night before. Gent came in and got up next to me.

"Hi ya boy. Want to nap with dad," he licked my face and whined. "It'll be ok. I'll be all right. Don't cry boy." At which point I did cry holding Gent by me.

I rolled over, looked at the clock, and realized it was time to go to work. I had cried myself to sleep and slept all day. I got out of bed and showered. Driving to work I hoped Marc would just come and get his things. Not pull some stunt of leaving his stuff here to assure us having to see each other.

My work day passed rapidly. There were many customers and I was so busy that when I noticed it was time to close, I was astonished and relieved. I hadn't had time to think about much of anything. I closed up and drove home.

As I walked in the door, I was afraid of seeing Marc, or Marc's things still sitting there. On the counter were the keys and a note. *"Darrin-- I do still love you. I never meant to hurt you, but I did. I respected your wishes. All my belongings are gone. I'm staying with my parents if you want to call me. I think I need sometime to get it together before I do anything else. I'll call you in a week. Love, Marc."* I crumpled the note and threw it out. He needed time! He was the one that created this situation.

I walked through the house and took note of the bare spots. The places where things of Marc's used to be. I needed to rearrange so the missing items weren't apparent, but not tonight! Gent came bounding to my side and I let him out. I walked in, turned on the television and sat down. At least he had moved his things. It didn't make me feel good. But I don't see how I could have continued to live this way either. It was over.

I had to start a new life style. It hurt. It stung. I loved Marc, I still loved Marc, but there wasn't any returning to what was or wasn't. It was a scary thought to start over again. I heard Gent barking, I got up and let him in the house. I went back to the living room and turned off the television. I snorted a line of coke and did a shot of JD. I was repeating last night. It numbed the pain and made it possible to forget for a while. What I wanted to do next was a void. Twenty-four hours ago I had plans, some strange, but I had plans.

Now, I couldn't generate enough thought to have a plan. I just didn't want to have to feel or think. So, I did another line of coke and another shot of JD. Life certainly wasn't fair at times and this was one of them.

Then there was the fact Marc was going to call next week. I didn't particularly want to deal with that either. I'm over it and I want to just move on. Not deal with the past. Perhaps when he calls I'll state that fact loud and clear. I drank another shot of JD, and reclined on the couch.

Again I woke up to realize it was morning and I had passed out somewhere between shots and lines. I got up, dressed, and took Gent for a long walk. When we got back home, I went into work early to reorganize the shelves and the stock room. I created a unique new display for our greeting cards.

The rest of the week I did spend staying at home and working longer hours at the store. I continued my numbing routine of shots of JD and lines of coke. It all seemed to blend together. I even went in on my two days off and worked for my relief man. It gave him sometime off. It was a way to get through being alone and angry.

The end of that week the phone rang. I hesitated to answer it. It would probably just be Marc.

"Hello."

"Hi Darrin, its Marc. How are you?"

"Fine, and you?"

"Oh, ok. Darrin, I miss you. I'd like to stop by and see you." Marc pleaded.

"Marc, I don't think so. What's done is done. I have thought about it and I don't want to see you right now."

"I wish you would. I feel like there are some things we still need to settle. We need to talk." He said.

"Marc, we can talk over the phone. What things need settled? You have another love interest. We broke up. I believe it is settled."

"I don't Darrin. I'm not seeing my new love interest for a while. I want to work things out between you and me. I want to try again."

"I don't Marc. I'm over it. You had a chance. You didn't take it. What's done is done. End of story."

"But, Darrin ..."

"But, nothing Marc. Someday perhaps we can be friends, maybe. Some day. For now, I want no contact with you."

"You are being totally unfair."

"Am I? And what were you, a saint? I'm not giving in Marc. That is my final decision. Goodbye." And I hung up before he could say anything else.

I walked into the bathroom and caught a glimpse of myself in the mirror. I looked like shit. In the past week I had abused my body so bad. I had chewed my nails so that there weren't any nails left. I had sat and pulled my moustache out of my face one hair at a time. So many lines of coke, shots of JD had gone through my body. I couldn't even begin to count them. I looked old and haggard.

If I was going to make a change, it was time to make a positive one. It was time to get off the pity pot. I decided to get myself tan. Time to get back to being me and a tan was a good beginning point. I put my swim trunks on, got a towel, went out to the yard and sat in the sun. If felt so good to be in the sun, getting tan. It gave me some time to think. I decided I wanted to call Marshall and go have a cocktail with him. Begin to do things with friends again. I had put in some extra days. I could take a day off. I finally felt like having a day to do nothing. I was beginning to feel like I had enough sun, so I went in. I picked up the phone and called Marshall.

"Hello."

"Yo, Marshall, Darrin. How you doin'?"

"Ok and you? Marc at work?"

"I'm ok. Marc is why I called. We broke up. I was wondering if you could meet me for lunch or a cocktail sometime today guy."

"Sorry to hear that Darrin. Yea, I have today off. You could come by here if you want. Or we could meet somewhere."

"Coming over to your place sounds real good Marshall."

"How about one or so?"

"I'll be there dude." I replied.

"See you then Darrin. By by."

"Later, by." I went back out to the yard. Lunch with Marshall should be fun. I was looking forward to that. Not to mention a home cooked meal. Better than the fast food Mexican places I'd been hitting the last week. I sat back down in the sun to make sure I would have some color.

I woke up to Gent barking. Unfortunately I fell asleep in the sun and I ran into the house to see the time. It was noon. I had to hurry, take a shower and get to Marshall's. When I was in the shower, I realized my chest and legs were a little reddish. Perhaps I had over done one side! I hoped it wouldn't hurt or peel. From the looks of things, it would do both. I got dressed and drove to Marshall's.

On the way over, my waist began to hurt from the rubbing of my jeans against my skin. I began to feel that hot stinging sensation of sunburn. As I walked up to Marshall's front door my knees and calves began to sting from my jeans. I had a sunburn.

"Hello Darrin, come in."

"Hi Marshall. Smells good. What's cooking?"

"I made enchiladas for lunch. I know you like Mexican food."

"Thanks Marshall."

"What happened to you and Marc?" Marshall turned and walked into his living room.

"To make a long story short, he was seeing someone else. I told him I wanted him out."

"Marc! Seeing someone else? Are you sure?"

"Yes, Marshall, I am sure. You know he's been accusing me of having an affair. Well, it was him, not me. Any way, we've been apart a week dude."

"Do you really want it that way?"

"Yes, I do. I felt really down this week. I'm beginning to feel better. Today is really the first day I've made much contact with the outside world. I do feel better."

"I'm sorry Darrin. I hope you made a good choice. I know, when Craig and I ended it, it was a tough decision. I hurt for a long time. Sometimes I still miss him. Hey, have you been out in the sun? Your face is bright red!"

"Yea, this morning. I fell asleep in the sun. My back does not match my front."

"You are really red. Bet that's going to sting later."

"It already does!"

"I have a cream I use when I sunburn. I will give it to you when you leave."

"Thanks guy that would be great." We walked to the kitchen and Marshall served lunch. We discussed Marc and work. It was a good afternoon. I was glad I was there. Marshall talked about how lonely he felt when he left Craig. It made me feel more normal. As I was leaving, Marshall ran and got his cream for my sunburn.

On the way home I stopped and rented a movie to kill the evening. I was beginning to feel down again. Seeing

Marshall and talking about he and Craig, reminded me of doing things with Marc. I needed to do something for myself. But right now I just needed to get through one day at a time.

My sunburn hurt. I used the cream Marshall gave me. It hurt to put it on my skin, but felt cool after it was on. I used the cream for the next few days, I did peel and itch. But I ended up with a nice tan on one side anyway. It was the beginning of getting back to my own life. The next few months I had periods of being at work constantly and periods of being with Marshall or Colt. I worked on maintaining my tan on my days off. I worked some long hours and the time I spent at work paid off. I was promoted to manager of the store. Spending time with Marshall and Colt made me feel good. I had made the right decision about Marc, much as it hurt.

I began to do things for myself. I ran across an old Lincoln for sale, one I had always wanted, and bought it. It wasn't in too bad of condition. The engine and transmission had just been rebuilt. The interior and the paint were in bad shape. But, I decided I would have them redone and the car would be as it had just been driven off the showroom floor. That project gave me a mission and made me feel good. My friends began to refer to the car as "Dos Boat" it was so big. I enjoyed driving it, big or not.

For the next month or so my time was spent getting the interior replaced and having the exterior repaired, painted and polished. I was so happy with the end results. My new project got me through a rough time.

I hadn't heard from Marc, after all his I love you statements, since the phone call the week after we broke up. I hadn't seen him either. That was just fine. It seemed like we had just split up yesterday in some ways. Yet it had been three months. I couldn't believe it was October already! Then one day at work a voice I vaguely recognized came from behind me.

"Hello Darrin, how are you?"

I turned around and looked to see Mat standing there, "Well, hello, how are you guy?"

"Fine. It's been awhile. So, how are you and your lover doing?"

"We split up three months ago, dude."

"Sorry to hear that. Must be difficult?"

"It's getting better. Turned out he had an affair going on the side. I figure it was only a matter of time anyway. And you, still single?"

"Yea, Prince Charming hasn't ridden in on his white horse yet."

"Maybe one day soon. May I show you anything?"

"Not really. I was thinking about you, had the day off, and took a chance you'd be working. I came down to see you."

"Why? Something I can do for you?"

"Actually there is. You were direct and to the point with me. Let me be direct with you. I want to take you home and 'fuck your brains out' I believe you put it."

"You do? What if I'd still been with Marc?"

"It was a chance I had to take. I really wanted to see you again." Mat said.

"I'm flattered. I am ready, willing and able, tonight too soon?"

"Not soon enough. What time do you get off?"

"Eleven. Takes me about twenty minutes to close the place down and clean up."

"How about just cutting to the quick? Why don't you come by my place after work?"

"How about you coming to my place this time?" I said.

"Ok. I can. Give me the address, an arrival time, and I'll be there."

"I should be home by quarter of twelve." I gave him the address, with a few directions. He left with a smile on his face. I couldn't believe he had actually come to the store to see me. Lifted my mood. I was feeling skinny and ugly. I'd forgotten how attractive Mat was. I began to remember the handcuffs. The wild first time we had. I never expected to see him again! Now I was not only seeing him, but meeting him at my place. To have an intimate moment, how bizarre!

The rest of the afternoon and evening the store was busy. It was so dead near eleven I closed up a little early. As I cleaned up the store, I played back the night I met Mat in my mind again. I left to be home before Mat arrived. On the drive home I thought about what tonight would be like. When I got home, I realized the house was a little messy. I hurried and picked up little messes, like yesterday's clothes and the day before that. Took a quick shower, dressed and put Gent out. As I walked back through the kitchen, the doorbell rang.

"Hello Mat, come in. Have any trouble finding the place?"

"Not at all. Your directions were great. This is an older duplex. I didn't realize they had built them for so many years. Leather furniture, huh."

"I've always been fond of black leather. Want a cocktail?"

"Sure. Can I see the rest of the place?"

"I'll fix cocktails and then I'll show you around. You like dogs guy?"

"Usually. Why?"

"I have a big happy dog out back. He'll want in soon. If you don't like dogs, we'll have a problem."

"Let him in."

"Get ready. He's affectionate." I went to the door and let in Gent. Mat followed me to the kitchen. Gent jumped up on me and I introduced him to Mat. "Mat, meet Gent, Gent, meet Mat."

"Hello there kid. How are you?" Mat put his hand out for Gent to sniff. Gent barked and jumped up and down. Then ran over and jumped up on Mat. He licked Mat on the face. He wagged his tail and ran around in circles. I went to the counter and fixed cocktails.

"He likes you. That's good."

"He seems friendly. A big white huge cotton ball on legs. Darrin, I have an over night bag in the car. May I bring it in?"

"Oh, an over night bag. Planning ahead? A little pushy aren't you?" I grinned, and felt my face turn red. "I'm just teasing. Go get it."

"Thanks. I'll be right back." He went to his car and I made cocktails. He walked back into the kitchen to be greeted by Gent again. I handed him his cocktail.

"Here you go. You can take your bag with you as we walk through the house. Then you can leave it in the bedroom."

"Ok. The cocktail hits the spot."

"Well, you've walked through the living room and the dining room. This is the kitchen. Let's go upstairs." We walked up what I called the back stairs to the spare bedroom and then down the hall to the master bedroom. Mat sat his bag by the dresser and we sat on the bed.

"This place is bigger than it looks. I like the Jacuzzi in the bathroom. It's a great idea."

"I've enjoyed it. Want to try it out dude?"

"Sounds fun, sure."

"I'll go run the water. The tub can fill while we finish our cocktails. I'll fix us another to take into the bathroom."

"I'm game."

I walked into the bathroom to run the water and Mat followed me. He watched me and smiled. I hadn't used the Jacuzzi since before Marc left. I forgot about it.

"Darrin, I want to get something clear and up-front. I came here tonight mainly because the men I've been with lately are jerks. I remembered how much fun we had. I wanted to repeat that experience. I'm not here to start dating or anything like that. I'm here to have a good time. I've also turned up HIV positive and I knew that wouldn't bother you."

"I am sorry to hear you're positive. I'm not sure Marc is far enough behind me that I am particularly ready for a relationship right now any way."

"Just so we understand one another." He said seriously.

"I think we do. Finish your cocktail. I'll make another." He drank the rest of his cocktail and handed me his glass.

"Here you go."

"If you'll watch the water level, and turn it off when it's full, that would be great."

"No problem."

I went down and fixed another cocktail. While I was putting ice into the glasses, I heard the water shut off. When I walked back into the bathroom, Mat was in the tub.

"Here you go. I see you wasted no time getting in the tub. I'll join you."

"I like your straight forward approach. I have adopted it."

I got undressed and slipped into the tub slowly, the water was so hot. "Ready for the jets to be turned on dude?"

"Yea, I want to feel the sensation!" Mat said excitedly.

"Ok. Here you go." I turned the jets on. The water started bubbling up around us. I looked over at Mat. He had lost weight, still very stocky, but thinner. His chest hair was bobbing around in the bubbles. I felt his foot between my legs. He began to play with me. It felt good. I hadn't been with a man since him, the last time.

"The jets feel good." Mat said with a smile.

"Feels good to me, too guy." I laughed. Both the water and Mat's foot felt good. I slid my foot between his legs and began to play.

"Ever made it with someone in a Jacuzzi?" I asked.

"No, I haven't. But, there's always a first time." We played in the water and teased. We caressed one another. The sensation of the water, Mat's body, and his movements were so sensuous. It felt so good to be enjoying the Jacuzzi with someone. I continued to rub against Mat.

"I'm really hot. Not that I don't totally want to do what you are wanting, but I need to get out of this hot water and cool off. Can we get out of the tub?" Mat said.

"Sure we can get out and go to the bedroom."

"I would like to hold off on sex for a while, let my body temperature drop a little if that's ok." Mat grinned.

"Not a problem, there is no rush. We can go watch tv for a while." We got out of the tub and wrapped in towels. I noticed Mat's back was nearly as hairy as his chest. I hadn't noticed that before. We walked downstairs and I made another cocktail. Mat followed me into the living room. We sat on the couch.

"Want to watch a movie guy?"

"I guess. What's on tv?" Mat asked as he looked through the program guide.

"I'm not sure. I have many movies recorded. They are over there in the cabinet if you want to look."

"Any old comedies?"

"A few. Go look for yourself."

"I will. I'm in the mood for a laugh." He walked over to the cabinet and looked through the titles. He pulled one out and handed it to me and we sat and watched it. It was great to snuggle on the couch with someone and watch an old movie. We laughed and giggled and held one another tight. After the movie we went upstairs to bed.

"Darrin, this has been an enjoyable night. I'm glad I came by to see you today."

"I'm glad you did too, Mat." I slid my hands down his stomach to his legs and back. He kissed me. We began kissing and exploring the other's body with our hands. Again, we were into many positions so fast I couldn't keep track of them. I felt Mat lean over the bed once and shortly after felt a stinging sensation. I looked to see what was happening. I realized I was being masterfully whipped.

"You little devil you. Your overnight bag seems to have had more in it than a change of clothes!"

"I told you the first time we were together I had many more talents to show you. This is just the beginning." And it was. He had so many toys and moves they were astonishing. We played and experimented for hours. I had never been so stimulated by one man. He could put on a condom so fast you didn't have time to realize what he had done. We were so exhausted we fell asleep beside one other. I felt Gent licking my ear and pushed him away. It was daylight again.

"Thanks a lot Darrin. I'm just trying to be sensuous is all."

I rolled over and it was Mat, "I'm sorry I thought you were Gent dude!"

"I feel the same as the dog?"

"Well he licks my ear when he wants out. I thought you were him!"

"Ok, I guess, this time." Mat went back to licking my ear and playing with my body. He used some new talents this time. It was very different and very stimulating. We ended hugging and laying there.

"Mat, you are amazing. I enjoyed that little surprise."

"Glad you did. I enjoyed myself."

"Want to take a shower?"

"Sure. Want to join me?" Mat said.

"I was thinking of fixing coffee while you showered. Since you put it that way, I'd like to join you." We got into the shower and explored various parts of each other while playing with the soap. We managed to wash each other fairly thoroughly in the process. We dried off and sat on the bed. Mat stared at me.

"Something wrong guy?"

"No, not really. Why?" Mat asked.

"You are sitting there looking hesitant."

"Darrin, I want to ask you something. I don't want you to take it wrong, is all."

"So, ask. If I take it wrong, tell me."

"I was wondering if you would mind spending the rest of the day together. Before we have to go to work."

"Sure. How could I take that wrong?"

"Because, I don't want you to think I'm talking about seeing each other all the time."

"I thought we settled that yesterday."

"As long as we both agree that's my main concern Darrin."

"I think we do," I walked over to the closet and got two robes, "want to wear this?"

"Sure. Anything you would like to do?"

"We could eat breakfast, watch game shows, or go out. I don't care."

"You like game shows?" Mat asked.

"I get a charge out of them. Marc said I'm a game show junkie. What would you like to do?"

"Breakfast sounds good. Even sitting around watching games shows sounds exciting."

"Let's go to the kitchen and start with breakfast. It won't be much. I'll do my best." We walked to the kitchen and I looked at what supplies I had. I grabbed a box of cereal, milk, and sugar. I got out some juice and put coffee on to brew. I remembered I had a grapefruit, so I got it out and cut it. That was breakfast.

"Here you go. Not fancy, but food."

"It's fine with me. Looks like that robe has been one you have had for a while. Fond of it?"

"That's the nicest way I've ever heard anyone say it's an old tacky robe. I just love it, and even though it's worn, I keep it around." We ate, cleaned up dishes, and walked to the living room. I turned on the television and flipped through the channels. All I could find were soap operas, talk shows, or news. No game shows. I pulled out an old movie from my private collection I wanted Mat to see.

"Since I can't find any game shows, I want you to see this movie dude."

"What movie is it?"

"Just wait and see. I think you'll like it."

"Ok, let it play."

"Let me know if you don't like it. I'll stop it." I pushed play and waited. I was anxious to hear the comment. The credits rolled by and then the action began. I expected a comment at any moment.

"Where in the world did you get this? It's got to be one of the oldest skin flicks I have ever seen!"

"Some guy came into the store with a collection of old porn films he'd transferred to video. He sold the collection to the owner of the store. I had to have this one. It's probably the original leather film made. And this guy, right there, reminds me of you. Especially the movements he has. Just watch guy."

"I'm embarrassed. You think I did it like that?"

"That is the image I had in my mind when you hand cuffed me that time."

"Ok. Do you have many of these films?"

"That entire cabinet is full of them. I buy all the newest ones we get into the store. I am buying that old collection one at a time. They are my retirement. I figure when I am in my sixties they should be worth money."

"You are probably right."

We watched the film for a while and then Mat stood up, right in front of me.

"Let's go back to bed. I want to try out that last scene in real life." Without a word we walked to the bedroom. He repeated the scene exactly as it was filmed. It was great.

The rest of the day we sat around watching game shows and some of my private videos. We laughed and teased. It was a pleasant afternoon.

"Darrin, I need to get going." Mat sighed. "I need to get ready for work."

"This has been fun." I said.

"It has. I'm glad I looked you up again."

"Me, too." We got dressed, and I walked Mat to the door. We hugged.

"If you ever want an encore, let me know, dude."

"I will Darrin. Have a good afternoon."

"You too." When Mat left I felt a little lonely. I walked back into the house. I got ready to go to work. It had been a great time. Almost better than any of the time Marc and I had. But Mat and I weren't romantically involved either. That was probably part of the difference.

After that night with Mat it was work, friends, and to the bar to play pool. Seemed like it was Thanksgiving before I knew it and then Christmas, I spent time with my family on both holidays. I got into a routine of going to work, eating at fast food chains, and going to the Circle to play pinball or pool. I had taken a couple men home. No one I wanted to see again.

The car was cluttered with sales slips, sacks from drive-up window food purchases and paper cups from pop and coffee purchases. It was getting to a place I was battling a shower of debris coming out of the car every time I opened the door. I needed to clean out the car. More like shoveling it out. Nevertheless, I procrastinated.

Valentine's Day I got around to that task. As I began cleaning out the car, I was thinking I didn't want to be out in the bar crowd that night because I knew it would be geared more for couples. But I didn't want to be home alone either. I decided I wanted to spend time with a friend, instead of being alone. I called Colt before he went to work, to see what he was up to for the day. He was single at the moment as well.

"Hello."

"Yo, dude, how are you?"

"Hi Darrin. Fine and you?"

"Oh, ok. Just the normal routine of work and home. What are you up to?"

"Not much different. Work and home. Kind of dull."

"I was wondering if you would do me a favor?"

"What's that Darrin?"

"It's Valentine's Day and I don't really want to go out, but I thought maybe you could come over here and we could do something."

"I don't have any plans, sure. What time?"

"Whenever you'd like. I'm off today, so whenever you get home from work."

"I get home around four. Name a time."

"Let's say about five. I'll even throw something together to eat."

"Such a deal. Ok, then, around five. See you then."

"See you Colt."

I got off the phone and looked at the house. It was pretty trashed as well. I needed to clean it up too. I had many things to do before five. At least having Colt over gave me the motivation to clean up a little. I did laundry, shoved the messes into cabinets, closets, trashcans and tidied up so it looked clean and the messes were out of sight.

I took the car to the car wash and shoveled out the remaining debris. I went to the store and got microwave meals of Mexican food and a few other items. I was beginning to look forward to a Valentine's Day with a friend, rather than a lover. It would be different. This would be fun, and a change. I was glad I had invited Colt over. The house looked good for a change and there weren't bags, sales receipts and cups falling out of the car when you opened the door. I guess I needed a reason to clean up. I was putting my laundry away and I heard the doorbell and went to the door. Gent bounded ahead of me.

"Hello Colt, come in."

"Hi Darrin. How are you? Hello Gent."

"Fine. What's this?"

"Since we are neither one dating, I brought these for you. I figured we are good friends and friends are as important as lovers."

"That was sweet of you. A rose and box of candy. I feel like I'm in the fifties and this is our first date. How traditional guy, you trying to date me or what?"

"Oh good grief Darrin let's not go over board with the whole thing."

"Seriously it was a nice surprise." I said.

"So, what's new, or should I say who's new?"

"Not much and no one. I haven't met anyone I have found interesting. I've just been spending time alone. And you?" I said.

"About the same basically, school, home, school."

"Exciting lives! You hungry dude?"

"Yes. What are we having?" Colt asked.

"You have a choice. Either tacos or enchiladas, I only have to zap them, so it won't take long."

"I thought you were really going to cook something. Tacos sound good."

"Good, I wanted the enchiladas!" We walked to the kitchen. I put the frozen dinners in the microwave. Colt petted Gent and played with him. While it cooked we set at the table.

"Darrin, you really haven't met anyone you are interested in?"

"Not really. I did have fun with this one guy a couple of times. We made an agreement that we would not become involved, we would just have sex now and again."

"Oh. So, if you found him interesting, why make that agreement?"

"The first time we got together was the day before Marc and I split. The second time he walked into the store and asked to see me. Neither time was a place I wanted to get involved. That's how that happened."

"What about now? Why don't you call him?"

"For one thing, I never got his number guy."

"That was bright. Don't you have any way of getting a hold of him?" Colt suggested.

"I've been hoping to see him at the Circle, but I haven't."

"There is no other way you could get a hold of him?" Colt pursued the topic.

"I do know where he lives. I guess I could just drop by."

"It's up to you. Do you have an interest in him?"

"I think so. That's the microwave, wait a minute." I got our dinners out and sat them on the table. "I'm not sure Colt that it isn't just because he was very compatible in bed."

"That's a start. Better start than some people have."

"That's true. I guess I could go see him. Last time he found me. I was so surprised, he's so attractive. I'm so tall and skinny. He's stocky with this great bushy moustache."

"You are not skinny, you are a slender build. Anyway it's worth a try. This looks good Darrin, even if it is zapped!"

"Skinny telling skinny he is slender build. Funny, very funny. Hey, just be glad I'm even feeding you dude. So what about you guy. No one has sparked your imagination?"

"Kind of. There is one guy that is a friend, but I think that is all he wants."

"God Colt, he could be sending all the signals and you'd be so worried he wouldn't like you, you'd miss them all. Take charge of your life guy."

"Not everyone is like you Darrin. We don't all just take the world by storm."

"Well you would all be happier if you did. Ask him out for a drink, or a cup of coffee or dinner or something. When you are out point blank tell him you are interested in him."

"I can't just do that. What if he isn't interested in me?"

"If he is not, then you will know. Mystery solved. You can't get anywhere if you don't take a chance you know dude."

"I know." Colt said with a sigh.

"I got your Valentine's card. You had to get it at the store. You must have snuck in on my day off. We are the only store I've seen with the whips and chains cards."

"I did. Wasn't easy, but I managed to go in one day you weren't there. Fortunately no one recognized me."

"It made me feel good to get a card. Thanks." We finished dinner. The rest of the evening we played games. I beat Colt at all of them. He said it was because I had more practice. I told him I was just more skilled. It was a different evening. I needed time with a friend.

I decided to go by to see Mat at his apartment only to discover he had moved. I was disappointed, but there wasn't much I could do about it. The new tenant didn't know where Mat had moved. I was back into the hope I'd see him at the Circle. I began to work longer hours. I rearranged the store so it was more "eye-catching" to the customer. I was working, going home and only going out on my "weekend" nights.

I felt good about the improvements I was making at the store, gave me a new project, and a new outlook on life. It was nice to be alone for now. Coming and going as I pleased. Sleeping in if I chose, getting up in the middle of the night to watch television. Doing whatever I wanted to do.

I was given the opportunity to buy into the store. I had some savings, I had not been spending much of my paychecks, and with the over time, it gave me some money in savings, and I was able to buy into the business. It was a nice birthday gift to me.

Now I was even more interested in making the business bigger and more successful. I drew up plans to open a second store. My boss took the idea with great enthusiasm. I searched for the right location, negotiated a deal for the building rental, and organized the plans for opening. In July we had the grand opening and it was a blow out. We had so many customers. Many were friends that were there to support my idea. But, many were new faces to the store. I was very pleased.

The store was making good money by the middle of July. I was relieved. Because of my idea, and its initial success, I was given a higher percentage of the ownership. The owner was at a point he was looking at retirement. So I became the sole manager of the two stores. My former boss, and now partner, was traveling.

I was enjoying the challenge of running two stores. I was spending time between the stores, making sure they were keeping up with inventory, making the stores more appealing to the eye and checking on employees. I was at the new store one afternoon at the end of our first month. I was checking the storeroom when I heard a familiar voice.

"Could you tell me if Darrin is in the store today?"

"Yes, sir, he is. May I tell him your name?"

"Mat."

"I'll go get him." As the clerk walked back to get me, I was walking out front. "Darrin, there's a guy named Mat to see you."

"I heard him. Thanks Freddie." I had recognized that husky voice and walked out front and over to Mat.

"Well hello dude. How are you?"

"Hi Darrin I'm fine. How are you?"

"Great. I tried to find you a while back, but you had moved."

"So I heard. I ran into the guy who rented the place and he said someone was looking for me. By the description he gave, I knew it was you. I went over to the other store and they told me you were here. I didn't even know you opened another store."

"About a month ago. Where did you move to guy?"

"Close to your house. I'd had it with the apartment. A little house a friend of mine owned became vacant. So I rented it."

"You could have come by you know!"

"I know. I didn't want to be an intrusion."

"You wouldn't have been. Come on back to the storeroom. We can talk while I check inventory."

"Sure. I've never seen the store room before."

"Nothing special, I can tell you guy!" We walked back to the storeroom and sat on some boxes. It was great to see Mat. He was a little heavier, but looking as good as ever.

"So, Darrin, what did you want?"

"The night before I dropped by I was talking to a friend, Colt. I told him I kind of wanted to see you. He suggested I just drop by, so I did."

"Oh, ok. I've thought about you often. I haven't been going out much. I've been working overtime to make some extra money to afford that house. Kind of adjusting to being HIV positive, the cocktail of pills, I get tired of having to explain that."

"I hear you there. I've been working long hours. I was the one who suggested we open another store. So, I've been working hard to make this store a success."

"Looks like your hard work paid off. What are you doing after work?"

"I haven't any plans. Why guy?"

"You said you wanted to see me. I thought we could get together late tonight."

"Sounds good. Since I've been working as manager, I can make my own hours. I could wrap up what I have to do by nine."

"That's good for me. Where did you want to meet?"

"Why don't I pick you up and take you to a late dinner?"

"Great Darrin. I haven't been taken to dinner in a long time."

I got Mat's address. We talked a little longer and he left. I finished the inventory. I went back to the other store to check on inventory there. I did some of the ordering that needed to be done. I couldn't really concentrate on my work. I was more excited than I had expected to be seeing Mat again. I had given him up as a lost cause when I found he had moved. I hadn't seen him out either. I got inventory closed out and headed for home. I was anxious to spend an evening with Mat.

"Hello Gent. Dad doesn't have time to play tonight. I'll let you out in the yard and you can run around. Ok?" Gent went bounding into the yard. He bounded up and down. He wanted to go for a walk. Not tonight. I went up and got ready to get Mat. I was excited. It had been a long time since I had been this excited. I realized I was thinking of this as a date. Mat and I had agreed long ago that we weren't going to date. I felt like this was an honest date. Wonder how Mat would feel about that. I went down, let Gent in, and left for Mat's. The drive wasn't very long. He did live just a couple blocks away. I walked to the door and rang the bell.

"Hello Darrin, come in."

"Hi Mat. Long time, no see. How are you?"

"Fine. What do you think?" Mat said nodding to his living room.

"From what I can see, it's a nice place. May I see the rest?"

"Sure. Follow me." We walked through the house. He was right. It was little, but cute. It was a lot bigger than his apartment, but that didn't take much. It was very homey.

"Looks great Mat. It is very homey."

"I like it. Want a cocktail?"

"Only if you do. We could have a cocktail after dinner guy."

"That sounds better. Let's go then."

"Ok. After you." We walked out to my car and got in. As we drove to the restaurant, I thought about telling Mat how I felt. He needed to know.

"This isn't the car you had before is it Darrin?"

"I'm not sure. When I bought it, the exterior and interior were in terrible shape. I had it repainted and the interior done over."

"Yes, I can see. Sales slips, food sacks, beverage cans, and a few plastic cups. Original idea."

"Very funny. It does need cleaned out, but I like it. I've just been really busy lately dude."

"I understand. It does look show room new, if you look under all the junk in here." Mat grinned.

"That's what I wanted it to look like. Mat, I want to be honest with you."

"I can see you haven't changed."

"I believe in the direct approach. It saves time and energy. I feel like this is a date. No, I want this to be a date, to tell the truth."

"I thought we agreed we wouldn't get involved."

"We did. But, that was back when Marc was around. I've been single for quite a while now. I have been out with a number of men and I always think of you. I really would like to date."

"Why do you think I looked you up the last time? I wanted to start seeing you."

"I wasn't sure why you looked me up. We talked that night and you said no strings attached. I figured you had no interest."

"I was checking to see if you were interested. It appeared you weren't. I guess I don't take quite the direct approach you do."

"No, not quite. Here we are, ready to eat guy?"

"Sure am. I love this place. I haven't been here in a long time!"

"I'm glad you like this place." We walked into the restaurant and were seated. We both looked at the menu and each other. The waiter returned.

"May I get you gentleman something from the bar?"

"Yes, I'll have JD and Coke," I said.

"Make that two."

"I'll be back to take your order." The waiter said.

"What are you going to have Darrin?"

"I think the Mexican combination, you?"

"I think the roast beef."

"I'm glad you came into the store today." I said.

"I was hoping you would still be single and want to go out. Have you heard from Marc?" Mat asked.

"No, I haven't. I've heard he and his new love left town. But I don't know that for sure. I haven't talked to him since we broke up."

"I guess that is good."

The waiter returned with our cocktails. "Here you go gentlemen. May I take your order?"

"I'll have the Mexican combination."

"And you sir?"

"I'll have the roast beef, medium."

"Your orders will be up shortly." As the waiter walked off, we stared at one another for a few minutes. I thought about how I had forgotten how attractive Mat was. I remembered how attractive I thought he was that first night. He was just as attractive now, if not more so than before. I was glad he had caught up with me once more.

"What you thinking about Darrin?"

"You. I was just thinking about the night we met."

"You certainly were up front and honest that night!"

"Yea, I remember." The waiter returned with our orders. We ate in silence. Dinner was good. It could have tasted terrible and I wouldn't have noticed I don't think. From here I would like to go home, but I thought it would be better if we went out. For a while anyway. We finished dinner, paid the check, and went to the car.

"Where to next, Mat?"

"I don't care. What would you like to do?"

"How about going to the Circle for a while guy?"

"That's a good idea." We went to the Circle and had a few cocktails. We played pinball and pool. Mat had obviously been practicing, because he wasn't so easy to beat.

We heard last call, and ordered another cocktail. It didn't seem like we had been there that long. We finished and walked to the car.

"So, where to? What next?" I was hoping home together.

"I guess the age old question, your place or mine?"

"Since I have Gent to consider, how about mine?"

"Sure. I'd like to stop by my place and get my car and some clothes."

"No problem guy." We drove to Mat's. He got his car and clothes, and followed me home. I walked in the door with Mat right behind me.

"Imagine that. Meeting you here at my door."

"Imagine that!" We walked into the house and were greeted by Gent. He seemed to remember Mat.

"Hi ya boy. Remember this dude?" He jumped up on Mat and licked him. "Guess so, huh."

"Darrin I think he is just friendly to anyone you bring home."

"No, he really isn't."

"I don't know if I believe you or not."

"It is true. Want a cocktail, or would you rather hit the bed and have wild and crazy sex?"

"Why don't you let Gent out while we have a cocktail? And you cool your jets a little."

"Awe, you're no fun. I'll fix a cocktail." I let Gent out and fixed a cocktail. Mat had walked into the living room. I joined him there.

"Here you go sir."

"Thank you. How about a game?"

"Ok, which one?"

"Doesn't matter."

"Tax man then." We played a couple of games. I got up and let Gent in, and we played another game. I was getting anxious to take Mat to bed, so I picked him up, cocktail and all, and carried him off to the bedroom. I laid him on the bed.

"You do have a kind of romantic side, don't you?" He laughed. "I couldn't believe that you carried me up the stairs!"

"I told you I could be romantic. I want to make love to you this time. You can do all the moves you want, but this time I am not just having sex."

"Sounds serious. Guess I'll just wait and see." At that point, I leaned over Mat, put his cocktail on the dresser, lit the few candles I had in my room, and began to make love to him. This was the best time of all. Mat used some maneuvers. We had surpassed first two times and extended them into an absolutely different experience!

"I don't know about you, but I feel wonderful," I whispered to Mat.

"Me, too," he whispered back. "Why don't you blow out those candles and cuddle up next to me?" I got up and blew out the candles. We cuddled together and fell asleep. In the morning we woke at the same time. We showered together and went downstairs to the kitchen. I put on a pot of coffee and Mat came up behind me and hugged me.

"How about if I fix you breakfast?"

"If you can find enough supplies in this kitchen to fix breakfast, go for it guy." Mat looked through the cabinets and the refrigerator. He pulled out supplies from both. He made bacon, eggs, and pancakes. I didn't think I had enough groceries to do all that. It was a feat of magic.

"Thanks Mat. That was considerate of you to make breakfast. I can't wait to taste it."

"Sit and eat. It is ready." I sat down at the table. It was different to eat breakfast with someone again. I was feeling very comfortable.

"Darrin, last night has convinced me that we should see each other more, or date I think was your word. I would like to do that and see where it leads."

"I would, too Mat. I feel very happy today, happier than I have in a long time. I'd like to see where this feeling goes."

"Just remember, I think we should take it slow and easy. I really do enjoy being around you, but, so far we have really only been together for the purpose of sex. I think we should spend a weekend together soon and see if we get along in other areas of life. It is a good next step to take, I think."

"I agree Mat. We could even go away some place and be alone for several days. We would find out fast, that way, if we got along or not!"

"I've got some vacation time. I could use it. We could go away for four or five days if you would like," Mat said.

"I could get off. Being manager, I can just get one of the other employees to cover for me for a few days. Where did you want to go dude?"

"It doesn't have to be far away. Just some place we could walk during the day and relax at night. It is still summer. We could enjoy the warmth of the evenings."

"Sounds good to me."

"Why don't we just drive to one of the small towns between here and no man's land and rent a room? We can spend a few days alone."

"Let's pick a week to go," I said.

"Next week is fine with me."

"I'll check at the store today, see if I can get someone to cover next weekend, and the next two days."

"I'll put in for vacation time."

"Why don't you just follow me to the store first? Just to make sure I can get off. Then you can put in for vacation time guy," I said excitedly.

"Good idea. What time?"

"If we get dressed, you could follow me to work and I could know before you even go in. My hours are of my own making now."

"Let's get dressed and go."

We got ready and drove to the store. I checked with one of the sales clerks. He was more than willing to cover the shifts I had been working. I was so excited. Mat seemed just as excited. He went to work early to see if he could take his vacation time. He said he'd call me back at the store.

Waiting for Mat to call seemed endless. I got busy with restocking shelves, checking our inventory, the orders made recently and making sure the store was in good shape. I paced for a while. I found myself gnawing at my fingernails. Finally the phone rang and it was Mat.

"Yo, Ins & Outs, Darrin here. How may I help you?"

"Yo, Mat here dude. I don't need your help. Maybe your body."

"So, do you know yet?"

"Yes, I do Darrin."

"Don't keep me in suspense! Can you?"

"Well, it was tricky, but yes, I can. I had to pull a few strings."

"I'm glad. All we have to do is pack and leave. That's a relief guy."

"I'm relieved, too. I've got to run. See you later tonight?"

"Yes, we have to decide what to pack and where to go. I have so many things I want to do with you. See you tonight."

"Later then Darrin."

"Later dude."

After thinking about our choices, we decided to just drive until we found a place that looked interesting and stay for the four days. The week at work seemed to drag. Mat and I spent every night together planning things we wanted to do. Organizing what we needed to take. I needed to have someone check on Gent. I decided to see if Derrek or Colt would. I didn't want to board him.

"Hello."

"Yo Derrek, this is Darrin."

"Hello Darrin. How are you?"

"Oh fine. And you guy?"

"Fine. So what is new?"

"That's why I called. Mat and I are planning on going away for several days. I was wondering if you would go by and check on Gent. You don't have to keep him at your place. I would appreciate it if you could just come by the house and feed him. Maybe take him for a walk a couple of times."

"I'd be glad to Darrin. He can just come here and stay with Clem if you want."

"No, he can stay at the house. I think he'd be better here. I've installed a dog door, so he can go in and out. If you would just come by and feed him, get him fresh water a walk a day that's all he needs."

"Yea uh huh sure, that is fine I can help you on that. Where are you two going?"

"We're just going to rent a cottage for a few days."

"What is with Mat? I thought you two were just friends."

"We did agree to be just friends. We just decided to spend some time together and see where it goes. That's why we are going away for a few days dude."

"Sounds really good. I am happy for you. I hope it all works out."

"Me too Derrek. I'm looking forward to the weekend. If we can get along all weekend, Mat feels we have a good chance dating. We'll see I guess."

"Well, good luck on it. Give me a call the day before you leave and I will pick up the key. I will check on Gent daily."

"Will do. Thanks Derrek. I appreciate it."

"Yea uh huh, no problem."

"Ok, later dude."

"By."

With Gent taken care of, I felt better. I was so primed to go I couldn't wait. Mat was just as excited. I hoped I could prove to him that we did have similar interests, and could get along alone together.

On the morning of our vacation, I was a wreck. Mat had spent the night with me. We had packed the car. All was in order, except I was nervous. I checked and rechecked the luggage. Wrote a note for Derrek. Checked the windows, the doors. Mat was calmly getting his things together. I was in a panic.

"Darrin, are you ready to go?"

"I guess so, Mat. Let me check to see if I locked the back door."

"You've checked it three times in the last ten minutes. You have checked everything several times! Moreover, Derrek has a key. If he notices anything wrong, he will take care of it. Let's go!" Mat said as patiently as he could.

"I guess you are right. Let's go. Gent, dad's going to be gone a few days. Uncle Derrek will be over to visit you. Be good, ok?" I leaned down and hugged him.

"You treat that dog like a real child. It's unbelievable to me."

"You ought to see Colt and Derrek with their dogs. They are just as bad. Even Marshall and his cat have the same basic relationship."

"I didn't say you were the only person on this planet who treats their pet as a real person. I just said you do." We walked out to the car and left. We both remained silent for a long time. I was thinking about the vacation. I was hoping being alone wouldn't get boring. Or that we wouldn't get tired of each other.

"Mat, I have to tell you I'm excited and nervous."

"I am, too, Darrin. I want this to be a pleasant vacation. I think it will be. We have spent a great deal of time together recently. We got along fine."

"True. I'm still nervous, though guy."

"Me too. It will be fine Darrin."

The rest of the drive we listened to music and enjoyed the scenery as we drove. The music helped pass the time. We looked for a place where we could go for walks, be by ourselves, and enjoy nature. As we drove along the highway we saw a sign for cottages for rent just up the road. We stopped when we saw them and pulled in to take a look. They appeared to be just what we wanted. The cottages were small, but nice, and there were places to go walking and swimming. We checked in and drove to our cottage. It was very small looking from the outside.

"Darrin this looks like a cozy little place!"

"It does, Mat." I unlocked the front door and we walked in. It was a little place with a loft bedroom, a kitchen, a small living room, and a bathroom. Small but cozy and even a fireplace. It was too warm to use it, but it had one. I checked the deck out and Mat went up to the loft.

"Darrin, come up here. Look at this bedroom. It's got a view you wouldn't believe!"

"I'll be right up. This is a cute place." I walked up the stairs to the bedroom. When I got upstairs, Mat was standing in the middle of the room naked.

"Look at this view."

I stared at him, "Is this the view you wanted me to look at?"

"No, look out this window. This view just made me feel like being all natural, so I stripped."

"Nice view," I turned and looked at him, "but, I like this one better dude." I also stripped. I hugged Mat. Things were off to a good start. Matt just stared at me for a while.

He looked me in the eyes and said, "Darrin, I had never really noticed until just now how hairless your chest is." He said as he ran his hands all over my chest.

"Well guy, not everybody has a hairy chest." We made love and then looked at the view from the bed. I had to admit. It was beautiful and peaceful.

"Want to go for a walk?" I asked.

"Sounds like fun. Let's see if we can find a spot to picnic later this afternoon."

"Some place secluded and quiet Mat."

We got dressed and went for a walk. We found a little path and walked along it for a while. As we walked, we found a place where we wanted to picnic. It was flat, secluded, and sunny. There were enough trees around that it had some shady and cool spots as well. We found a pond and a stream and played in the water. In the distance we could see a lake. We decided to go swimming. No one was around so we went skinny-dipping. We hugged and caressed while we swam. Getting tired, we got out put on our pants.

"Too bad we didn't bring a blanket," Mat sighed.

"I know. I think this would have been a good spot to make love guy."

"You read my mind. It's so quiet and pleasant here."

"It is. I didn't realize how much I needed a vacation." We grabbed our shirts, walked back to the cottage, and gathered up supplies for a picnic. We made sandwiches, packed a blanket, and a bottle of wine. We changed into shorts and T-shirts.

Walking back to find our picnic site we enjoyed the scenery. We spread out the blanket and ate lunch. After lunch we laid in the sun. At first we laid in our shorts. But I felt so sexy being in nature. I stripped. Mat, seeing I had stripped, did the same. The sun felt good on my skin. I was so relaxed. I almost fell asleep. I felt Mat's lips on my leg. He used his tongue to excite me. Nature took is course.

Afterward we lay there looking at the view. It was nice to be away from the daily routine of life.

"Let's go wade in the pond. I want to see how deep it is." Mat suggested.

"Ok, let's go." I got up and ran to the pond. Mat ran after me. We played in the water and enjoyed the peacefulness. Our skin began to wrinkle from being in the water so long, so we went back and sat in the sun. It was so soothing. We were getting along fine so far.

"Darrin, remember that stream we saw this morning?"

"Yes, why dude?"

"Let's walk beside it for a while."

"Ok. I think I'm going to put on my shorts. I don't want to get sunburned in certain places. It would put a damper on making love to you." I commented.

"Guess we should be careful." We walked up the stream, talked and laughed. We got absorbed in looking at nature and lost track of time. We had walked for quite a distance.

"Mat, the sun is beginning to go down. I think we should head back."

"You are right. We've been walking longer than I realized!" On the walk back we found a place where there was a small waterfall and many rocks. We took note of the place so we could come back tomorrow. When we got to the cottage Mat said he wanted to take a long bath. I told him I just wanted to sit down.

While Mat soaked in the tub, I changed into a jockstrap. I mixed us both a cocktail. I went up to the loft. When Mat got out of the tub, I yelled at him to come upstairs.

"Woo, aren't you sexy? Just a jock, huh."

"I thought it was so warm that I'd wear the least possible. Here, I fixed you a cocktail."

"You do look sexy." He walked over and sat in the chair beside me. We sipped on our cocktails and looked outside.

"Why don't you come join me in the chair guy?" I suggested.

"Where am I going to sit?"

"Oh, on my lap would be fine."

"Oh really, sounds almost romantic, are you sure?"

"I am. I've told you I can be romantic." He walked over and sat on my lap. I put my arms around him and hugged him. He put his hands on my arms and leaned back against me.

"Feels like someone wants to do more than just sit here and relax!"

"My body just reacts to you. Actually I really just want to sit here and enjoy your bare skin next to mine."

"That sounds fine to me." Mat sat on my lap and we just relaxed. I guess I fell asleep, the next thing I knew Mat was shaking me.

"Hey you, if you are that tired, let's just take a little nap." Mat suggested. We climbed into bed.

When we got up we fixed dinner. We ate by candle light, in the buff. We enjoyed the peaceful atmosphere. After dinner we played cards. It was slower paced than bars and games. But, it fit the mood of the cottage. It was different and fun. We had several cocktails and went up to the loft. We looked out at the sky. We had a view of the moon, with the moonlight shining into the loft. The day had been a good one. I felt relaxed and at ease.

The rest of the vacation went much like the first day. We went for walks, discovered areas of the countryside to make love in. We enjoyed being together. I discovered the second day when we went for a walk Mat had brought his toys. They took on a special meaning in the outdoors. We got along well. We both liked to go for walks. We both enjoyed being in nature. Mat did most of the cooking. I did most of the tidying up. We found we were compatible.

The morning we packed and left, we were both sorry to have the vacation come to an end. We decided to extend our vacation by two more days. We had a wonderful time. When we finally did drive home we were still sad to have the vacation come to an end. We drove home in silence, remembering the things we had experienced. It had been a great vacation. When we got to the city we both sighed.

"Back to reality I guess, Darrin."

"Back to reality. I wonder how Gent did?"

"We'll find out soon."

"I can hear him barking now." I said as I drove into the garage. I went into the house, Gent jumped up on me and licked my face. Then ran to Mat and licked him. He proceeded to run around the house and bark. He was glad to see us both.

"So, you missed dad, huh. Were you a good boy for Uncle Derrek?" Gent barked more, ran over to me and sat. I saw a note from Derrek on the counter.

"Darrin & Mat-- Hope you had a good time. Must have since you stayed two extra days. Gent was great. We went for a walk a day. I feed him this morning. He did fine. Give me a call later. Derrek."

"I guess you were a good boy. A walk a day huh? Uncle Derrek has spoiled you!"

"That doesn't surprise me, Darrin. At least you know he was cared for."

"I knew he would be. So, after six days alone with me, what do you think?" I quizzed.

"I think I've fallen in love with you. That's what I think. And you, after six days of me?" Mat asked.

"I know I've fallen in love with you guy."

"That makes me feel good. I still think we should take it slow and easy. I don't want to rush into anything. I don't want you to rush into anything." Mat said.

"I agree. I do love you though. Coming home I realized that you will be going home and to work. Made me aware just how I feel."

"I know. The idea of going back to work doesn't excite me at all. I do need to go home and check my house. It's not that I don't want to spend the night with you Darrin, but I think that maybe it would be best if we were apart. Just to see if it was just the romance of the vacation, or if we really feel the way we do."

"I guess. I just wish you wouldn't go. I'd rather you stayed. You have a point though."

"I think I should go home. I'll give you a call in the morning."

"I'll talk to you later then. Let me walk you to the garage dude." We hugged. Mat got in his car and drove off. I began to feel very alone and sad. I don't think it was the romance of the vacation. I went back to the house, unpacked my things, and started laundry. I needed to get things ready for work. Back to the grind. It didn't sound good at all. I sat to watch television. I hadn't done that in six days. I flipped through several programs. None looked interesting. The doorbell rang. I wondered who it could be. I considered not answering it. But, I thought it might be Derrek returning the key. Walking to the door, I wondered what Mat was doing now. I opened the door to find Mat standing there.

"Hello, I missed you so much, I decided to surprise you and come back. Is that ok?" Mat grinned.

"Is that ok? Of course, come in! I was just thinking about calling you. I didn't want to pressure you."

"I decided if it was the romance of the vacation that caused the feelings I had, I wanted to enjoy it for the rest of the evening."

"I'm glad you did."

"I can't follow my own advice." We walked into the living room. We sat and watched television. Mat laid his head on my lap. Shortly I heard him snoring. I was tired, so I shook Mat to wake him.

"You fell asleep."

"I was just resting my eyes."

"Oh, sure you were. Let's go to bed. I'm tired and with you here, relaxed enough to sleep."

"Let's go then." And so we did just go to bed and sleep. In the morning we got up and prepared ourselves for the return to the routine. We showered together, dried one another off, and stood and hugged each other as long as we could before we had to get dressed and leave.

We both got back into the routine of work and home. We began to spend every night together. Even all of our common days off were together. I had arranged my schedule so that I had the same days off and the same hours as Mat. He stuck to his idea of taking it slow and easy. We lived separately and stayed back and forth between our houses.

Through September and October we went out after work to the Circle on the weekends. We stayed home weeknights. We went to movies, and out to dinner, once a week or so. We both agreed we were in love with each other. We were still in the "courtship" stage as far as Mat was concerned. His lease was up at the end of November, and we were at a point of facing a decision whether to live together or not. Mat and I decided it was time for him to just move in with me. At Thanksgiving Mat had me over for dinner. We had a great time. The next weekend we moved his things to my house. It was a natural flow since his lease was up any way.

We rearranged furniture, got rid of some of our personal things. We made the house a combination of both of us. I enjoyed having a partner again. I got into a habit of waiting in a jock for Mat when he came home from work. Sometimes with a cocktail fixed, sometimes just watching television and waiting. He liked walking into the house seeing me in nothing but a jock. He said it made him forget his problems at work.

Christmas we spent time alone. We went back to the cottage we had rented in the summer. We had our own Christmas celebration. New Years we went to a party at the

Circle. Work got busy for both of us after the first of the year. I was drawing up plans to open another store out of state. Mat was trying to get a promotion.

Through the winter we were into a regular routine of daily life. We were happy with our lives. There were a few arguments about staying home verses going out. We had a few arguments about cleaning house, somehow my theory of just making things look good didn't blend well with Mat's ideas about actually cleaning. He wanted things to be cleaned, not glossed over. We compromised and managed to work things out.

Mat's birthday was in April. I wanted to make it unique. He had hinted around about taking a few days off work and going to the cottage again. I called and made reservations. It seemed like the best surprise I could plan.

Several times before his birthday I almost slipped and ruined the surprise. The night before his birthday I packed the car while I was waiting for him to come home from work. That way I was ready to leave in the morning. It would make it more unexpected. I just hoped he wouldn't miss anything I had packed. I almost forgot to get into my jock. I was changing as he walked in the door.

"Hi honey. I'm home!"

"Hello. How was your day?"

"Ok. I'm glad I have the next three days off!"

"Me too. I will be glad to have some time off."

"Did you want to go out tonight?" Mat asked.

"No, I thought we could stay home tonight and watch tv. I figure we'll be out tomorrow night to celebrate your birthday."

"Ok. Anything good on tv?"

"No game shows. There is an old classic on cable. I thought you might want to watch that." As I finished my sentence, Mat took all his clothes off. I sat on the couch, and he sat on my lap.

"Can the birthday man have a pre-birthday wish?"

"I guess it would be ok. What?"

"Let's go sit in the Jacuzzi. We haven't done that in a long time."

"Oh I think I can grant that wish." I said.

"I'll go fill the tub, if you'll make cocktails."

"I'll bring them right up, Mat." He went upstairs, and I went to the kitchen. I made the cocktails and went upstairs.

"Here you go."

"Thanks. I wish this tub filled faster. Let's sit in the tub while it fills."

"It does take awhile. Let's get in." We climbed into the tub and sat there. It reminded me of the first time Mat was at the house. We had a good time that night. Not that we hadn't since then, this just reminded me of that night. I started to play with Mat's legs with my feet. He played back. We drank our cocktails and played more. We ended making love in the tub. We got out and fixed dinner. Then watched some television and went to bed.

In the morning, I woke up before Mat. I went down to check on Gent. I started to write a note for Derrek and while I was writing the note, Mat came into the kitchen.

"What are you doing?"

"Oh, leaving a note for Derrek. I have made plans for your birthday. Happy thirty-seventh."

"Thanks. What kind of plans?"

"You'll see. We need to shower, get dressed, so I can take you for a drive guy."

"Why are you leaving a note for Derrek?"

"We are going to be gone for three days. He's watching Gent, again."

"Where are we going?"

"You'll have to wait and see."

"Ok, then let's get going. I want to see where you are taking me." We got ready and left. As we drove out of the city, I knew Mat must realize where we were going.

"We are going back to the cottage aren't we?"

"Yes we are. You hinted at the idea enough dude."

"I did not. I'm glad we are going. We have spent so much time there I think we should have part ownership in the place."

"Yea, we should." We rode up the rest of the way in silence. The drive seemed quick. We had gone there often enough. It was a familiar experience by now. When we got to the cottage, we unpacked, went for a walk. We went back to where we had picnicked and walked to the lake.

When we went back to the cottage, I sent Mat to take a long bath. While he was in the tub, I got out things for his birthday. I had brought a card, a bottle of champagne and leather chaps. I put them on the table in the kitchen. I changed into my jock and sat waiting. Mat walked into the kitchen.

"Your birthday suit huh guy."

"Well, it's my birthday. I felt the birthday suit was an suitable choice. What's all this?" Mat asked.

"Your birthday supplies, a card, a gift, and a bottle of champagne to celebrate."

"What did you get me?"

"Open it and find out." He tore the package open. He pulled out the leather chaps and held them in front of him. Then he slipped into them.

"My old ones never fit. How did you get such a good fit without me being there?"

"I took your old ones with me and told them where they didn't fit. They made these from your old chaps and my suggestions."

"They, and you, did a good job. Thanks." He walked over and kissed me. He started to play with my chest and rub my back. "Thanks for bringing me up here honey. I like this place so much."

"You are welcome. I enjoy this place. I also enjoy seeing that hairy butt of yours hanging out in the breeze." We opened the champagne and drank a toast to Mat's birthday. It started to rain. Mat sat on my lap and we watched the rain. It was slow and soothing. Mat kissed me again, and started playing with my chest again. We ended making love on the kitchen table white it was raining slow and easy.

"Let's go walk in the rain." Mat grinned.

"Let's go guy." We slipped on jeans and shirts. We walked up the path outside the cottage and got drenched. Mat started taking off his clothes.

"What are you doing?" I shouted.

"I'm drenched to the skin. I might as well just get good and wet."

"Isn't it cold dude?"

"It's not bad. Try it yourself." So, I did. It was a little cold at first, but I got used to it. We walked to the lake and went for a swim. The rain started to come down harder. We ran back to the cottage. Neither one thought about the fact we ran back naked until we were in the cottage, putting wet clothes on chairs to dry.

"Do you realize we just ran all the way back without a stitch on?"

"Not until we walked in the door Mat. I wonder if anyone else is up here and saw us?"

"Who knows? With the rain, anyone up here is probably inside and not looking out anyway."

"That's probably true. I'm kind of chilly. Let's take a hot bath."

"I just took one Darrin! I guess it would warm me up. I see we have splashed mud on ourselves as well." I followed Mat to the bathroom. We ran a tub of hot water. I put in some bubble bath I had brought. We sat in the tub and got warm. We always did such unusual things at this cottage. Mats birthday weekend we walked, swam, and just had a good time. It was hard to leave, as usual.

Work moved us through the end of April and through May. It seemed like only a few days had passed and June arrived. Mat had been making statements about some surprise he had in store for my birthday. I wasn't sure what to expect. I just prepared for almost anything. I took two days off work, as per his request. He had also taken off two days. When I woke up the morning of my birthday, I really expected something strange to happen. Mat was already downstairs. I went down cautiously to see what he was up to down there.

"Mornin' honey."

"Happy thirty-first."

"So what are you up to?"

"Oh, just fixing breakfast." He walked over and hugged me. Gave me a big kiss.

"What are you fixing?"

"Mexican omelet."

"Smells tasty."

"Sit down. I'll get you a cup of coffee." He poured a cup of coffee and walked over and handed it to me. He kissed me again and went back to the stove.

"What is this special surprise of yours guy?"

"You'll see later on. Don't worry. It's nothing terrible."

"I'm not worried. Just curious."

"Here's your omelet. Eat while it's hot."

"You eating dude?"

"Yea, I just fixed them one at a time so I wouldn't ruin one. Mine will be done shortly. Go ahead, eat. I'll join you in a minute."

I began eating my omelet and Mat did join me shortly. He cleaned up when we finished. He walked back over to the table.

"Let's get ready for the day. I want to go for a drive."

"Whatever you say." We got ready and left. We headed downtown. I wasn't sure where we were going. I couldn't tell by the direction Mat was taking. I wasn't sure what he was up to. We pulled into a parking lot.

"If you will follow me please."

"Sure. The curiosity is killing me!" We walked down a couple of blocks. Then I realized where we were going. We were headed for the leather shop that we used at the store. The place I had Mat's chaps made. I knew where we were going, but not exactly why. We walked in and Mat went to talk to the clerk. He motioned me to come over.

"They need to measure you for a pair of chaps and a vest. Since I didn't know how to do this, I had to bring you in to have your exact measurements taken. This is the surprise I was talking about."

"I'm surprised. A leather vest *and* chaps?"

"Yes, made to your specifications. Choose whatever you want." The tailor took my measurements. I looked at all the available styles. I picked what I liked best and the order was written up. We walked back to the car.

"Thank you honey."

"I didn't know what to do for sure. I wanted to take you in earlier and have you measured so you would have the vest and chaps for today. Yet, I wanted it to be a surprise. So, I made the choice to make you wait, so it would be a surprise on your birthday."

"I'm glad you waited. I wish I had them today, but I like the idea of surprise. Why did you have me take two days off?"

"Because, I do have one other thing planned. In the trunk are our bags. Colt has a house key and is going to watch Gent. I've rented a cottage, but in a different place. One of the guys at work was telling me about this other place he had been to. So, I made reservations there. We're not headed home. We are headed out of town."

"You are sneakier than I am. Another cottage huh. I do enjoy getting away from the city for a couple of days."

We listened to music, talked a little about the new place we were going. We commented on whether or not it would be as much fun as the old stand by. The ride was enjoyable. Arriving at the new cottages, we noticed one instant difference. There was a main lodge, with little cottages surrounding it. It wasn't as open or as rustic as the place we usually went. We checked into the cottage. We found another difference. The cottage was all one level. There was a large deck off the back of the cottage. It overlooked a lake. The cottage was a little more modern. We unpacked, went out to the deck and sat.

"I don't know if I like this place or not Darrin. I guess I should have just stuck with the old place."

"It's always good to try out new places. This is very different, Mat, but we haven't gone exploring yet. We may like this better in the end guy."

"That's true. Do you want to go explore?"

"Might as well. Let's see what the place has to offer."

As we walked around, we found this place was a little more organized. You could rent a sailboat for a day. You could rent horses. There were guided tours of the countryside. The lodge had a restaurant. This was set up with planned activities, rather than the self-exploring at the other cottage. We found a path to walk. It had little places where you could stop and read signs and find out about the history. Overall, it was a place where things were planned for your entertainment. Instead of you left to fend for yourself. We agreed that the next day we would rent a boat and go sailing. We spent the rest of the day walking on the "guided" path and reading up on the history of the place. It was as pretty, but not as secluded.

We went back to our cottage and sat on the deck. Mat made us a cocktail and we looked out at the sailboats on the lake. It was very much the opposite of the cottage we usually went.

"Darrin, I'm going to go in and change. I'll be back in a few minutes."

"Ok, I'll sit here and watch the boats. I'm looking forward to sailing."

"Me, too I haven't been sailing in years. My parents used to go sailing every summer. I'll be right back." Mat walked out of the room.

I looked out at the boats. I had been on a motor boat before, been water skiing, but never sailing on a sailboat. I was looking forward to that.

"Darrin, could you come in here for a minute?"

"Be right there." I walked into the bedroom, and found Mat naked on the bed. He had written on his chest in icing "*Happy 31st*", and had covered himself in whipped cream from his stomach to his thighs.

"I thought I would be your birthday cake."

"Nice birthday cake. Good looking. Only one candle guy?"

"You get the idea."

"Yes, I do." I walked over to Mat and began eating the frosting off the hair on his chest. Then I managed to get my face covered in whipped cream as I moved down his body. I was having so much fun I didn't care. I took off my clothes.

"Mind if I blow out the candle?"

"No, not at all." I put my lips on the "candle" and it tasted like mint.

"How did you get a condom to taste like mint?"

"They sell these items at your store. Don't you even keep track of your stock?"

"Guess I missed that one." We made love. Mat never ceased to amaze me how he could make safe sex so stimulating. I admired and loved that about him. After, we were both sticky and gooey from icing and whipped cream. We took a shower together. We went to the lodge and ate dinner. After dinner we went for a walk around the lake. When we got back to the cottage, we went to bed.

In the morning we got up and went sailing. We did have fun. Mat remembered how to sail and taught me how to sail a sailboat. I missed the instant mobility of a motor boat, but it was fun to have the wind guide you along. We spent the day on the lake and didn't come back to the cottage until dusk. When we returned, we had dinner and went to bed. The next morning it was difficult to get up and go back to the routine of home.

We had been home a couple of weeks when I got the call to come down, pick up my chaps, and vest. I picked them up and had them on when Mat got home. He was excited to see me in my new get up, since the vest and chaps was all I had on to greet him. We had one of our spontaneous lovemaking sessions.

For our year anniversary, I took Mat back up to our "new" cottages. I called ahead and rented a white horse from their stable. At a costume shop, I rented a prince's costume and packed it to take to the cottage. It had been a long week and when we arrived Mat laid down to take a nap. While he napped, I grabbed the prince costume, changed and walked up to the stables to get the white horse I rented. I got on the horse rode to the cottage and stopped out front. I began to yell for Mat. Finally, he appeared at the front door.

"Prince Charming here," I yelled to Mat.

"So you finally showed up. You took your sweet time arriving!" He called back as he walked up to the horse.

"Some things in life just take time." I said to Mat. "We made it for a year together. I figured I could count myself as your Prince Charming on his white horse. Happy first anniversary."

"Yea, I would say you were my Prince Charming!" Mat said.

I got down from the horse and kissed Mat. We walked together to return the horse to the stable and walked back to the cottage. Mat had tears in his eyes. He hugged me close.

"That was the damnedest thing I have ever seen. And one of the most romantic gestures anyone has ever done for me." Mat kissed me. "Thank you so much. You are truly are my Prince Charming. You never cease to amaze me with the things you do."

Mat took me by the hand and we walked to the bedroom. He pulled a box out of his suitcase and handed it to me. I opened the box, inside were two rings.

"What's this guy?" I asked.

"What does it look like?" Mat grinned.

"Wedding bands." I said.

"Correct. I know we are not able to legally marry, but I wanted us to have a symbol of our relationship to carry with us. I thought if we had a wedding band to look at when we were apart, it would be a reminder of our relationship." Mat explained.

"Well guy, now that is very touching." I said. I pulled the rings out of the box. I took Mat's ring and put it on his finger. "With this ring I vow my devotion to you."

Mat took the second ring and slid it on my finger. "With this ring I unite with my Prince Charming, for better or for worse."

We had a very romantic weekend. I had deeply touched Mat with my Prince Charming routine. He had deeply touched my heart with the rings.

The business just continued to grow. We merged with another company, but I maintained my part ownership with the merger. We made plans to open a store in Arizona. We actually bought the land and built a new store on the site.

That was three years ago. We were about to open yet another store. I was going to be the one to open that fifth new store, which would be the second store in Arizona. That would be in October or November. Mat was coming with me. I would be gone a month while I trained employees and helped set up the new store. It would be almost like a vacation.

Our only problem would be Mat getting the time off to go. I was sure he could get at least two weeks. I was hoping he could stretch it to at least 3 weeks. If we liked Arizona, we could move there, I had been given the choice. We would just have to play it by ear and see what happened. Mat would have to find a new job, but he was ready to take that challenge. Life had certainly taken another turn for the best. I looked forward to each and every day with Mat in my life.

Interlude II Zee Gang

I handed everyone their drinks, everyone gathered up another plate of food to eat.

"Mat and I probably are going to be out of town for a month or so opening a new store. The business is going well right now," Darrin said.

"Seriously?" Derrek asked.

"Seriously Dude," Darrin answered, "you wouldn't want to baby sit Gent would you?"

"I could if you want me to." Derrek replied.

"Or, I could." I replied.

"They deserve combat pay," Marshall replied.

"Funny Marshall. Don't hear any offers from you or Sampson," Darrin teased.

"I told you, Tom and I are moving to California."

"In a condo down town? Gent the bounding cotton ball!" Sampson responded. "Are you out of your mind? Don't answer that, I know that answer."

"Sure, you both have flimsy excuses!" Darrin laughed.

"Gent can be a real bundle of joy to deal with," Marshall said. "Derrek and Colt are either crazy, or very generous."

"He's not that bad," Darrin defended his dog, "Sampson, what are you writing about now?"

"Darrin, I'm working on a novel that combines various parts of each of your lives in a racy little story."

"How is that Sampson?" Derrek asked.

"I've taken key events about each of you and put them into one character that portrays the beginning of a relationship. I've used little pieces of all of your lives. Be glad I am not naming names in my book."

"What parts of our lives are you using?" Marshall asked.

"Many parts. I've taken my own life, and the four of yours, and tried to compile a character with the trials and tribulations of meeting someone, falling in love, and beginning a relationship. I have used things I know about each of you to make the character more plausible."

"Sounds interesting. I've always wanted to write a book," I said.

"So, write one! You've had enough experiences in your life Colt to write a book," Sampson said.

"I'd hope!" Darrin teased, "Or a soap opera!"

"I bet you could do it," Derrek added.

"I just may." I said.

"Yea, you could write a book Colt. Back to my question, what parts?" Marshall asked.

"It's hard to explain, Marshall. For example, I took from each of you the beginnings of your relationships. Each of you had different starts, but in some ways they were similar. Wanting to be alone, wanting to be with that person, having different problems with the sexual side of your relationships. The difficulty of getting to know someone, their habits and your habits, those first few months of living together and getting your boundaries and role in the relationship established. I took the similarities and used them to make a character and his lover."

"In other words, we have to wait and read the book," Derrek said.

"I guess that's what I'm saying, although Colt and Marshall will wait for the movie version to come out!" Sampson said. "However, there is one thing I can share with you. We have all had various reactions from our families about being gay. I tried to show that."

"Derrek, speaking of which, how did your parents take the news? I heard you recently told them." Darrin quizzed.

"Not so well. They would rather I was a criminal than gay. My brothers and sister were relieved I finally told everyone. I think my parents will come around eventually." Derrek explained.

"Sounds like my parents. When I visit them or talk to them, as long as I don't mention Ron, or any other topic that relates to my life, we are fine. I mention Ron, AIDS, anything gay and there is dead silence." Sampson said.

"I guess I'm lucky. My family accepts me for what I am," Darrin said. "One of my sisters is even involved in AIDS benefit projects."

"Mine accept me," I said. "My sister even stopped dating a man once because he didn't want to be exposed to the faggot in the family. I guess I am lucky."

"What about you Marshall?" Derrek asked.

"I haven't told either one of them. I know they suspect because of Craig and Tom." Marshall said.

"Well, that's one of the topics I used you four as a reference. One of the characters had total acceptance from his family. The other one does not." Sampson explained.

"Why don't you just use your relationship with Ron?" Marshall asked.

"Because, I wanted to write about a character that wasn't solely based on me, I wanted to have a character that was representative of a gay relationship. One that had generic qualities all gay men could relate to, I hope. I just put things from all of our lives that were similar into print. It makes it more varied, yet authentic."

"Yea, uh huh, I suppose. You and Ron's relationship would be interesting," Derrek said.

"Mainly he didn't want to write an entire novel about a queen!" Darrin said.

"The juicy details only," Marshall added.

"Sounds like you have an audience here," I said.

"Yea, sure. Like I said, Derrek and Darrin would buy the book, and you and Marshall would wait for the movie version," Sampson quipped.

"Still be a profit, right?" Darrin explained.

"I guess that's true, Darrin," Sampson said.

"How long have you and Ron been together anyway?" Marshall asked.

"Little over a year. It still feels like just the first few months."

"That is good!" Derrek said.

"Anyone need food or beverage?" I asked.

"I'm fine," Darrin replied.

"Me, too," came from Sampson.

"I'll take a beer," Derrek added.

"Oh, what the hell, me, too," Marshall joined, "I'll have another Manhattan as well."

Sampson and Ron

My first impression of Ron did not amount to a long-term relationship. I had just resolved to go celibate for at least a month. I had decided that there had been way too many one-night stands, way too many attempts to try to make a relationship work. I was determined to take a break from the meet, drink, grope in the dark, have sex, and never see one another again cycle.

So from now on, it was going to be out for cocktails with a friend on weekends only and home early in the evening. To begin my month of celibacy I asked Colt to go with me to Bobs for cocktails and a relaxing evening away from all the daily drudgeries. We were standing watching the men dance, drinking our cocktails. Ron walked up to me and asked me to dance. He said he had danced with me before. With his looks I knew he hadn't. He had the kind of looks I wouldn't forget and he was too young for my taste. At first I thought it was a come on of some kind. As the evening progressed, I realized that he was honestly interested in me.

"He's a good looking man, Sampson," Colt said.

"Yes, he is. Very young though. I'll bet he's barely twenty-one."

"Worse things could happen. At least he can country dance!"

"He also can carry on a decent conversation. It's good to have someone who not only can dance, but who can converse on top of it!" Ron walked back to me and asked me to dance again. I told Colt to stay put, gave him one of my glares that I meant what I said, and went to the dance floor with Ron.

"Sampson, you do look like someone I have danced with before." Ron said again.

"Ron I would remember dancing with you if I had. I have a good memory for the men I have danced with before. And I seldom ever dance with someone as young as you are."

"You are a good dancer. Better than the guy I thought you were." Ron commented.

"Thank you Ron. I enjoy country dancing. Mainly because you can dance close to the man you are with." We danced to several songs. I was impressed with the dancing ability Ron had. He was a good dance partner. "Shall we sit this one out? I need another cocktail."

"Sure. Let me get you a cocktail. What are you drinking?" Ron asked.

"Vodka seven." Ron walked to the bar and I went to find Colt. He was standing talking in the same place I left him. He understood my glare.

"Hi again, Sampson. So, how's it going?"

"Fine Colt. He's an excellent dancer, easy to talk to as well. He even went to buy me a cocktail."

"That was considerate." Colt teased. Ron walked back and handed me my cocktail. He put his arms around me and hugged me.

"Thank you sir." I replied.

"You're welcome. I'm going to play a game of pool. You going to be here a while?"

"Yea, I am."

"I'll be back again to dance if you want." Ron said as he turned to leave.

"I'll be here somewhere. If you want to dance, I will."

"Ok. I'll be back." Ron walked off and I began to think about how young he was. I enjoyed his company. Few younger men could I actually talk to and enjoy, usually they were just airheads.

"Looks like he has an interest in you, Sampson."

"You think. I don't know. He's awfully young. You know I don't get along well with younger men. That instant

275

message generation, sex is a strip and cum routine, no sense of making it something special. Besides I have gone celibate, remember?"

"Yea, like you could remain celibate for more than twenty-four hours! Besides there's always a first time for everything you know. Perhaps Ron will be the boy to prove your theory about boys to be wrong."

"This is true. We'll see what happens."

"Don't judge him by his age. He seems nice."

"I won't, I said, we'll see what happens. I'll do a card reading on myself and see what it says." Ron walked back and asked me to dance again. We danced to several songs and talked. We played pinball and had a few more cocktails. Ron even bought Colt a beer. Somewhere between dances and cocktails, Ron suggested we go home together.

I warned him that all I was going to do was cuddle and hug. I had a new outlook on going home with someone, no more casual sex. I explained to Ron I had ridden in with Colt, so I needed to prepare him for the fact we were going home together. Ron was the typical young man, no car, had hitched a ride with a friend. I walked through the bar and found Colt.

"Colt, would you mind taking Ron and me back to my place?"

"Sure, no problem. Going to stay celibate?"

"Yes I am! I already told Ron just hugging and cuddling nothing else."

"Sure, I'll believe that when I see it." Colt chuckled.

"You just wait Colt. I can handle it." Ron walked up to us and we left. Colt dropped us off and gave me one of his grins that he gives when he doubts I will keep my word. Ron and I walked into my condo and sat.

"A penthouse condo! Interesting place."

"I like it. Do you want another cocktail?" I asked.

"Yea, and to see the rest of this place, if you don't mind," Ron asked. "I have to ask, what is with this cocktail term. Why not just call it a drink?"

"Well for one thing, I don't consider alcohol a drink, water, iced tea, lemonade, those are a drink. For another it sounds classier. Besides, look at the play on works, cock and tail in the same place. How much better can it get?" I went and made us both a cocktail and then showed Ron through the condo. We came back to the living room and sat.

"You have some great art pieces."

"I travel a great deal and I have collected them over the years. If I see something unique that I like, I buy it."

"You write I gather. Up in your loft I noticed by your computer several manuscripts."

"I do. Magazine articles, short stories, plays, novels."

"I'd like to read them sometime. I like this place. The high ceilings make it feel spacious. It's fancy, but cozy.

The plants are uncommon too. You have quiet a flair for colors."

"I try. Need your cocktail freshened?"

"Sure. I should tell you, I am only twenty. If that makes you uncomfortable serving a minor, I will understand."

"I knew you were young. How do you get into the bars?" My suspicions were right.

"Well, I have a fake ID, and most times I don't get carded." Ron replied.

"Lucky for you young man, I am not sure I should be serving a minor!" I snapped.

"Well, I can certainly walk down to the liquor store and buy my own booze if you'd like," Ron said.

"No, no, it's your life, your decision." I freshened Ron's cocktail and sat next to him again. He put his arms around me and started to kiss me. I kissed him back, but held a certain reserve. I had warned him, cuddling, but that was all. He began to play with my ear. His tongue was piercing, but I resisted.

"You are determined aren't you?" Ron observed.

"I told you Ron, cuddling, hugging, and that is all. I meant that!"

"I can see. You're so tall that it is difficult for me to reach the erogenous zones on the back of your neck. I know I could seduce you. However, I will not. Just how tall are you any way?"

"I am six foot one in my stocking feet, and six foot six in my heels," I said thinking I could distract his intentions for a while.

"Your heels? What do you mean by that?" Ron asked.

Ah, success, the child was side tracked. "Well, I do a comedy routine, in drag once a month."

"Wow, really? What name do you use, maybe I have seen your perform," Ron asked.

"I go by Ruby Balls," I said.

"No, I guess I haven't seen you, why Ruby balls? Some Christmas theme?" Ron seemed confused.

"Well dear child, think about it. I have reddish hair, and the slang for having sex is balls and the slang for testicles is balls, so Ruby Balls." I explained.

"Oh, I get it, very clever. So what's your act, lip-syncing like all the rest of the drag queens?"

"No, no, I don't sing. I said I do a comedy routine. I just do a stand up bit, but dressed as a woman. I think it gives it more class."

"I would like to see you perform sometime," Ron said.

"Perhaps one day you will." We cuddled on the couch hugged and kissed. Ron seemed to be respecting my wishes.

"I'm a little drunk, or should I say, cocktailed and tired. Mind if I sleep with you? I won't do anything. I promise!" Ron grinned at me.

"As long as you understand that we SLEEP and that is all."

"I understand." We went to the bedroom and went to bed. In undressing, I noticed Ron's youthful tight body. It would be difficult just to sleep. When I woke in the morning, Ron was still sleeping. We did sleep side by side and that was all. I told Colt I could stick to my decision. I got up, went to the living room and smoked a cigarette. Ron came into the living room while I was smoking.

"Morning. Sleep ok?" I asked.

"Yes, I did. I didn't believe you were serious about just cuddling, but you proved you were."

"I told you that in the bar last night. Do you want to take a shower?"

"If you don't mind. Then I need to go home so I can change for work."

"You work Saturdays?" I quizzed.

"Yep, I work at a bank, we are open on Saturday." Ron replied.

"Well then I guess you best get moving." We walked into the bathroom. I showed him where the towels, soap, and shampoo were. He took a shower while I looked over one of my manuscripts. While I was reading, Ron came up to the loft and hugged me.

"You are so tall. I like that. I see in this light you have green eyes. Very seductive. You mind taking me to my place now. I need to get to work."

"So a compliment to get me suckered up to take you home?" I snapped.

"No, no, I meant that, I didn't notice your eyes last night. They are sexy." Ron said calmly.

"Yes, I can take you home, we can leave now. I'd like to jump in the shower first however."

"Go ahead. I'll have a cigarette and check out some of your art pieces." Ron replied.

"Wow, a man of your generation that smokes. I thought you were all so health conscious and anti cigarettes."

"Not all of my generation, obviously." Ron replied. I went in and took a quick shower. When I came back to the living room, Ron was looking at one of my plants. I walked over to him and hugged him.

"Ready?"

"Yea. You don't mind do you?"

"No, not at all. I actually have to say to you that in your actions you have earned my respect. I am very touched that you respected my wishes."

"There is no use pushing someone to do something they don't want to do. I think it just opens the door for trouble and I don't want trouble." Ron replied. We went down to my car and I took Ron to his place. He didn't live far away. We were silent on the drive. We both smoked a cigarette and sat thinking.

"Want to come up and see my apartment?" Ron asked eagerly.

"Sure, why not." I parked the car and we hiked back to his building.

"I have to warn you, I have a grumpy roommate and he gets moody. He may be there." Ron cautioned.

"I can ignore him." When we walked into Ron's apartment, his roommate left. He did appear to be rather grumpy. Ron took me through the apartment. We went to his bedroom so he could change. I sat on his bed while he got clothes out of the closet. He had stripped to his underwear and walked over to the bed. He sat next to me. A cat walked into the room and jumped up on the bed.

"Sampson, this is Stud, my cat," Ron explained, "Stud, Sampson."

"Hello Stud." He jumped off the bed and ran out the door.

"I did enjoy last night. I haven't enjoyed myself that much in a long time." Ron said, "It was a fun evening, and nice even without having sex at the end of the evening."

"I enjoyed myself, too. Every encounter you have with another man doesn't have to end in sex." He began to kiss me and pushed me back on the bed. Before I knew it, I lost my celibate thoughts and we were beyond cuddling. I lost my bet with Colt. Ron had gotten to me! Ron rolled over to look at the clock.

"It's so late! I've missed my bus. I'm going to be late for work!"

"I could take you to work. Even though I shouldn't since you persisted in having your way." I quipped.

"You know, you can't seduce the willing. I'd appreciate that, if you wouldn't mind taking me." Ron dressed in a hurry and I drove him to work. I gave him my number so he could call me on his break.

On the drive home, I thought about Ron. I could just hear Colt with his I told you so. At home, I went to the loft and worked on my latest manuscript. Off and on I took a break as my mind drifted back to Ron. I had done so well when we got home from Bobs. Then this morning I went back to my normal self. Yet it was great. It was worth it. I'd see if Ron called me or not. I was so wrapped up in my work I forgot Ron for the time being and the phone ringing brought me back.

"Hello, Sampson, it's Ron."

"Hello, Ron. What's up?"

"I'm on break. It's been a wild morning. I was wondering if you would want to go out again tonight."

"We could. Where would you like to go?"

"I guess we could go back to Bobs."

"That sounds ok. When did you want to go?"

"Any time that's good for you," Ron said.

"The bar doesn't get busy until after ten."

"That's true. I guess I could meet you there then."

"What time do you get off work?" I asked.

"Oh, three, three-thirty today."

"Why don't I pick you up at work? We can go out to dinner or something."

"Ok. Be a nice change from riding the bus."

"I'll see you at three thirty then." I said.

"See you then. I'll let you go, by."

"Goodbye." I hung up the phone and remembered I was going to do a Tarot Card reading for myself. Colt was about the only person who ever really trusted my readings. Marshall in a pinch would ask. Everyone else called it hocus-pocus, but for me I always found great insights to my life. I shuffled the cards and thought about Ron until I felt comfortable. I laid out the cards and began to read.

This does show a man, a relationship, some conflict, a move, new home, and a partner. I laid out some more cards, romance, work, travel. Nothing really negative, perhaps Colt was right, I should give this young man a chance. I spent the rest of the afternoon writing. Some of what I was feeling made what I was writing come to life a little more. I was still amazed I had given in to Ron, I was disappointed with myself, but I didn't feel bad. Going out to dinner would give me a chance to see how I felt today. I checked the time found it was mid afternoon. I showered, dressed, and went to pick up Ron.

While driving to Ron's work I wondered if he'd remember the car and if he would be on time or not. Pulling up to the building, I saw he was standing on the sidewalk waiting. He walked to the car as I pulled to a stop and got in.

"Hello Sampson. I appreciate you picking me up at work. I was trying to remember if you had a green sedan or not."

"Hello Ron. Your memory was correct. Any place special you'd like to go for dinner?"

"Before dinner, I'd like to go home and change, if you don't mind."

"Sure, fine it is early. We can stop by your place first." I drove to Ron's. He asked me to come up while he changed. I hoped his roommate wasn't home. We walked into the apartment and I didn't see his roommate. I hoped he wasn't there.

"I'll be as quick as possible Sampson."

"No hurry Ron." I looked around a little and then I walked into the bedroom. There stood Ron in underwear and socks. He looked frustrated. He turned to me.

"I can't decide what to wear. Are we going any place fancy?"

"It's kind of up to you. If you want to, why?"

"Well, I thought if I knew where we were going to eat it would help me decide what to put on." He walked over to me and put his arms around me. He kissed me on the chin. His bare skin felt soft and warm. He stood looking up at me waiting for an answer.

"Dress casual, then we can go some place that isn't fancy."

"Ok, I will." He continued to stand there holding me. He kissed my chin again and then my neck.

"I thought you were going to get dressed!"

"You said no hurry. I feel good standing here holding you. You could undress, too." Before I could answer, I felt my shirt being unbuttoned. As we continued to kiss as I felt my shirt being removed.

"I guess I don't get a chance to answer?" I replied.

"You weren't resisting, I thought you had answered." Ron continued to undress me, and before I knew it, we were in bed. He was very skillful in manipulating me to the point I lost control of my thoughts. He felt so good to touch. We just fell back on the bed and lay there quietly. I heard the door of the apartment open. It had to be his roommate. At least we were in Ron's bedroom.

"You home Ron?"

"I'm in my room. I have company."

"Oh, ok. I'm going to shower and go out."

"Fine," Ron yelled and then lowered his voice, "he can be a sweet heart, but he can be such a bitch. Let's stay in here until he leaves."

"It's ok with me." We snuggled on the bed and listened to the shower. I kissed Ron and started to play with his body. I looked to see if the door was closed enough that you couldn't see in the room. It was. For the first time, I took a good look at this young man's body. His hair was coal black, like I had always wished my ruby red hair had been. The very top of his chest and his legs were so hairy they could pass for a rug.

I began to play in that mat of black hair on his chest and found two large nipples to pinch. I aroused Ron so much, that while his roommate took a shower, we finished our passionate moment. After we heard his roommate leave, we showered, dressed, and walked to a nearby restaurant.

"Ron, I'd like to compliment you on something."

"What's that?"

"Few men I have been to bed with practice safe sex. I always have to insist. You just automatically do. I find that very admirable."

"I don't know anything else. I guess I just never thought about not practicing safe sex, I value my health. When I became sexually active that was the decision I made."

"That was a very mature decision for one so young. I still find it a characteristic that shows concern, compassion, and respect for ones self."

"Thank you." Ron said with a grin.

"I have to ask, have you been tested for HIV?" I said bluntly.

"Actually yes, just recently I went in and got tested, and you?" Ron responded without a complete answer.

"You didn't exactly give me a complete answer yet, are you positive or negative?" I continued on.

"And you didn't exactly give me an answer either," Ron quipped back, "I am HIV negative he said with a smile."

"Well, now see how easy it was just to answer the question. I am as well, and I would very much like to keep it that way thank you. And while we are on the topic of sex, young man, I call your age group the instant message generation. Your quickie sex encounters are fine, but your generation has no idea how to have a fulfilling sexual encounter. If we continue to see one another, one day I will have to show you what slow and easy can do for you."

"Well, old man, I guess I have something to look forward to then, slow and easy. From what I could see, my *instant message* method wasn't being pushed away."

"No, I said it was fine, just not as exciting as taking your time." We ate dinner, walked back to the car and drove to Bobs. We danced, had several cocktails, and ended back at my place. Ron stayed the night. The next week we spent time together either at my place or his. We watched movies, played chess, went out for cocktails, watched television, and continued to break my celibacy vow.

We spent so much time together that first week I had kind of lost contact with my other friends. So Ron and I decided to meet his friends and mine for cocktails and evenings out. Ron seemed to take a particular liking to Colt, and I took a particular liking to his friend, Jack. We seemed to end up with either Ron's friends or mine, but never mixed. We had hoped Jack and Colt would hit if off, but they did not.

I began work on a new comedy routine. I put it together and tested it out on Ron. He of course was very complimentary. I needed a bigger audience to play off to see if the routine would work. Colt had invited Ron and me to a party at his house so I did the routine for his guests. It seemed to go well. My reception was good, but I needed to change a few lines, make my delivery timing a little different, but I was ready to perform to a crowd of strangers and see how it went.

Ron and his roommate began to have many arguments. Nights we spent at his apartment became very tense. We never knew if his roommate was going to be upset or not. We had only been seeing each other for three weeks. Yet I felt this was the relationship I had always wanted.

Because of the difficulties where Ron was living, we decided it would be best if he moved to my place.

The one adjustment I had to make was Ron's cat. I wasn't used to having a pet at the condo. Moreover, I was not particularly fond of cats either. Still Ron moved in, cat and all. His first night in the condo we began to set our boundaries.

"Ron, I have to tell you it is going to take me some getting used to having your cat here. I've told you before I'm not fond of cats. I find kitty litter boxes appalling, but I am sure he'll grow on me."

"Oh, he's such a good kitty. You'll get used to him. He's going to enjoy exploring the place. And I will keep the liter box clean, I promise."

"I'm sure you will. Are you sure he remembers where his litter box is? I don't want to walk into any surprises on my carpets!" I snapped.

"Yes, he always is good about that."

"I have something in the kitchen for you." I said. We walked to the kitchen and I got out the bottle of JD I had bought as a moving in gift. He preferred to drink JD and coke and I seldom had that in the condo. I handed it to Ron.

"JD, you listen well. How nice!"

"I thought we could celebrate your moving in with it." I explained to Ron as I hugged him.

"Thank you Sampson. It's nice to have someone do something special for me." He kissed me on the cheek. I poured us each a shot of JD and we drank it.

"Good grief I don't know how you stand that stuff, it burns going down!" I remarked. Ron just laughed.

We walked back out to the living room with our glasses and the JD. I filled the bowl on the bong and we smoked it in celebration of the move. Ron snuggled up next to me on the couch. We hugged each other. Stud crawled up next to us. We began to play and ended up making love. I did enjoy Ron's company.

"I am glad you moved in here," I said softly.

"Me too. It is a good feeling."

"Yes, it is." We got up and went to bed. It was pleasant to have someone in the condo, someone who cared about me. I watched Ron as he fell asleep. He was so young. I swore I would never be with anyone younger than me. This was certainly not what I ever planned on having happen to me.

I poured myself into my comedy routine trying to perfect it. I had decided to do a performance at a local comedy club and then repeat the performance at Colt's Halloween party. I bounced lines off Ron, but I really needed an audience to see a crowd's reaction. Ron and I began to spend time with friends, as well as alone. We were beginning to get into a routine of our own, establishing our boundaries and our roles in that relationship. Ron was very mature for his age and we seemed to have similar ideas on time together and time alone.

I invited the gang, and people I had worked with, to the comedy club to see my performance, and Ron invited his friends. I was so nervous about this particular performance I couldn't believe it. We had the gang meet us at the condo and go downtown with us. We had a couple of shots before we left.

There was quite a crowd at the club when we arrived. It looked to be a sizable group to be here so early. I sent the gang out to their seats and walked back stage to dress and put on my makeup. I waited for my intro. When I got the intro, I walked on stage to perform with butterflies, no large moths, in my stomach. I hoped I could pull myself together.

Good evening ladies, gentlemen, and fellow queens. I'd like to introduce myself to you all, I am Ruby Balls, and dam proud of it. Ah, I see a few of you had to ponder that one. You do know why gay men wear a moustache don't you? To hide the stretch marks! I saw a gay family moving today. It was so touching to watch two hunks, two dogs, one cat, known as two point five pets, and forty houseplants parade into their new home. Lovely family. You know you can divide the gay male community into four basic groups. You have the GQ males. They stand in front of the mirror all the time; at the gym, they position themselves in front of the mirror. In their homes there are mirrors every five feet, can't miss a chance to stand and model, you know S&M. Ah, which brings us to those butch leather boys. They love to parade around in their leather with their bare ass hanging out for all to see. Oh baby, whips and chains, tie me down. Then we have the Levi boys. Always in a pair of faded blue jeans and a tight t-shirt, that leaves little to the imagination. You know those 501's, five buttons, oh unbutton me, one dick and sssuck! Then you have the fems, you know the men with manners and good taste? The ruler of that group is the queens. We queens do love a mystery, we like keeping you guessing. Hike that dick up the crack of my ass, put on a dress and let you wonder what is under it all. Say, I went to the park today to hang out for a while. Only thing was, the police officer I ran into found my hanging out to be indecent exposure. I thought I looked pretty decent myself. Ever notice at a party how you can always tell the gay men? You know the ones with cigarette ashes all over their shoulders. (So far, there had been few laughs from the crowd.) *Oh, this is a tough crowd, are you all breeders from Kansas or something? Speaking of Kansas, you know this isn't Kansas any more, because the scare crow is the man you find next to you the morning after bar cruising and just grabbing the closest live body you can at last call; the Lion is the hunk you tried to pick up all night but he already had a boy friend; and the tin man is the bartender that told you the bar was closed it was time to get the hell out and go home. You know I have found myself dating again. I've been out with a number of younger men. I like to call them the instant message generation. They do not talk to you in person. They have to instant message you or text message you on your cell. They even prefer to have their sex on line. Come to discover they have sex the same way in person. Their pants come off and in an instant they are done. Know what separates a gay relationship from a straight relationship? Straight couples count the years, gay couples count the months. Well, I would like to leave you with one final thought. A good man is hard to find, but a hard man, is good to find. Good night all.*

I got a loud round of applause. I was disappointed I didn't get more laughs, but I was nervous and my timing was off, which made the routine feel as if it wasn't as good as it could have been. Everyone I invited said I did well. I wasn't as sure as they were that it had gone well. However, I was the one on stage. We all went back to Bobs to celebrate after the performance. We had a good time. It seemed like between that night and the night of Colt's party time just snapped by.

Ron and I seemed to be spending "our" free time with friends and none of it alone any more. We had been together nearly two months now. I wanted to celebrate that event. The problem was it was the night after Colt's party. We would be caught between all the Halloween celebrations at the bars, and Colt's. I wanted to do something special and alone. I needed to talk to Ron.

I got busy writing on a new manuscript and rehearsing my comedy routine. I wanted the act to flow smoother than it had. I was thinking of changing a few lines, adding some new stuff. I also wanted to talk to Ron about being alone for a couple of nights. I got to the point where it was so important to me that I thought I was going to explode. One evening when I heard Ron yelling for me I decided we needed to chat.

"Sampson, Sampson, where are you? I'm home from work!" Ron's voice came booming from the front door. I started down from the loft.

"I'm up here Ron. I'll be right down." I hurried down the stairs as Ron was coming up the stairs. He greeted me with a kiss and a hug. "I'm glad you are home. I want to talk to you. How was your day?"

"Not too bad. I might get a promotion. I'm in line with two other employees." Ron said out of breath.

"That's good. Where do you stand with the other two?"

"Well, I'm not sure. I think my age is against me with this promotion. I would be working more directly with clients from the company's accounts. I think the big boss feels that an older person with more experience would do better." Ron explained.

"If he does, don't let it get you down. I hope you get it. Did you want me to read your cards?"

"No, I will just wait and see if I get it. So, what'd you want to talk to me about?"

"I'm feeling like we haven't spent much time together alone for the last couple of weeks. We have got caught up with friends and going out. I'd like to spend some alone time together."

"Well, we can. We have several commitments coming up soon though. Colt's party, we promised Jack we'd go out with him, your comedy act, and our friends at Bobs we promised to see. What did you have in mind?"

"Frankly, I wouldn't mind canceling some of our commitments. What I was thinking about is that we have spent almost two months together, and I'd like to spend time alone with you to celebrate that. I enjoy our friends, but I'd like to enjoy you alone. That is more important to me right now."

"Sounds fine. I don't mind spending time alone. It's just nice to have people over and go out with them. What did you want to do for the second month alone?"

"Be together mainly. Just not out particularly. Some ALONE, together activity."

"You haven't got an idea?" Ron asked.

"Not exactly I am toying with a couple of ideas."

"Ok. Sampson, I have something to ask you. Stud gets lonely sometimes when we are gone. I was wondering how you would feel about getting another kitty. He'd love a playmate."

"Where did that come from? I thought we were talking about us spending time alone."

"You told me something that was bugging you. This is bugging me. Equal time I guess?"

"The answer is no, Ron. One cat is enough. I wouldn't mind a dog though. That I could handle."

"So, can we get a dog? I think Stud would enjoy that."

"I'd like to Ron. Perhaps we could go shopping tonight." I said.

"Could we really?" Ron said with a smile, he was eager to go.

"Yes. I'm interested in getting a dog."

"Great. What kind?"

"I need to look around. A smaller dog I don't want a big dog!"

"Then let's go looking!"

"Would it be possible to eat first? I am rather hungry and I don't think the dogs in the pet stores are going anywhere in the next hour." I tried to slow Ron down.

"Yes, we can eat first. I just am excited about getting Stud a pal." We fixed dinner and Ron hurried through it like a little kid hurrying to go out and play with friends. When we cleaned up dinner, we went to pet stores. I didn't see any dog that I liked at the first store. At a second store, I found a dog I liked, but it had just been sold. I was disappointed, but not as much as Ron seemed to be. We looked most of the evening, but I just didn't see a dog I liked. I wanted to get a dog that was friendly and intelligent. Ron tried to talk me into several dogs and several cats. I maintained my position and we went home empty handed.

For the next couple of days we talked about a dog and I thought about our anniversary. My mind was on our anniversary, I was thinking about dinner out, and then home to watch a movie and snuggle on the couch together. I was hoping Ron would like the idea.

Ron was thinking about dogs, he was barraging me with ads about dogs. His thoughts were solely on a new pet. My thoughts were on a romantic evening home alone! For an entire week the only conversation Ron had was about finding a dog. I was thinking about our alone time, he was tracking down dogs to look at. He came home one night excited about something. He ran into the condo out of breath and tracked me down. He cornered me at the computer.

"Sampson, I have the greatest news!"

"Must be good, I didn't even get a hello, or a kiss. Let me guess, you got the promotion?" He gave me a quick kiss and hug.

"No, someone else got it. There are other chances coming up. No, I'm excited because my mom found a dog that I think would be perfect for us. It's a terrier and it is a female, like you wanted. She won't get too big. Can we go look at her? Can we tonight?"

"Not tonight. But, I'll have to see her before I decide."

"Can we go tonight?" Ron pleaded again. "Mom is keeping her for a friend who wants to find her a good home. I don't want to loose this opportunity!"

"YOU promised Colt we'd meet him at Bobs tonight, remember?" I quickly pointed out to Ron.

"We could still go. I'll call Colt, he'll understand. Can we?"

"Let's stick to our original plans. We can go look at her tomorrow, can't we?" I suggested.

"I guess. I just know you will like her." Ron prodded.

"Like I said, I'll have to see her first. Then I'll decide." We ate dinner and met Colt at Bobs. I had a feeling Ron wasn't going to let this subject rest.

"Hello Sampson, Ron." Colt greeted us. Ron went to buy a cocktail and left me to talk to Colt alone.

"Hi Colt. How are you?"

"Oh, fine, and you Sampson?"

"Fine."

"Here you go Sampson," Ron said as he handed me my cocktail.

"Thank you hon. That was quick."

"There was no one at the bar. Hey, Colt, did Sampson tell you? My mom found a dog I think will be perfect!"

"No, he didn't. Have you looked at him or her yet?" Colt asked.

"No, it's a she, I wanted to tonight, but we promised to meet you here."

"Like I said, I can't decide until we see her. We can go tomorrow Ron." I said.

"What kind of dog is it?" Colt asked.

"It's a terrier, female, and she won't get real big. Just what Sampson wants."

"You could have gone to look at her. I wouldn't have minded." Colt said innocently. I thought to myself, Colt would have to say that.

"See, Sampson, I told you!" Ron said.

"I know, but I felt like we needed to keep this commitment. You don't just change your plans when they involve others at a moment's notice."

"So, why don't you go ahead and look at her?" Colt added.

"Well, she's at Ron's mom's house. We didn't tell her we were coming over and it's late." I said trying to get Colt to take the hint I would rather go tomorrow.

"I could go call her. She stays up late!" Ron said excitedly.

"Oh, all right. Call her and see if she's going to be home." I sighed.

"Ok, I will. You want to come along Colt?"

"If you don't mind, sure I'd like to tag along." Colt agreed.

"I'll be right back." Ron ran off to call his mom. Colt and I went to buy another cocktail.

"How are things going with the comedy routine?" Colt asked.

"Before I answer that, couldn't you see the signals I was giving you? I really didn't want to go see this dog until tomorrow."

"Sorry, I just thought Ron was so excited that you could at least look at this dog tonight. It won't kill you to go look," Colt responded.

"I am aware there will be no harm in looking. I just think Ron is way to wound up in this dog search. He certainly could have waited one more day." I explained.

"He is young and he is just trying to make you happy. So, back to my question, how's the act coming?" Colt continued.

"My act, I am doing fine. I have most of the act in my mind. I haven't really written any new material yet. You still want me to do two performances?"

"Yea, I do. I'm excited about the party. Are you worried about performing twice in one night?"

"I'm a little nervous. I've got mixed feelings about this act. I hope it goes over." As I finished my sentence, I saw Ron coming back with a big grin.

"She'll be home, and up late working, so we can go over any time." Ron announced.

"Let me finish my cocktail. Then we can go." I sighed.

"Hon your glass is half empty, I am sure you can just swallow that down." Ron said impatiently.

"You know young man I do not like to be ordered about." I snapped back.

"Boys, boys, lets just chill out here, Sampson sip your drink, Ron, calm down we will get to your mom's tonight." Colt said trying to sooth the rough edges.

I downed my cocktail and we drove to Ron's mothers and looked at the dog. With pressure from Ron, and even some from Colt, we took the dog. She was cute and seemed intelligent. After we came home, I began to remember about puppy training. You have to watch every move they make, be on top of them every moment. They have endless energy and a propensity for making messes.

We discussed several names and ended up with Roberta. I would allow her to be called Berta or Rob, but not Robbie. She was very affectionate. It took Stud and Roberta awhile to get used to one another, but they were doing better by Colt's party.

I was fond of Roberta, but not so fond of her necessary walks and all the training that went into house breaking her. The condo I had loved was now a place I was not so pleased with any more. I wished I had a yard. All the walks I had to go on could be simplified to just opening a door and letting her out in the yard. I was beginning to understand what Colt had to go through with Max daily.

I decided to use the routine I did at the club for Colt's Halloween party and it went well. Not many of his invited guests showed up, so I played to a small audience. I carried the act off great, but the audience was so small it was difficult to tell how I did. I at least had some ideas of what worked, and didn't work with my timing, not being so nervous this performance.

The night of our second month anniversary, I had made reservations at the Fez, and rented two movies while Ron was at work. I bought Ron a card and another small bottle of JD. We hadn't really discussed our plans. I had mentioned I was planning on dinner out and home for a change of pace and Ron had agreed. I was determined to make tonight alone and distinctive. When Ron got home from work, we changed and went to dinner. We were seated at our table and I was contemplating the menu.

"So, what are you having honey?" Ron asked.

"I'm not sure. I want to ask the waiter what the chef suggests. I'd rather have what Marshall has prepared particularly for tonight."

"That is a good idea." The waiter walked up as we were discussing dinner.

"May I take your order?"

"I'd like to know what the chef suggests."

"Well, sir, the chef's specialty tonight is Chicken Cordon Blue."

"I'll have that then," I replied.

"And you sir?"

"I'll have the same."

"May I get you anything to drink while you gentlemen wait?"

"Bring us a vodka seven, JD and coke please."

"Certainly sir. I'll be right back with your beverages." The waiter walked off. I wanted Marshall to know we were here, so I decided I would send the meal back no matter how it tasted. I knew it would bring him out front to see what the problem was. I was deep in thought about the rest of the evening.

"Honey, I just wanted to thank you for taking me to dinner. I hadn't realized how much time we were spending with other people until I was sitting here with you alone able to talk to you without waiting for a pause in a conversation." Ron said as he squeezed my hand.

"You're welcome. I was feeling like we hadn't spent any time together. That's why I wanted tonight to be time alone." I was comforted he was feeling what I had been feeling. He redeemed himself with that comment.

The waiter returned with our cocktails, "Here you go gentlemen. Your order will be up shortly." Along with the cocktails, the waiter placed a bowl of shrimp on the table to eat while we waited for salad and main course.

"A toast to our second month," I saluted.

"Our second month." We touched glasses, sipped our cocktails. Looking at Ron here alone made me feel very content. He looked so naive and so young. I still was flabbergasted that a man of merely twenty had captured my heart. I swore I would never date someone younger than myself.

"What ya thinking about?" Ron asked.

"You. I am still amazed that someone as young as you has come into my life."

"Best thing that ever happened to you isn't it old man?" Ron teased.

"Well, boy, aren't you the modest one? Yes, it is."

"You are the best thing to come into my life, too, Sampson." The waiter delivered our salads. We ate in silence, looking at one another. I put my feet next to Ron's under the table and he winked in acknowledgement. The waiter returned with our dinner. He sat it on the table and I hurriedly tasted the meal.

"Waiter, I have a problem," I called as he walked off.

"What is that sir?"

"Tell the chef that this meal is unacceptable."

"But sir why?"

"I don't believe it is cooked properly. Tell the chef it is unacceptable! Tell him I want to speak to him in person." I said sternly.

"Sir, Monsieur Marshall doesn't leave the kitchen, ever."

"Tell him I want to see him. You go back and tell him right now!" I demanded.

"Yes sir." He reluctantly went to the kitchen. He looked afraid to enter.

"Sampson, why did you send the waiter to get Marshall? The food is marvelous."

"I just wanted to give him a scare. Just a little joke on Marshall."

"Oh, I was wondering what you were doing." I watched for Marshall. Shortly the door flew open and he stormed out of the kitchen door with a scowl on his face. The waiter pointed him to our table. As he walked over, he began to grin.

"What the hell do you mean the food is unacceptable?" Marshall grumbled.

"Exactly what I said, it is unacceptable." I laughed.

"I was very upset when I heard someone had complained. When I walked out and saw you I was relieved."

"I just wanted to give you a scare. It's our second month anniversary. I wanted you to know we came here."

"Well, I'm glad you did. How are you Ron?"

"Fine and you?"

"Ok. I've been busy."

"This is really great Marshall. I have to admit, you are a great chef." I said.

"Thank you Sampson. I'm glad you are here. I hope you enjoy your meal."

"We will I am sure. We should let you go. Sorry if I gave you a scare."

"You did, but it's ok. Enjoy."

"Thanks. Hope to see you soon." Ron added.

"Happy second month. See you later." Marshall went back to the kitchen. Ron and I enjoyed our meal. We talked about work, our pets, and life in general. The waiter came back to our table as we finished dinner.

"Monsieur Marshall sent this to you, with his sincere congratulations."

"Thank him for us." I said. The waiter placed a dish of chocolate mousse on the table. Attached to it was a little note, "*Happy second month. A little something special for you to enjoy. M*"

"That was nice of him." Ron said.

"It was. Let's taste this and see how he did." We ate the mousse and enjoyed the treat.

On the way back home, I thought about how often Ron could read my mind and save himself from a severe tongue-lashing. I guess he knew me better than I really thought that he did. At home Ron went to change into something more comfortable. I went to the kitchen to get out my surprise. I gathered up the JD, the card, and movies. I walked back to the living room and placed the gifts on the coffee table. I sat and filled the bowl. Ron came back in baggy shorts and a muscle shirt and sat. He noticed the JD and the card. He picked up the card.

"A bottle of JD and a card!" He opened the card, read it, "*To the man who broke my celibacy. I love you, Sampson.*" He gave me a kiss. From under his muscle shirt he pulled out a card and handed it to me. I opened it to read it and a picture fell out. The picture was of a painting I liked.

"What's this picture for?" I asked.

"I remembered you liked that painting. So, I went to buy it for you. Unfortunately, it can't be delivered until the end of the week. So, I enclosed the picture for you to see."

"Thank you!" I leaned over and gave him a hug. I poured a shot of JD for us both. "To our second month!"

"Our second month!" We downed the shot.

"Good grief," I said coughing, "I tell you I don't know what you see in this stuff. It burns all the way down."

"So you have said that before. You'll get used to it. Doesn't bother me!" Ron sassed.

"I doubt I ever get used to it. I rented movies to watch. Want to watch one of them now?" About that time Roberta was at my side. She needed to go out. Stud came up and sat on the couch. The pests had invaded.

"Here, let me take her out. You get the movie ready and we can watch it when I get back." Ron said.

"I won't argue with you." Ron and Roberta went out the door. While he was walking her, I undressed and put on my robe, sat back on the couch, and lit a cigarette. I decided to start a fire in the fireplace and sat in front of it while it started to burn. Roberta bounded back into the living room. Ron followed close behind.

"Changed I see. You look more comfortable. And a fire, that's romantic. And warm. A little chilly out there for a tank and shorts." He sat beside me and we snuggled close. "It was just a little cooler out there than I thought. The fire feels good."

Ron removed his muscle shirt while he sat by the fire. We watched one movie with Roberta laying on Ron, and Stud laying on me. Even alone, we weren't alone! Before the second movie, I got up and disturbed everyone. I fixed cocktails and popcorn. I was forgiven by all when the popcorn arrived. We were enjoying alone time in our house. No friends bothered us and we had an evening without interruptions, for the most part. The dog and cat had to move around, play and make a commotion. It still felt good to lie next to Ron.

When the movie was over, I reached over to get the remote and was greeted by a kiss from Ron. "Thanks honey that was a good movie. It feels nice to be here alone for a change." He reached up and kissed me on the cheek.

I leaned down and kissed him on the lips.

"Oh, I see something hanging out of your shorts, looks like someone is excited." Almost instantly we were in a passionate embrace. My robe seemed to fly off and Ron's shorts seemed to disappear. It was romantic in front of the fire.

"I swear I can't keep condoms in the correct room of this house no matter where I put them! I think from now on I'm hiding a supply in every room in the house." Ron complained.

"Go ahead. Let's hope a guest doesn't stumble across them!"

"Who cares if they do, it's not a secret we have sex!" Ron said as he disappeared into the bedroom for a condom. He returned in a flash and we picked up right where we had left off.

"What an appropriate ending to our second month." I said.

"Who said it was ended?" Ron replied.

"Well, no one I guess. It has been so nice to have you all to myself. I have enjoyed the evening so much."

"I'm not ready for it to end yet."

"What did you have in mind?" I asked.

"I don't know exactly. I would like to do something else."

"Not go to a bar I hope!"

"In a way a bar doesn't sound bad, but no, we wouldn't be alone." Ron answered.

"I was afraid you'd say that. I'm glad you ended that sentence with being alone. So what would you like to do?"

"Something special. I don't exactly know."

"It's late, why don't we go down to the indoor pool and skinny dip?" I suggested.

"That sounds like fun. Okay, let's go!" We got up and put on robes. We grabbed a pair of swimming trunks just in case we ran into someone. We went down to the pool, no one was there. We took off our robes and dove in. The water felt good on my bare skin. I came up for air and looked for Ron. I couldn't see him anywhere. I felt hands on my waist, and knew where Ron was. We played and teased in the water for quiet some time. I was exhausted, so I got out and sat on the edge of the pool to rest.

"What's wrong hon, tired?" Ron teased.

"Just a little. I wanted to catch my breath. Why don't you come and sit by me?"

"I guess I could." He swam over to me and stood in the water below me. He looked up at me and smiled. Then he pulled me into the water. We swam and teased each other in the pool. Being naked and alone was new to me at the pool. I got out of the pool and this time sat away from the edge.

"That was worth coming down for!" Ron said as he climbed out of the pool. He walked over and sat beside me. I leaned over and kissed him.

"I do love you. Too, bad we didn't bring our cocktails down with us."

"We should have. We could go back and get them." Ron suggested.

"No, it would spoil the moment to go up and come back."

"I guess it would." We sat side by side and just enjoyed dangling our feet in the water. I watched waves in the pool slowly calm down to the point of not seeing any motion at all.

"Let's go back up and fix a cocktail," Ron finally broke the silence.

"I guess we should go back and check on the pests anyway." We put on our robes and went back to the condo.

When we walked in the door, the pests were fast asleep. We left them that way. I went and fixed another cocktail. I took them out and joined Ron. He was sitting in front of the fireplace, a fire burning again. He had a towel wrapped around him. Soft music was playing in the background. I sat beside him and kissed him. He hugged me close.

"This has been a special evening. Thanks. It's made our second month feel so good."

"I wanted it to be special. I'm glad you feel that way." I replied. I was glad he enjoyed this evening.

"You know Sampson I don't want this evening to end. Can we just lay here and stay up for a long time?"

"Sure. You are the one that HAS to get up in the morning and go to work."

"I was thinking of taking the day off. You don't have any pressing appointments or deadlines to meet do you?"

"None that I can't change."

"Good. Then I'll take the day off, if you want. We can extend this evening into tomorrow as well."

"Ron, you know I'd love it. That sounds good to me!" It was the reason I wanted this evening in the first place. That wasn't a hard choice.

"It's a deal." We lay in front of the fireplace for hours, watching the fire, adding wood, holding each other. Ron fell into a deep sleep and I carried him to bed. In the morning I vaguely remember hearing Ron get up and call work. Then he crawled back into bed and snuggled up next to me. I fell back to sleep.

Roberta woke me up a second time. I snuck out of bed and took her for her walk. While we were walking I got the idea to go on a picnic. The morning air was warm for the fall and it felt like it was going to be a beautiful day. One we shouldn't waste indoors. When I got back, Ron was still sleeping. I packed a picnic lunch and put it in the refrigerator.

I went back to bed and started to play with Ron's body. He pushed away at first, then rolled over and was very receptive. We wrestled in bed and had a pillow fight. We were laughing so hard. This is the kind of thing I was wanting so bad.

"Shower with me?" Ron commanded.

"Is that a question or a command?" I said sarcastically.

"A command!" Ron joked. We showered together. Again, we wrestled, teased, and sprayed the shower massage on each other. Eventually we did take a shower. We dried one another off and wrapped in towels. Ron went back to the bedroom and looked out the window.

"Looks like a beautiful day, especially for the fall."

"It was warm when I took Roberta outside. I thought it would be a good day to picnic, so I packed some things for later."

"What a great idea! Where do you want to picnic?"

"I thought that little park just down the street from here would do fine."

"Yes, it would. Want to get ready now?"

"I have a few calls to make first. Then we can leave. Why don't you go fix a pot of coffee while I make my calls?"

"Certainly." Ron went to the kitchen and I went to the loft. I called and changed the appointments I had for the day and went to the kitchen. I sat at the table and Ron brought me a cup of coffee. He sat and lit a cigarette. I, in turn, did too.

"Want to take Roberta with us?" He asked.

"I guess we could. She might enjoy that."

We dressed and gathered up the supplies for the picnic. Ron got Roberta and a bowl of food and a bottle of water to take with us. We walked to the park, spread out a blanket, and set the supplies on the ground. We walked Roberta around the park, talking and enjoying the afternoon. We ate our lunch and spent the afternoon lying in the sun. Late in the day we picked up our supplies and headed home. When we got home we were tired. We sat on the couch.

"I don't know about you," I said, "but I could take a nap."

"I was thinking the same thing. Let's." We went to the bedroom and lay down. Stud had beaten us to the bed. Roberta wasn't far behind. We were sleeping in a matter of minutes. Again, I was disturbed by Roberta. I looked at the clock to find we had slept through to late evening. I got up and took Roberta outside. Ron was watching television when I returned.

"I was startled when I first woke up. I figured Roberta must have gotten you up."

"Yes, she had to do her duty. It's rather chilly out. Looks like it could rain. I'm glad we went on a picnic today."

"It was fun. There's an old movie on cable I thought we could watch. Want to order a pizza and just watch tv?"

"I guess. Tomorrow brings the work schedule back. We might as well enjoy the rest of the evening."

"Which brings to mind the telephone. It hasn't rung all day has it?" Ron asked.

"I couldn't tell you. When we went into nap, I turned the phones off. I haven't checked to see if there are any messages since we got up."

Ron walked over and checked the messages on the landline. Sure enough there were many. Friends that wanted to stop by, or wanted us to meet them for cocktails. A message for me that I needed to go to New York to meet with the producer about my play. Another from the publisher wanting to meet with me about one of my manuscripts. Real life had just re-entered our household. We both checked our cell phones. Mine had a repeat of the same messages. Ron had messages from his friends asking if we wanted to meet for a cocktail.

"Save all the messages. We will deal with them tomorrow. It's late let's just spend the rest of the evening together in seclusion."

"I guess you are right," Ron sighed. We ordered the pizza, watched the old movie, and finished the evening alone. The next day our lives would return to normal.

And they did. We met friends for cocktails, had friends over. The painting Ron bought me arrived. I put it up in the living room and Ron was thrilled where I placed it. I went to New York and then to Chicago. It seemed like November just flew by with little time alone with Ron.

Thanksgiving came faster than I had anticipated. The spirit of the holiday season caught up with me. I found myself inviting many friends over to spend the day with Ron and me. Between Thanksgiving and Christmas, we were busy with friends and preparing for the holiday season. We had a tree trimming party. We spent Christmas Eve with Derrek, Jason, and Colt. Derrek and I surprised Ron, Jason and Colt with a carriage ride. New Years Eve the five of us got together again. After the first of the year, I began to feel like Ron and I had lost track of one another again. We had been together, but so much of the time was spent with friends or relatives.

Things calmed down. Our fifth month anniversary was close at hand. I needed some time alone again with Ron. It was the cold of winter, so I made reservations to go out of town, out of the cold belt. I booked us on a flight to Mexico. I thought Ron would enjoy the surprise. All I had to do was keep it a secret and get Ron to go without asking too many questions. One of the gang would watch Stud and Roberta. I was sure. I only had to clear my schedule and make sure Ron didn't make thousands of plans with friends and relatives. That particular weekend I wanted free and open so there were no ifs ands or buts from Ron.

I kept the secret fairly well. Ron thought we were repeating the seclusion of our two-month anniversary by just staying home alone. But, little things, like packing were a problem. I kept turning down plans for the end of January. Ron began to be suspicious. We had been asked to go with friends for that weekend. We were invited to parties, dinners, movies. I turned them all down. Ron began to suspect something was going on. I just hoped he wouldn't figure it out. I got Colt and Derrek to watch Roberta and Stud. They both promised to keep their big mouths shut. A couple of nights before we left, I had to prepare Ron to at least pack some clothes and find his birth certificate. The problem was he had to have his birth certificate.

"Ron, I have a surprise for the weekend. I have to reveal part of it now."

"I knew you were up to something. Tell me, what is the surprise?"

"No, I am not revealing all of it. I will tell you that you need to get off work at noon on Friday. You also need to pack some clothes. You need to pack things for a warmer climate. I also need you to locate your birth certificate."

"Why, where are we going?"

"I'm not telling you. Just trust me. Pack some summer clothes, locate your birth certificate. That's all I'm going to tell you."

"Please, tell me. Please."

"No, it will ruin the surprise. Just pack for three nights, four days, take a personal day off on Monday. That is all you need to know."

"Come on, please tell me!"

"No, I won't. Just pack!"

"Well, we have one slight little problem. I need to run to mom's to get my birth certificate. You mind?" Ron responded.

"It isn't a matter of my minding or not minding, you have to have it, so let's go get it." We drove out to Ron's mom's place. She wasn't there, so we were able to run in, locate the document and return home quickly. For the rest of the evening, and all the next morning Ron pestered and implored me to tell him the surprise. I held out, difficult as it was.

I called a cab to pick me up and then pick Ron up at work. When Ron got into the cab, he started in again. All the way to the airport he begged. I told him he'd have to wait. When the taxi dropped us off, my surprise was soon to be unveiled. We'd have to check our bags and then he'd know. We walked up to baggage check and Ron discovered where we were going."

"Mexico! I was thinking maybe Arizona, Florida, Southern California, but, Mexico! Wow. If we weren't in the middle of the airport, I'd kiss you!"

"Go ahead, I don't care," I quipped, "so, my choice for vacation is acceptable?"

Ron kissed me, "Acceptable! It's terrific."

"I'm so glad you think so!" It seemed to take forever to board the plane and get into the air. Even the flight seemed to take forever. When we landed and got off the plane the warmth made the entire wait worthwhile. We even made it through customs in record time. Ron now understood why he needed his birth certificate.

"This is beautiful and so warm. I can't wait to see our hotel!" Ron gasped.

"You will shortly. I'm anxious myself."

"I'm so excited. I've never been to Mexico before! Thanks honey." We got our luggage, got on a shuttle bus to the hotel and checked in. The room was beautiful. A bottle of champagne and a basket of fruit were in the room. I was excited to be alone with Ron again. Every other time I had flown out of town on business, Ron had to work.

"It's beautiful Sampson. I love it. I can't wait until tomorrow to go to the beach and go swimming."

"I thought for tonight we could unpack and go be typical tourists. Look around for a while. Maybe have a cocktail somewhere."

"Sounds like fun. I'd like to take a shower first and change. I feel grubby with my work clothes still on!"

"Go ahead. I'll unpack. I'll see what I can find out about the area around the hotel from the desk clerk," I said. I called the clerk while Ron showered. He told me that down the street from the hotel there was a nice cantina. He said everyone usually enjoyed the place. He felt it would be a good place to start for the evening. I wanted to freshen up too.

"What do you think I should wear?" Ron shouted from the bathroom.

"Jeans and a shirt I would think would be fine."

"Is that what you are going to wear?"

"Basically. I might wear slacks instead of jeans. It doesn't matter that much."

"I'll be out shortly!" He yelled.

"No hurry." I choose the clothes I wanted to wear. While Ron dressed I took a shower. It was so good to be away for a few days. I got dressed and went to join Ron.

"Ready?" Ron asked as I walked into the room.

"Ready as I am ever going to be."

"Did you find a place we could go?"

"The desk clerk said there was a cantina down the street from here. I thought we could go there."

"Let's go then. My only question is do you speak any Spanish?"

"I think enough to get us by," I replied. We left. On the way the conversations we heard made it clear we were out of the states. Mixed English and Spanish conversations and accents, it was a great awareness of being some place different. We found the cantina and went in to have a cocktail. We sat at a table and a waiter walked up to us.

"Speak Espanola?" The waiter inquired.

"Poco," I answered.

"Well, you are in luck senior, I speak English. What may I get you senior?"

"I'll have a Margarita."

"And you senior?"

"The same please." As the waiter walked off, I turned to Ron. He asked, "Why did you order a Margarita?"

"I ordered something that I thought might be made a little better here than back home. I see you blindly followed my lead."

"Well, I thought it was a good idea."

"Not like bars back home. It's long and small. I like it though. Lots of colorful tiles everywhere"

"It is different. It's just good to be away from home for a weekend, Sampson."

"Yes, it is, in the warmth. The conversations in Spanish make me aware that we are indeed away from home."

"Here you are senior. Did you want a tab?" The waiter asked.

"No, we'll pay for these."

"Here is your check then senior." He walked off.

Ron sipped his Margarita, "Tastes great. Maybe it's my imagination, but it does taste different."

"It's the tequila."

"I suppose it is."

"Well, it's true. We should buy a bottle to take home with us." I thought aloud.

"I suppose you are right." We finished our cocktail and went for a walk. While we were walking taking in the sights, we bought a little bottle of tequila and a lemon for our room. When we got back we had several shots of tequila and passed out. We were both exhausted. The next morning I woke up to Ron shaking me.

"Sampson, it is so beautiful out. Let's get dressed and go to the beach. I want to be in the sun."

"All right, I'll get up. What time is it anyway?"

"It is eight."

"You could have slept in a little longer you know."

"I'm too excited. I wanted to get up and go to the beach."

"You know Ron," I said as I got out of bed, "I don't think it is quite warm enough to lie in the sun yet. Look out at the beach. Do you see many people there?"

"No, but that doesn't mean it isn't warm enough to be there."

"True. Let's do this. Let's go eat breakfast and go for a walk. See how warm it really is. If it's warm enough we can come up and change. Then go to the beach."

"Ok, I guess. I'm going to the shower then."

"Ok, go ahead." He left the room. I got up and got in the shower with him to surprise him.

"What are you doing? You startled me!"

"I thought I'd surprise you and shower with you. Is that ok?"

"Yes. I didn't mean that it wasn't."

"I wondered. Hand me the soap, please, and I'll wash your back." Ron handed me the soap I washed his back. We ended up making love in the shower. I found that more important than going to the beach. We got dressed and went to breakfast. We ate in the hotel diner to save time. Then we went for a walk. Ron was so excited.

"I guess it probably isn't quite warm enough to lie out in the sun yet. It's much warmer than home! We can walk around and see the sights first I guess."

"I thought you'd feel that way once we got outdoors. See, we could have slept in longer."

"I know, I know." We walked around the resort walked in and out of shops. Ron ended up buying a poncho and a wedding vase. We took that stuff back to the hotel. Ron was tired, so we took a nap. I felt like I had just fallen to sleep when Ron woke me up to go out in the sun. We went to the beach. It was warm. The sun felt good.

"It's warm enough now. It feels so good. I want to be dark when we leave. I just want to sit here and get a dark tan."

"I want to be tan, too. It does feel good." I laid there enjoying the warmth and thinking about how to add this event to one of my books. Visiting Mexico in January.

Ron interrupted my thought, "Be nice if the gang was here."

"Why, you aren't happy being here with me for our fifth month celebration?"

"I didn't mean that. I was just thinking about how the gang would act. Bet Derrek and Colt would be throwing a Frisbee. Marshall and Darrin would be checking out the men. Jason probably would be reading a book. Tom would be bitching at Marshall about how horny he was. Jack would be trying to learn enough Spanish to impress his friends at home. I'm not sure about Mat."

"Probably sitting here in the sun with us enjoying his vacation." I guessed.

"I suppose. Wonder why Colt hasn't found anyone yet? He's a nice guy."

"For one thing, he was involved for nine years. For a second, he just has no self-confidence. Men give him all kinds of signals, but he doesn't see them."

"I didn't realize Colt had a lover for nine years. That's interesting."

"Before Tom, so did Marshall. He and Colt had lovers at about the exact same time. Marshall went on to meet Tom. Colt went on to date a number of men, but none of them worked out."

"You learn something new every day."

"That gives me an idea. I was just sitting here thinking about writing a story that included this vacation. I could roll the other four into one character and write a story."

"That could be interesting. I don't know how you would roll the four of them together into one person, but it would be quite a character. Want to go for a swim?"

"I'll race you to the water." The ocean was a little cool. We were determined to swim, so we did. We spent the afternoon playing in the ocean, laying in the sun, and enjoying the vacation. We both were tired so we went back to our room. While we were changing, I noticed a definite tan line. Or should I say red line. Ron did too.

"Ron, you look like a lobster!"

"Speak for yourself. You are rather red. It doesn't hurt though."

"Let's hope it doesn't. Sunburns are so painful!"

"I know. I don't think I've ever had a sunburn in January."

"Me either." We left to go eat dinner. We walked around and looked for an interesting place. We found a little place we liked the looks of and ate there. After we ate we continued to walk. We both began to feel a slight stinging sensation. The sunburn was beginning to catch up with us. When we got back, we soaked in a tub of warm water and baby oil. It helped relieve the sting.

When we got up in the morning, we took another oil bath. We hadn't slept well. It was due more to the excitement than the sunburn and knowing we had to leave tomorrow. We couldn't go back to the beach again being sunburned. We walked around for a while, wondered in and out of shops. In one shop the woman behind the counter noticed our sunburn.

"Senior, you are so red. I have Aloe Vera lotion that works well on a burn." She said. "You like to try it?"

"Well, I suppose." I said. She squirted some lotion into my hand and I rubbed it on my arm. What a cooling sensation. "How much?"

"Four American dollars." She said.

"I will give you three." I replied.

"Gracias senior." She responded.

As we left the shop Ron could barely wait to be out the door. "Why did you pay less than she asked?" Ron demanded.

"Because it is part of the culture here to barter." I responded.

"Oh!" Ron replied. "You could have told me that before now! I might have been able to save some money."

"I thought you were bartering," I replied. We walked back up to our hotel room.

"Strip young man." I said to Ron.

"What? Why?" Ron asked.

"Just follow orders and don't ask questions." I ordered. So he did and I rubbed the Aloe Vera lotion all over his body. I then stripped and he rubbed the lotion all over me. All the rubbing caused us to do a lot of rubbing of our bodies together and we ended our last day making love.

In the morning we had to face the reality of packing and flying back. We neither one hurt much, the lotion seemed to do its trick. We were kind of tan when we got home. I wished I had bought several tubes of that lotion. We had definitely had some signs of a tan.

The next few weeks we got back into the old life style again. We were spending little time alone together. I was busy with a new novel. Ron was trying for another promotion. It seemed like we had just got back from vacation and it was my birthday. I wondered if Ron would do something or not. I was going to be thirty and he would probably do some old man thing.

My inquisitiveness was resolved quickly. Ron began to leave little hints that something was planned for my birthday. On my computer I found messages like, "*On the twentieth you will be thirty, you old man!*" Or notes like, "*Age is how you feel, and in your case thirty is old*". Most were references to old age. I didn't care for most of them. The teasing about being over the hill was not as funny to me as it was to Ron. He obviously had something in mind.

The morning of my birthday, I heard Ron call in sick. When I went down to the kitchen to get a cup of coffee, there was a card labeled, "*The first of 30*". The card said, "*Once you're over the hill . . . You pick up speed. Love ya, Ron.*"

"Thanks for the card. Not as bad as I expected."

"You're welcome. I decided to take the day off. You are stuck with me all day. I have twenty-nine more things for you to find."

"That will be interesting. Any clues I need?"

"No, you'll find them as the day goes by."

"Okay. I can hardly wait." Roberta came bounding in for a walk.

"She's your daughter. You walk her." Ron said.

"Oh thanks. I thought since it was my birthday you'd walk her for me."

"Wrong. You go right ahead. You old duffers need your exercise." I choose to ignore that crack and took Roberta for her walk. When we returned, the table was set, and a breakfast was waiting for me. On my plate was a note that said, "*Number 2. Breakfast just for you*". Ron served me breakfast and cleaned up the dishes. After breakfast we sat in the living room.

"How about watching some tv?" Ron asked.

"I'm really not in the mood."

"Oh, come on honey. Just one show."

"Do I have a choice? I suppose." He handed me a card as he reached for the remote, the card said "*This is number 3, a movie just for you . . .*" He pressed the remote, the television came on and the *Wizard of Oz* began to play, one of my favorite old movies. We watched that together and at the end of the movie another card was handed to me. "*Better check your novel. You may want to make an addition*".

"What's that supposed to mean?" I asked.

"Go find out." I walked up to the loft. Sitting on top of the computer was a box. It had the message, "*This is number 4. I don't want to hear any more bitching about your novel.*" As I opened the box, Ron came to the loft and stood behind me.

"A picture of a computer? And your point would be?" I said confused.

"Well if you look in that closet over there you will find a new computer and a new monitor. Now you won't have to bitch and moan about your old computer freezing up." Ron said like a sales clerk.

"What a wonderful gift. I have been fighting the old computer for months."

"I know. I was afraid you would go out and buy this for yourself before your birthday came."

"I almost have. I'm glad I waited." I turned to Ron and kissed him. I went to the closet and got out the boxes. Ron helped me unpack them and move my old computer. We got the new one set up on the desk. I configured the computer and then loaded my files. It would save so much time. I looked around to demonstrate how fast the new machine was and Ron was gone.

I got up to find him. He was in the bedroom on the bed. He was wearing a sign that read, "*This is number 5, if you think you can handle it.*" The sign was all he was wearing, very strategically positioned.

"I can handle it. Being thirty doesn't mean my sexual ability has left me!"

"Well, I wasn't sure. Thirty is pretty old." I walked over and he began to kiss me. He slowly removed my clothes. We made love like the first time Ron seduced me.

We were still in bed when the door buzzer went off. I wondered who that could be.

"Go answer it." Ron commanded. I figured this must be a part of his plans, so I grabbed a robe, and answered the buzzer.

"Hello."

"I have a delivery for Sampson Dae."

"That's me. I'll buzz you in." I went to the door to wait for the knock.

"Hello, Sampson Dae?"

"That's me."

"Here you go sir."

"Thank you." As I closed the door I looked at this large collection of balloons. Some said, "*Over the HILL*", others said, "*Happy Birthday*", and others said, "*Happy 30th*". Many were black balloons. There was also a card attached. It read, *"Hopefully this is surprise number 6. Happy Birthday"*.

"That was timed perfectly," Ron said rather confidently.

"Yes, it was. Thanks."

"You're welcome."

"What am I going to do with these?"

"You could tie them to the stair case I guess."

"That's not a bad idea. I'll do that. Thirty balloons certainly take up a great deal of space!" As I tied them to the banister, I saw another envelope on the stairs. It said, "*This is number 7. Open carefully*". I was almost afraid to open it. It was awfully large. I wondered why I had to be careful opening it. It was very thick. I was afraid it would explode. As I tore the envelope open a long paper fell out of it. On it were birthday wishes from my friends. Messages signed to a long banner that said, "*Happy Thirtieth Birthday*".

"How did you do this?"

"It's taken awhile. I have been calling your friends and having them drop by here when you weren't home to get this signed. I'm not sure I got everyone, but I tried to get the most important friends."

"That's an original idea." I sat on the steps and read the various messages from friends. It was like having them all here. I couldn't imagine the time it must have taken to get all these people to sign and to keep it a secret. As I read, I noticed Ron walking up to me with a box. He handed it to me. It was labeled *Here is 8, 9, 10, and 11*. I opened the box do discover a shirt, slacks, under shorts, and socks.

"You have nineteen more things to give to me? I can't continue to say thank you that often. I'll wait for number thirty and say one big THANK YOU then."

"Yes, there are nineteen more! You can save the thank you until number thirty. That's fine."

Through out the rest of the day Ron kept guiding me here and there and gifts would appear. In the bathroom I found twelve and thirteen, a bottle of cologne, and after-shave. In our closet I found fourteen, fifteen, a sweater and a tie. We went for a drive, and sixteen was lunch, and seventeen a cocktail. Eighteen was time in a tanning booth. Nineteen was an oil massage by Ron. Twenty was thirty spring flowers delivered to the condo (They had a tacky note attached with something about it almost being spring, but me being too old to spring any more.) Twenty-one was a bottle of vodka. Twenty-two and twenty-three were a new mini music player and a portable drive for my computer. Twenty-four was a new lighter. Twenty-five was a collection of photographs of our seven months together. Twenty-six was a leather wallet. Twenty-seven was a key chain. Twenty-eight was a birthday cake via Marshall. Twenty-nine was dinner out. I couldn't wait for thirty. I wondered if it would be something extra special. It would be hard to top the gifts of the day.

"So, what's thirty Ron?"

"You'll have to wait and see. I'm not telling you the final surprise!" We went for a walk with Roberta, watched some television. I began to wonder what thirty was. Finally Ron spoke up.

"Let's go out for a cocktail."

"That's thirty isn't it?"

"No not really."

"Then what is it?"

"Just wait and see." We went to Bobs and I discovered thirty. When we walked into the bar there were my friends waiting for us at the pool table, all dressed in black. Colt held a sign that said, "*And for the final gift, number 30, here are your friends to help conclude the celebration for your birthday old man*".

The end of the evening was fun. Talking to friends, having cocktails, Ron had made my thirtieth very special. After the bar closed we went home. I was exhausted, but happy. "Ron, you made my birthday special. THANK YOU!"

"You are welcome. I hoped you would like the day."

"Oh, I did." I ended with gift thirty-one. Ron made love to me again. Since it was after midnight, it didn't count he said. It was a delightful day.

Ron's birthday seemed to be the next event that happened. The month between his birthday and mine was busy. I had been to New York a couple of times to help coordinate the opening of my play. Ron got a promotion and was working longer hours to learn his new job. I had planned something for his birthday I hoped he would like as much as I had enjoyed what he did for me. He was going to be twenty-one. I knew I'd have to be in New York the week of his birthday, but I didn't tell him that. I told him I had a plan. He kept asking what I was doing but I wouldn't tell him. He had to wait just like I had.

The day before his birthday, while he was at work, I packed things for both of us. I wasn't going to tell Ron what was up. I didn't want him to know we were leaving town until the morning. I was hoping to be as sneaky as I had been with the Mexico trip. When he got home from work, we ate, met some friends for cocktails, and went home. In the morning I woke Ron early.

"Take a shower, get dressed, and meet me in the kitchen."

"Why, what's up. This is a vacation day, AND my birthday. I would like to sleep in!"

"Sorry. Unfortunately you can't. Part of your birthday gift causes me to have to make you get up now." Reluctantly he got up and took a shower. While he got ready, I fixed him breakfast and put a birthday card on his plate. He came to the table and sat. He opened his card.

"*Happy twenty first. Now you can legally drink the booze you have been drinking since I have known you!*" He read aloud. "Hey, yeah that's right. You made breakfast?"

"What's it look like, dinner?" I scoffed.

"Just asked." He discovered the second envelop on the table. He opened it. It had a ticket to fly to New York. "New York! We're flying to New York today?"

"Yes, we are. I've already packed your bags and called a cab. We are spending three days there."

"This is my birthday present?"

"Part of it."

"There's more?"

"Yes, there is. Now eat so we can get going."

"Ok, ok. Can we hit a nightclub in New York to bring my twenty-first birthday in with style?"

"Well, I don't know that you would want to hit a nightclub, that could hurt, but we certainly can go to one and have twenty-first birthday cocktail." I quipped.

"Oh you and your play on words," Ron replied. He ate and we got our bags and went to the airport. The entire flight Ron kept asking me to tell him what was up next. I just kept telling him he'd have to wait. We landed, checked into the hotel, and began to unpack. As Ron unpacked his things, he looked at me puzzled.

"A package? A birthday present?"

"Open it and see."

He tore open the box and smiled, "What a camera! A video cam, with tape, battery pack and all. Thanks!"

"You're welcome. I thought you could tape the places we go while we are here. Our old camera doesn't take the greatest pictures anyway."

"Let's test it out!" We went walking around New York. I think Ron video taped every building we passed. He went through enough tapes. I feared his tape would not turn out it was dusk, but he had fun. When we got back to the hotel room we collapsed. I began to kiss Ron and undress him at the same time. I made love to him in a way we had never done before. I had told him often I wasn't from his instant message generation of zap and you are done. I showed him what I meant about slow and easy.

"What an experience. Stopping, starting, moving so slow, I thought I was going to explode several times. I've never taken that long to make love before!"

"I know. I've been telling you . . ."

"You aren't of the instant message generation. Some things are done better the old fashion way. I know. I get the point now."

"I hope so! Did you enjoy it this way?"

"I have to admit, I did. I didn't think I could make it this long! What else do you have planned?"

"You'll see. How about a short nap before the evening's festivities?"

"I am tired. I guess it couldn't hurt. I'm dressed for the occasion. I didn't want to get up this morning anyway."

We took a thirty-minute nap. We needed it. When we got up Ron went to take a shower. I had bought him a new suit and I put it out while he was gone. When he came back to the bedroom, he wanted to know what to wear. I pointed in the direction of the suit. He stared for a minute.

"Another gift? A new suit?" He walked over to look at it. He got dressed and finally noticed the ticket in the suit pocket. "This is to your play isn't it?"

"Yes, it is. Tonight is the opening night. I thought you might like to be there." I said.

"Yes, I would. I forgot your play opened this week. I want to see this. After all the moaning and groaning you've done, I'd like to see how it actually looks performed."

"I'm glad. I need to get ready. I'll be right back." I went in to take a shower. I thought I heard something. I turned around to see Ron with video cam in hand taking a video of me in the shower. I should have been more prepared.

"Making your own porn film? This had better not be on the public viewing of this vacation, or I'll burn all the film!"

"Relax. It won't be. I just wanted to test it out indoors is all."

"Sure you did. I mean it, you show that to anyone, and I'll burn all the video tapes!"

"I won't!" Ron yelled.

I got ready and we went to the theater. I was worried because when we arrived the next surprise wasn't there. It was supposed to be. We were seated and I was a little angry. My anger subsided shortly. Jack came walking in and I was relieved.

"Jack, what are you doing here?" Ron shouted.

"Wishing you a happy birthday. Sampson sat this up. I have the room next to yours. I'm part of your birthday surprise."

"Thank you honey. This is wonderful." The curtain opened and we watched the play. I was in agony. I hated opening night. Listening to the audience's reaction and worrying about critics. It was always a tense event. I listened to hear comments, response from the audience, as the production continued. Most of what I heard was positive. You never knew about the critics. At intermission we went into the lobby of the theater.

"Ron, this will be your very first legal cocktail. Why don't you go get us one so you can flash your ID?" I said.

"Great idea, my first legal cocktail, in New York City, in the theater!" Ron excitedly took off to go buy a cocktail for us all and announce that he was twenty-one today. We had our cocktails, did a toast to his twenty-first birthday, and returned for the remainder of the play. I was never so glad when the curtains finally closed. We left the theater and had cocktails at nightclub to continue to celebrate Ron's twenty-first.

"Sampson, this is like an old movie. I didn't realize playwrights really were so tense opening night." Jack said.

"Well, they are. The critics can make a play or break it."

"Are we going to wait up for the reviews like they do in the movies?" Ron asked.

"It's not quit the same as in the movies and my work is off Broadway, but I thought we would wait up and see if any of the trade rags have any reviews." We had cocktails with the cast and crew from the play and waited for the reviews. When they finally arrived, I was relieved. The play had fair reviews, ones I could live with. The celebration really began. A cake was delivered for Ron, and the cast and crew sang him happy birthday. We went back to the hotel exhausted.

"Gentlemen, I don't know about you, but I need some sleep. Thank you for including me Sampson. I had a great time. Happy twenty-first Ron." Jack said.

"You're welcome Jack," I said.

"Thank you Jack, Sampson, it's been a great birthday." Ron answered. Jack went to his room and we went to ours. "Thanks honey. This has been a very exciting day. I've enjoyed it. It was an exciting way to bring in twenty-one. I'm glad your play was a success."

341

"You are welcome. I'm relieved my play is a success. Means we can continue to spend money like water." I laughed at myself.

We spent the next two days touring New York. Jack had to leave the morning after Ron's birthday but saw some sights with us. We spent late hours in the bars, went to various parts of the city, and ate in several fancy restaurants. I believe Ron took enough video tape to make a four-hour documentary. I was sure our friends were in for one long boring night of his twenty-first birthday vacation. Our last night there we celebrated our eighth month together. It had been a great vacation.

Coming back from New York was a let down. Getting back into the routine of life was difficult. I began to conclude a condo and a dog just don't work. Roberta's need for a walk came at very inopportune times. If we had a house with a yard to let her out into, life would be much easier. Ron and I began discussing selling the condo and buying a house.

As spring turned to summer, we began to look for a house to buy. Some we looked at I felt were overpriced. Some were just not in the area of the city where I wanted to live. I had to take several trips out of town for books, magazine articles and the play. Ron was able to join me a few times. Summer was fun and warm. Ron and I took two weekends in the sun and out of the city to relax. We began to balance our time with friends and time alone. As our first year began to come to a close, we talked about how much we had changed individually, as well as a couple.

Ron put together a DVD from his tapes of our New York trip. We had friends over to view his DVD. I was afraid it would be awful and be just shots of buildings. However, he did an excellent job of editing. Our shower scene was not among the scenes in his movie thank goodness. Everyone thought he had a great talent in producing his vacation movie. I had to admit I was incredibly impressed with the work he did with the movie.

At the end of August for our first year, we took a short vacation to the cottages Darrin had suggested to us. I had wanted to go some place like Hawaii, but I had commitments to be places and I couldn't take the time we would need for a trip like that. We had to put those plans off until the fall. We settled for the short vacation near home and planned a long vacation in the fall.

So we drove up to the cottages Darrin suggested. As we pulled into the drive, I wondered why I had agreed to go here. They looked rather rustic and there certainly weren't any restaurants or stores anywhere close. Ron on the other hand seemed pleased.

"Sampson, look, it is so rural and out in the open. I love it!" Ron squealed.

"I can't say as this is looking wonderful to me hon but we will see." I retorted. Walking into the cottage, I felt another sinking feeling. It was small and not really modern. I looked around and wasn't sure I could make four days here.

"Oh, Sampson, look at this view it is just so wonderful." Ron gushed.

"It is quaint." I managed to say. I unpacked while Ron explored. He was off and running like a child at a playground. I was glad he was so excited. I was just hoping I would be able to find the charm he found.

"Sampson, come out here." Ron yelled to me.

"What do you need, I am unpacking." I replied.

"Just put that stuff on hold and come out here please." Ron pleaded. Reluctantly I walked outdoors to see what had Ron so excited. He was pointing to a path and behind that was a body of water. "Look Sampson we could go for a hike and go swimming. Isn't it beautiful here?"

"It has its own charm." I said. "We could go walking, but I need to change before we do that."

"Well, get changed and let's go walking." Ron followed me back to the cottage. We both put on a pair of shorts, t-shirt and sandals. I grabbed the insect spray and sun tan lotion. Ron was out the door ahead of me, off on a walk. I followed behind, amazed at his excitement. He pointed out vegetation, views, animals, and birds as we walked. Eventually we came across this little stream. We decided to sit and take a break. I was glad Ron was so excited about this trip since this was my gift to him. I still wasn't so sure this was the place for me.

"Look, up the trail that looks like a cave. Want to go up there and look around?" Ron said eagerly.

"We can." I said. I wasn't sure I wanted to be in a cave, but new experiences can be good for a sole. We walked up the path to the cave. Ron explored in the cave and I explored outside of the cave. After a while he came running up to me just so excited.

"That cave is awesome. You should come and see. There is a little water fall inside and a little pond. It is beautiful honey." He said out of breath.

"I am sure it is beautiful, but it's getting late, why don't we just plan on coming up here tomorrow?" I said trying to avoid the whole thing, at least for today.

"You are probably right. But you will come up here with me tomorrow, right?" Ron begged.

"Yes I promise." I replied. We walked back to the cottage. I wasn't sure what to do about dinner. I decided perhaps we should take a drive and see what we could find. Ron agreed that wouldn't be a bad idea. Neither one of us were really wanting to cook.

We drove for a few miles and found an old restaurant. From the outside it looked like it should have been condemned years ago. But when we walked into the restaurant, it was very nicely done. There were tables with the loud red and white checkered tablecloths, candles and big huge wooden chairs at the tables with matching checkered napkins. A tall, elderly gentleman came over to us.

"May I seat you for dinner gentlemen?" he asked.

"Yes, that would be wonderful." I responded.

"Follow me please." He seated us at a window table that had a view of a valley in the distance. He handed us our menus.

"Something to drink while you look over the menu?" he asked.

"Yes, I would like a glass of white wine." I said.

"And I would like a bourbon and coke." Ron replied.

"Son, I will need to see identification before I can bring you a bourbon and coke." The waiter said to Ron. So Ron pulled out his wallet and flashed his identification. I quietly chuckled to myself.

"Thank you son, you don't look that old to me." He said as he handed Ron back his wallet. He left to get our cocktails and I finally let loose with a laugh.

"And just what is so amusing?" Ron grumbled.

"I just think it's a riot you got carded in the middle of nowhere, after all this time that you have been drinking under age." I laughed harder.

"Makes me feel good." Ron replied. The waiter came back with our cocktails and asked if we were ready to order.

"I am afraid we haven't looked over the menu yet. Is there a specialty of the house?" I asked.

"Our chili is wonderful and so is our BBQ beef." The waiter replied.

"Let us look over the menu for a few minutes please." Ron said.

"Certainly, I will be back in a few minutes." The waiter responded. Looking over the menu nothing really caught my attention. I could see Ron was flipping through the menu repeatedly as well.

"Why don't we try one of the dishes the waiter suggested?" I said to Ron.

"That sounds good. But which one?" Ron asked.

"I think I want the BBQ Beef." I said.

"That sounds good to me as well." Ron replied. When the waiter returned we ordered the BBQ beef and sipped on our cocktails while we waited. I looked around the restaurant and wondered how long it had been open. It was certainly a rustic location. Our wait wasn't long. The beef wasn't bad. The place had its own charm. Perhaps I could enjoy this location after all.

Back at the cottage Ron disappeared into the bathroom when we returned. I sat in the rocking chair and looked around the cottage. I was deep in thought about one of the pieces I was writing when I realized Ron's bare leg was resting against my arm. I looked up to see Ron standing beside me wearing nothing but a bow around his genitals.

"Are you having trouble keeping an erection in your old age?" I teased him.

"No, I am your anniversary gift. I am waiting to be unwrapped." He retorted.

"My anniversary gift hey. Well, let me take that bow off the package and see what you got me." I said as I pulled the end of the bow and it fell to the floor. I wasn't sure what Ron had in mind, but I found out shortly. He made love to me slow and easy. By the time we finished I was ready to explode.

"So, how was that for your gift?" Ron asked.

"Very nice. It appears being of legal age has helped your love making skills." I responded.

"I had this great teacher." Ron replied. We cuddled the rest of the evening and crawled into bed for a much-needed sleep.

The next morning Ron was up when I got up. He was bustling around the kitchen. I walked in to see what he was doing. In the kitchen was a breakfast sitting on the table. Ron was dressed in an apron and nothing else.

"Where did you find food?" I asked.

"I went for a walk this morning and found this little store. I just bought a few things to fix breakfast for you since this is our anniversary trip." He said.

"It looks wonderful." I said, "thank you." We ate breakfast and made plans for the day. Ron attempted to arouse me, but I resisted. I wanted to save that experience for later in the day. Ron insisted we walk back to that cave, so I packed the bug spray, a blanket, some water, a couple of rags, sun tan lotion, a flashlight in a backpack and we left for our adventure. On our walk up I had to admit it was a beautiful. The outdoors had rather grown on me over the last twenty-four hours. Ron was so excited he was walking way ahead of me to get to the cave. When I caught up with Ron he was headed into the cave. I was very reluctant to venture into the cave. In a few minutes his head popped out of the cave.

"Aren't you joining me?" He asked.

"Yes, I am, I just caught up with you." I said.

"Come on, it is beautiful in here." Ron pleaded. With great disinclination I followed Ron into the cave. There was a great deal of light in the cave. As we walked I realized there was a small opening in the cave where the stream flowed through and created the waterfall. It wasn't nearly as dreadful as I had imagined.

"Come over here and feel this water." Ron shouted. "It is warm. This must run through some hot springs or something."

I walked over and put my hand in the water. I was amazed, it was warm. "This is warm. I suppose there is a hot spring up here somewhere." I said. Ron was splashing under the waterfall. He looked so happy. I walked over and joined him. I let the water run down my face, across my chest and down my legs. The warmth felt good. I felt Ron's hand and then my shorts fell to the ground.

"Get naked honey, feel that warmth all over your body." I opened my eyes to find Ron naked and splashing around in the water. I took off my shirt let the water flow over my bare skin. It was very rejuvenating. I again leaned my head back and let the water flow over my body. I heard Ron splashing my way. I felt his lips on my chest. He slowly licked his way down my chest to my crotch. He didn't have to do much to have his way. We sat in the pond and just let the warm water touch our bodies as we laid back. Ron started, paused, started and paused so many times, I got to a place I just let go I couldn't last any longer.

"Ha, so the old man gave out!" Ron panted.

"I wouldn't say gave out, I would say came to a boil that boiled over." I defended myself.

"So the instant message kid was able to do the old fashioned love making again." Ron gleamed.

"Well, the old fart needs to finish the session." I said as I pushed Ron's body back and made my way to his crotch. The instant message kid fell back to his instant message style.

We sat in the cave for a while enjoying the moment. I was astonished with myself, I was finding the rustic outdoors a nice place to be after all. We pulled on our wet shorts and picked up our wet t-shirts. I gathered up the backpack and we took a leisurely walk back to the cottage. Once there we showered and changed. We decided just to sit back and watch the rest of the day go by. We seldom ever just sat and watched the world as it completed a day.

"This has been a wonderful first anniversary." Ron said.

"Very different than our first date I would say." I commented.

"That is true you were on your celibate binge then. We could only hug no fondling and NO sex. Yep very different." Ron mused. That night we repeated that first date. We cuddled, hugged and snuggled in bed together but we did not have sex.

For the rest of the weekend we decided to relax and enjoy the surroundings. By the time we needed to leave, I was so relaxed I really didn't want to go home. Nevertheless, life has to return to normal and we packed up and drove home. Back in the city our hustle bustle lives went back into full swing. Colt's end of the summer bash would be soon. I had work to do on a novel. Ron got busy with his job. We looked over brochures for our big trip. We settled on the island of Oahu in Hawaii. Life just keeps moving along, sometimes faster than we would like it to pass by.

Interlude III Zee Pool

I distributed everyone's drinks. We all filled another plate with munchies. Sampson lit a cigarette.

"It 'tis a butuful night," Derrek remarked.

"Yea, it is," Marshall agreed.

"Why don't we take our cocktails and go to the pool?" Sampson asked.

"Yea uh huh good idea!" Derrek said.

"I don't have any swimming trunks!" Darrin protested. "I suppose you told everyone else to bring swimming trunks except me, Colt."

"Yea Darrin, it was a private plot. And since when has that ever stopped you?" I said, "I've known you to either skinny dip, or wear your jeans into the pool.

"Don't be a party poop!" Sampson added.

"Oh, all right, I suppose," Darrin said, "but I can't wear my leather in the pool. I'll just sit and watch you guys."

"I have an old pair of trunks in the car, let me go get them." Derrek said as he left to go out to his car.

"You can just sit by us at the pool, that's a good idea," Marshall said.

"Ok, ok, I already said I would," Darrin responded.

Derrek came back into the house. "Here, Darrin, try these on," Derrek said out of breath.

"Thanks Derrek. Are these clean?" Darrin said. "I'm just not sure I want my boys to hang where your boys have been."

"Yea uh huh, they are actually a pair I have never worn," Derrek replied, "so your boys don't have to worry."

I grabbed some towels, my drink and headed to the pool. Everyone else grabbed their drink and walked with me. Derrek, Marshall and Darrin went for a swim. Sampson and I went to the hot tub.

"Max and I have enjoyed this hot tub this summer. It's been nice to have him around," I said.

"He's a nice guy Colt. I'm glad you finally met someone unique. Seems like in the last year the single part of this group settled down with someone." Sampson replied.

"Mind if I join you?" Derrek asked.

"Not at all," I said.

"Ough, this is warm!" Derrek said.

"Can two more fit in there?" Marshall asked.

"Oh, I'm sure we can make room," Sampson said.

354

"Thanks guy," Darrin said.

"It won't be the same next year with you moved to California Marshall," I said.

"Well, Colt, I can fly back for this event. We've done this for too many years for me to miss it," Marshall explained.

"We won't see as much of each other from now on," Darrin said, "no more frantic calls to take you to work 'cause the car wouldn't start!"

"That's true," Marshall said, "but we'll keep in touch."

"You expect me to believe you'll write? You don't even send post cards when you are on vacation!" Sampson teased.

"He uses a phone well," Darrin laughed.

"I know I don't write, but I will call and keep in touch. I just don't like to write letters," Marshall defended himself, "I don't even like to write emails."

"Oh, did we tell you, we all plan to visit you and Tom the last part of November, for Thanksgiving." Derrek teased.

"You can all come out to visit. I expect you all to come out. Hopefully not all at once, at least not the first time." Marshall said.

"So, what are the chances of you moving Darrin?" Derrek asked.

"Fair. It depends on me really. If Mat and I like Arizona, I have a job there. The company that bought us out has offered me the opportunity to open this store and then manage any other new stores they open in Arizona. I can either stay here or move to Arizona. Mat and I are waiting to see what we think of Arizona while we are there opening the new store." Darrin explained.

"So, two of the five of us could be moving out of state soon then?" I said.

"Looks that way," Sampson added.

"I think it's great we all have finally found someone to settle down with. Someone we each care about, that cares about us," Derrek said, "some of us took longer than others but, at the moment we all five seem to be very happy."

"Yea, good old Colt finally completed the group. I'm glad you and Max got together. He's a good man," Marshall added.

"Forget that part, Colt thinks he hot, that's all Colt looks at," Darrin added.

"So, how is your class this year, Colt?" Marshall asked, changing the topic.

"Like I told Derrek, it's been a good start so far. That's all I want to say. I know you all get tired of school stories." I said.

"Is it third or fourth grade?" Marshall continued.

"Fourth. I like the fourth graders better." I said.

"Do you remember the time you had that rabbit at school, and the art teacher had her rabbit at school?" Marshall asked.

"Oh no, here we go. If you get Colt shut up, then Marshall has to tell one of Colt's stories for him!" Darrin complained.

"How could I forget?" I said.

"Why what happened?" Derrek asked.

Marshall went on, "Oh, God, Colt called me at work one day hysterical. In front of twenty-eight third graders, his rabbit gave birth to six bunnies. He was hysterical because no one knew the rabbit was pregnant. I went over to his school to help him get the mother rabbit and her babies to Colt's house. She had rejected them because she was too young to be pregnant."

"Did the bunnies live?" Derrek asked.

"Yea, all six of them lived," Marshall explained, "Colt fed them every two hours with an eye dropper and I helped him a couple of times a day force feed them with the mother."

"Lord, what a two weeks that was! By the time they were old enough to eat solids, I was exhausted!" I replied, "And all the veterinarians said they couldn't be saved."

"So, how was she pregnant without anyone's knowledge?" Sampson asked.

"The janitor thought it would be fun to have bunnies. So, he put Colt's rabbit and the art teacher's rabbit together Valentine's weekend that year. Around Colt's birthday they were born." Marshall said.

"Well, at least you saved them, Colt." Derrek said.

"True. It did make me feel good to prove the vets wrong." I said

"Darrin, you remember when you had the flu so bad? You refused to go to the doctor. I went by to see him because his boss said he hadn't been in to work," Marshall said.

"Yea, well, I felt like I was going to die anyway. I didn't care." Darrin explained.

"Well, I went by and drug him off to a doctor. They said he should be in the hospital because he had dehydrated. The only way they would consider letting him go home is if I stayed with him and made sure he took his prescription and drank liquids. So, I did stay with him a couple days. He was a royal pain! I should tell Mat about that one!" Marshall said.

"I was not that bad!" Darrin protested. "Besides, I was sick, what did you expect?"

"That you would be sick enough your mouth would stop working." Marshall replied.

"Got the doctor to let me go home didn't it?" Darrin replied.

"Then there is Derrek who seems to not understand what a gas gauge is used for." Sampson said. "I get this phone call late one night from Derrek asking me if I can go buy him a gallon of gas. He had run out of gas on the Interstate."

"I know how to use a gas gauge! I just wanted to see how far I could drive before I ran out of gas." Derrek explained. "I was sure I could make it to the gas station."

"Blond I tell ya Derrick, blond!" Darrin teased.

"Sampson, remember when you came by and forced me to go out with you?" I asked.

"Yes, Colt, I do. I just hated to see you sitting home and feeling so down and hurt. You had just broken up with someone I think. I know you were down and out. I just knew if I could get you back into the swing of life you'd begin to forget and rebuild your life." Sampson said.

"I was angry at first, but I was grateful later on," I answered. "Because of that night that is actually how I ended up dating Max."

"Because you started going out again?" Derrek said How is that?"

"Yea because of Sampson being so pushy I did start to go out again. One thing led to another." I replied. "I eventually hooked up with Max because I started going places again."

Max and Me

I had known Max for a few years. Dating him didn't happen right away. Sampson had kept saying I'd meet someone from *the past*. I first met Max three or four years ago through mutual friends. We talked and went our separate ways. We saw each other frequently and even met once or twice for drinks. That was all that ever happened. I found Max to be extraordinarily attractive. But he seemed to have no interest in me. His slender six-foot body, blond hair, and brown eyes made him next to perfect in my book. Even his eyeglasses were so cute, tiny wire frames that just covered right over his eyes. One night we ran into each other again when I was out with Sampson.

"Hello Colt," Max's voice came from behind me.

"Hi Max," I turned around, with my intelligent reply, "fancy seeing you here."

"You look good tonight, Colt," Max said with a grin.

"You're lookin' good yourself," I replied, feeling myself blush.

"How are things going?" Max queried.

"Things are going fine. And you, Max?"

"Fine Colt. I haven't seen you in awhile."

"No, I haven't been out much lately." I said in truth. "Max, this is a friend of mine, Sampson. Sampson, this is Max."

"I wondered when you were going to introduce me, Colt." Sampson replied as he reached out to shake Max's hand. "Nice to meet you Max."

"Good to meet you Sampson. I've seen you out before with Colt I think." Max turned to me, "Want to dance Colt?"

"Sure, Max, why not." As we walked to the dance floor, I turned back to Sampson and shrugged my shoulders in amazement that Max asked me to dance. Sampson shooed me away with his hands and I turned and caught up with Max. A very slow romantic song was playing. I was dumbfounded and pleased.

When we got to the dance floor, Max held me tight. We danced close to one another without talking at all. He caressed my back and fanny and kissed my neck and ears. I responded by squeezing his fanny and kissing his neck. He smelled so good and felt so warm. When the song was over, I started to leave the dance floor. Max grabbed my arm.

"Let's stay and dance to this song, I like it."

"Sure thing!" We danced to that song and then the next one and yet another. We brushed up against each other as we danced. I was so excited to be this close to Max, to spend this much time with him. And at his request!

"Phew, I'm hot, how about you?" Max shouted to be heard.

"Yes, I am. Let's take a break."

Max grabbed my hand and led me off the dance floor. We stopped at the edge of the floor and he gave me a kiss, a hug and a smile. I melted.

"I'm hot and sweating. Want to go out to the parking lot to cool off?"

"Sounds like a good idea." Max once again took my hand. As we walked out to the parking lot, I couldn't help but to stare at Max's shirt sticking to his wet chest. We stood and let the night air cool our bodies holding hands.

"Excuse me a minute Colt." Max walked off and I noticed he walked over to a Porsche. He got a pack of chewing gum out of the car.

"New car?" I yelled at him.

"Yea, well, new to me, I just bought it last week Colt. Like it?"

"Yes, I do. I've always wanted to ride in a Porsche."

"I'll do you one better," and he tossed me the keys, "you can drive it." He said proudly. I walked over to the car

363

and got in. I was thrilled to have his keys and to be driving his car. I started it up and we were off. It had such a smooth ride compared to my truck. It almost felt like floating on air. I was enjoying shifting through the gears and listening to the sounds of the engine as it smoothly gained speed.

"I can sure tell you are used to driving a truck Babe!" Max pointed out.

"Why?" I said smiling at the fact he called me Babe.

"Well, you happen to be doing sixty-five in a thirty zone! You better be careful, two fags, one Porsche, and we've been drinking!"

"You are so right, Max. I guess I'd better go back to the bar. Besides, it is beginning to sprinkle, and I don't want wreck your new car."

"I doubt you would have an accident. But it is probably a good idea to head back. Gee, April showers just like in that old saying." Max mused.

"Bring May flowers." I completed that rhyme. I turned around and drove back to the parking lot. I pulled in and turned off the engine. I handed Max his keys and was met by a kiss on the cheek. It was followed by a long passionate kiss lip to lip. His arms wrapped around my shoulders and he pulled me closer to him. He put his tongue into my mouth and we kissed passionately. We kissed and hugged each other for a long time. I finally decided to interrupt the moment, to be daring and see if I could go one more step. I didn't want the evening to end. I hoped to prolong the time together.

"Max, how about coming out to my place for a night cap?" I said impulsively.

"Why not I'd like that. What about your friend, Sampson?"

"We can just go back inside and tell him we are leaving. He'll understand." I was caught up in the excitement Max had agreed to go back to my place.

"Ok, fine Babe. Let's go bid adios." We walked back into the bar, went back to the pinball machine and found Sampson there playing pinball.

"Well, if it isn't Colt and Max. I thought you boys had abandoned me, and lo and behold, here you are." Sampson said sarcastically.

"Yes, Sampson, here we are. However, I came back to tell you that Max and I are leaving, so that you wouldn't feel abandoned."

"Oh, sure, leave me here to fend for myself. You ask me out for a cocktail and then the first pretty face you find you take home. And leave me here all alone! You men are all alike."

"Gee, Colt, maybe we shouldn't go now," Max sighed.

"He'll survive, Max. Don't let him fool you. He just likes to give me a hard time, right Sampson?"

"Me, give you a hard time? Come now, me! No, really, go on and leave. Ron should be here shortly, if he knows what's good for him."

"I'll call you tomorrow Sampson."

"It was nice to meet you Sampson." Max said as we walked away.

"Nice to meet you Max. I'll be waiting for that call Colt!" Sampson said as he shot me his glare.

We walked to the parking lot hand in hand. When we got to the truck, Max once again held me tight and kissed me then a smile and a hug. I hugged him tight. We stood there for a minute just holding each other.

"Well, Colt, since I've never been to your house, I'll follow you home."

"Good idea, Max. Let me write down the address in case I lose you in traffic."

"No need, I'll keep up with you. No problem!"

"Ok, then, I'll see you at my place, shortly. Oh, by the way, parking is limited at my place. Just pull into the garage next to my truck."

"Will do." Max kissed me again. I got in the truck and pulled out of the parking lot, making sure Max was following me. He was. As we drove home I began to have the reality catch up with me. Here was a man I found so attractive, who I enjoyed as a person, actually following me home! Was I dreaming? Up to this point he lacked apparent interest in me. Now he was holding my hand, hugging me, kissing me, and following me to my house. We had to stop at a light. Max got out of his car and ran up to the truck. He came up to my window, gave me a kiss, and ran back to his car. I was melting inside but so confused, was he changing his mind and going home instead?

I leaned out the window and yelled, "What was that all about?"

"I just like to be spontaneous and I needed a kiss," Max yelled back. He got in his car and honked his horn. I realized the light had changed. The rest of the way home all I could think about was how romantic Max was. It was confusing to me how he could be so interested all at once. I pulled into the garage and in a moment the Porsche appeared next to the truck. We both go out of our vehicles and walked up the stairs together holding hands. We were greeted by my dog barking and wagging his stump, as only a Schnauzer could do.

"Well, Max, meet Max." Max barked more softly. Max stuck his hand out. Max sniffed him and jumped up on Max. A good sign I thought.

"Well, hi there guy. You've got a great name!" He leaned over and petted Max.

"I need to let him out to do his job. It won't take long."

"Go ahead, no problem." Max responded while I walked to the door and let Max out. I stood there watching to see when he was finished. I was being lazy by not walking him to the top of the hill to the canal path. I felt Max's arm go around my waist and his body push up against mine. He began kissing my neck and ears. He rubbed my stomach and held me so tight I felt so warm and happy.

"So what's up that hill?" Max asked as he looked out the door.

"There is a canal up at the top of the hill with a bicycle slash walking path that I usually take Max for a walk on last thing at night," I responded.

"That sounds like it would be a fun place to walk." Max replied.

"It actually is a great deal of fun," I looked out at my Max and yelled to him, "Hurry up child and do your thing. Then get in here." As I waited for my dog to finish his duty Max continued to kiss my neck passionately. "Max, you want a drink? And Max, get in here now! This is going to be interesting Max and Max."

"Yes it will be interesting. And if you mean me, yes, I'll have a drink because I am in here already." He turned as he spoke and looked up the staircase, "what is up these stairs here?"

"I meant you for the drink and up those stairs are the bedrooms." My dog Max came in. I took the human Max's hand and led him to the kitchen. "What would you like to drink sir?"

"If you'll show me where you keep your liquor, I'll make it for us," Max said, "guess you'll have to call us big Max and little Max."

"That's not a bad idea. You little Max and the dog big Max?" I said sassy as I pointed to the cabinet where the liquor was kept.

"Sure, Colt, whatever you want." This time I stopped big Max and gave him a kiss and a hug.

"Max what prompted you to come home with me? You never seemed to be interested in me." I thought I would just use Darrin's advice and be direct.

"Yes, I was. But every time I saw you out you were with someone else. I have kissed you goodnight several times. We've even met for a drink before. I never felt you were interested in me. I thought at first the men you were with you were dating. Then I realized you were just with friends. Last time we saw each other I was going to ask you out for a drink. I couldn't find you when I went to look for you. You had made some sarcastic comment about me ignoring you. It was then I realized there must be mutual interest. Tonight when I saw you I made up my mind I wasn't taking any chances. I was just going to take the more direct approach."

"I am certainly glad you did. You know every time we met for a drink it was through other friends. And the goodnight kisses came for the other friends we were with too. I always just thought you included me to be polite. I'm astounded. We were both so hesitant to tell one another how we felt!"

Max pointed to cabinets and shrugged his shoulders as I finished my sentence. "Oh, the glasses are in this cabinet, and the booze is under this counter. The ice is in the fridge freezer." I directed.

"I don't think I could have found the ice without that information." He laughed. "At least we are talking now. Let me make you one of my exclusive drinks. I think you'll like it." He made the drinks using what seemed to be every kind of liquor I had. I watched his movements and admired his body. He was like a dream come to life for me. Even little Max sat at his feet and watched him intently. He handed me my drink. I sipped it, and was astonished at how good it tasted, not like booze at all really.

"This is good! As I watched you mix it, I wasn't sure what to expect. What is it?"

"I like to call it Max's Hammer."

"Interesting name. Couldn't be because of the after effect could it?"

"Something like that Colt." As I sipped the drink, Max walked over to me and put his arms over my shoulders.

As I looked into those brown eyes, I felt his body next to mine and got lost in his face. His moustache was thick but almost invisible it was so blond. His eyes were so dark they put me in a trance. I put my drink down and felt his lips on my neck. I turned, put my lips on his and we kissed. I felt my body being lifted off the floor and carried across the room, then up the stairs, and to the landing. "This room right down the hall in front of us your bedroom by chance?"

"Yes," I sighed. We continued on into my bedroom as we continued to kiss. He laid me down on the bed so gently and started to unbutton my shirt. He was being so soft and tender as he slowly undressed me and kissed each part of my body. I worked at unbuttoning his shirt and jeans as he removed my clothes. I felt like I was fumbling compared to his gentle movements. The glimpses I saw of his chest exposed his chest's fuzzy blond hair that was barely visible and he was skinny, but firm. His body lived up to and surpassed my fantasies of it.

He stopped briefly and took off his glasses. "I am laying my glasses on the nightstand here, remind me later that is where I put them he whispered." He began to play with my body by licking my skin. It felt different than it had ever felt before. His body was darkly tanned, very slender and solid.

He moved to my feet to remove my socks. As he did I rubbed my hands over his back. He worked his way from my toes to my lips hitting every erogenous zone a body has on his way up. The glimpses of his body made my every fantasy come to life. He even managed to put a condom in place with the most sensual sensation I have ever experienced. The touch of his lips alone was enough to cause a climax of gigantic proportions. His hands had a soft tender touch, like velvet, his body feeling like a sun warmed rose pedal against my skin. The hair on his chest and legs rubbing against my body was soft and tender and I felt like melting butter. For the first time in my life I climaxed twice in a time period that felt almost simultaneous. I felt the same warmth from Max. He laid there and just kissed me gently and held me.

"Mind if I stay the night?" he whispered into my ear.

"Mind! If you leave I'll kill you!" I sighed.

He laughed. We rolled against each other. He put his arms around me and held me like a stuffed animal.

"Mind if I run down and get our drinks?" Max asked?

"Not at all." I said.

He brought the drinks upstairs and handed me mine. He crawled back into bed and sat beside me. I put my arms over his. "I know this will sound silly, but when is your birthday?" I asked as we lay there.

"July eighth," he replied, "why?"

"Oh, I just like to know what zodiac sign people are. A Cancer huh, water sign." I mused.

"Is that good or bad, when is your birthday?" He responded.

"It's not bad. My birthday is March twenty-second, Aries, a fire sign. As the saying goes, the fire creates steam, or the water puts the fire out, not much in-between." I responded. "You are in good company, little Max was born July first, and we get along."

"Oh we have more in common than just our names!" Max grinned. "Ok, my turn how old are you? I have a thing about age. I don't like younger men."

"Why, how old do you think I am?" I asked.

"Oh no, I know better than to go any where near that question. If I give an age and you are younger than that age, you will never forget." He replied.

"Ok, I'm forty," I said.

"You are shitten' me," Max responded.

"Why, too old for you?" I panicked.

"No, Babe, no, you just look so young, even with that sexy thinning hair of yours," he responded.

"Nope, I am the old geezer in the crowd, always have younger friends and lovers," I responded. "You can use the phrase balding by the way. So, how old are you?"

"I will stick with thinning hair. I would say guess my age, but that wouldn't be fair. I start my new age in January, even though it isn't official until July, I am thirty-five."

"Well, we aren't so far apart in age then I guess," I responded.

"I have always said it's not your age, but how you feel. Any other pressing questions?" he said.

"No, not that I can think of," I replied. We were so close to each other it felt like we were one. Little Max joined us on the bed. We finished our drinks and we all slept.

I awoke to a tongue licking me the next morning. I figured it was the dog. Opening my eyes, little Max was letting me know he needed to go out. Big Max still had his arms around me and I carefully slid out of his hold. I took little Max out for a walk. I made it a quick walk, wanting to return to bed before big Max woke up.

When we came back in I went upstairs to discover that big Max was still asleep. I carefully crawled back into bed and got up next to Max. I marveled again at the fact this particular man was actually spending time with me! He still had a sweet smell. As I looked at him under the covers I was aroused again. The night before had a memory that wouldn't leave my mind. I started to slide my head under the sheet when little Max jumped up on the bed. That woke big Max up and he looked at me. He realized I was awake and what I wanted to do. He put his body in a position that made it easy to accomplish my goal. He offered no resistance. We reenacted the night before. I was satisfied and in awe of the fact he was still in my presence.

"Horny little devil aren't you?" Max whispered into my ear.

"Let's just say you bring out the beast in me. You have to be anywhere special today?" I grinned.

"No, I don't. You?" Max replied.

"No, I'm free all day."

"Good, how'd you like to spend the day together?" Max asked eagerly. His tone of voice was equal to my desire he stay.

"In bed?" I answered excitedly. Spending the entire day with Max sounded wonderful. I felt very lucky and happy.

"Whatever you'd like Babe whatever you'd like!" He laughed and started to tickle me. Little Max at that point started to bark and growl.

"Protecting dad huh? Well, I'm not going to hurt him fella." He petted Max and he settled down. I rolled over and hugged big Max. He snuggled up next to me and we laid there. I felt so relaxed I fell asleep and so did Max. When I woke up I rolled over and big Max was still there. He also was awake. He kissed me.

"You been awake long?" I asked.

"No, I just woke up. I was looking at you. For a skinny older man, you have a nice body." That comment melted me.

"Thanks. I guess it's not so bad. I usually get the you are so skinny comment. How about a shower," I paused, "together?"

"Awe together huh, sounds kinky but why not!" We walked into the bathroom chuckling. I got the water running and warm and we got in the tub. I gently lathered Max up from his neck down to his toes. I lifted his feet and even washed between his toes. The lather gave me a chance to caress every inch of his body and touch him. I was taking in every inch of his naked body in daylight. It wasn't a dream, it was real, and Max was standing in the shower with me. He rinsed off and in turn lathered me up. He touched every part of my body. I tried to shampoo his hair, but he was so tall I couldn't reach his scalp. He laughed at me.

"Wait, Babe, let me bend down." He squatted down on his knees and I shampooed his hair. Max took advantage of the position he was in to arouse me. Between the touch of his lips and the sensation of the soapsuds, I was tingling. He stood up and pressed his body against mine. We kind of just stood there with water running over our bodies. "Just getting you warmed up for later."

"Oh I warmed up!" I said. I took the showerhead and rinsed off his body. Max took the shampoo and washed my hair. He turned the showerhead to a massage that was a pulsating jet of water. He rinsed off my hair and body and I again rinsed his body. We got out of the shower and dried each other off. We wrapped in towels and stood kissing. We walked back into the bedroom and sat on the bed.

"Want some breakfast?" I asked.

"Something besides you?" Max teased.

"Well, I was thinking of bacon and eggs."

"Oh I suppose," he sighed. "Do you happen to remember where I put my glasses he asked?"

"On the nightstand next to the bed," I answered. Max put on his glasses we went down to the kitchen and I fixed breakfast. I had many interruptions from Max in the form of kisses and hugs. It was the most fun I'd ever had fixing breakfast.

"Could you do me a favor and set the table please?" I asked.

"Sure. Point out the cabinet with the dishes." I pointed to the cabinet and Max set the table. As he finished, I put the food on to eat. We sat and as we put food on our plates I felt a bare foot pushing its way up my leg. I looked over to see a big grin on Max's face. With his toes he pulled my towel open. He put his foot up against my thigh.

"Good breakfast." Max beamed.

"It's just bacon and eggs." I said smirking at his move.

"It is still good." Max replied. He finished his plate and pushed back from the table. In the sunlight I could see his hairy chest and arms. His body was a little more slender in the daylight than it had felt in the dark, but it was still a body that sparked my sexual desire. I got up and started to clean up the dishes. I gathered up plates walked to the kitchen and began putting them in the dishwasher.

"Can't that wait until later?" Max begged.

"I guess so, why?"

"Oh, I thought I could take your naked body to the living room and we could go watch tv" he got up and started to walk to the living room "or maybe in the bedroom."

"You're on." Max walked up, put his arms around me, and gave me a kiss. He took my hand, we walked up the stairs holding hands, and somehow his towel fell to the floor as we walked. We lay down on the bed and turned on the television. We spent more time staring at each other than we did at the television.

"Max, can I ask you a serious question?" I said thinking aloud.

"Sure, sounds real serious?" Max cringed.

"It's serious. Have you been tested recently for HIV?"

"Yes I'm HIV negative. You?"

"Yes negative. I just wondered. I figure it is best to have that out in the open now. That's all." I leaned against Max.

"That is true, it's best to know now and not be surprised and feel betrayed or taken advantage of."

"Yea, I know the feeling."

Max smiled at me and said, "Anything else you wanted to get out of the way while we are doing the question and answer session?"

"No, sorry, I just didn't want to have that lingering in my mind I wanted it out in the open." I sighed. I guess to change the serious conversation, Max again started to tickle me. Little Max was asleep downstairs, I guess. He didn't interrupt this time. We wrestled around on the bed until we were both out of breath.

The phone rang twice. I let the recorder get it. My cell phone was turned off, fortunately. I was sure it was Sampson and he'd figure out what was going on. That day turned into two days. Days spent entirely together eating, sleeping, watching television, listening to music, and having sex. I dreaded to see Max leave. However we both had to go to work. It had been a wonderful weekend. As Max kissed me goodbye, I had a feeling that this was probably the first and last encounter we would have. And if it was, it was a beautiful moment to remember.

We stood kissing one another goodbye for what seemed to be hours. Finally Max said, "Babe, I have to go. We both have to get to work today and I need to get moving. I will call you soon. Now, one last check spectacles, testicles, wallet, cell and keys. I'm ready," Max sighed as he touched his glasses, his crotch, felt his back pocket, touched his phone and shook his keys.

"What is that all about?" I said.

"I constantly am leaving the house to discover I don't have my keys, or my glasses, or my cell phone or my wallet. One of my friends once joked I'd leave my balls behind if they weren't attached. So I created a little saying to help me remember the things I need most, and added my testicles for good measure." He said.

"Clever idea. Max, I have had a fabulous weekend. I will be waiting anxiously for your call."

"I had a great time Colt. I will call you later this week after I see how my schedule is for the week." He kissed me goodbye one more time. I hoped I hadn't been too pushy with that last statement. I walked Max down to his Porsche and waved goodbye as he drove away. After Max left I decided I had better get myself to work. The day seemed to drag by. My class was just off the wall but, I guess my attention to them was limited. When I got home from work I decided to call Sampson back.

"Hello."

"Hi Sampson, Colt."

"Well, that's all you are going to say, Colt, hi? I called both Saturday and Sunday, and your recorder was all that I got, and you obviously turned off your cell phone. So, what happened I want to know all the details?"

"Well, we spent the weekend together. It's probably the first and last time we will but, it was worth it," I said to Sampson.

"You are such a pessimist. What makes you say that Colt? From the look in the man's eyes Friday night I bet you will be seeing a great deal of him. Did he say he'd call?"

"Yea, he did later this week. I do like him. He's like a fantasy come to life."

"I think you more than like him. You have talked about him before. You've known him for quite awhile haven't you?"

"Yea, for three or four years we just never got past the hello how you are friendship stage. He said he's been as interested in me as I have been in him."

"See. I told you, a man from your past. See! Listen Colt, Ron and I are supposed to meet Jack at Bobs. Why don't you join us there? We can continue this conversation."

"No, I just want to stay here. I need to rest from the weekend."

"Awe, come on, go out with us!" Sampson pleaded.

"No, I want to stay home. Thanks anyway."

"Suit yourself. Talk to you later." Sampson jibed.

"Later." I said.

The other person I knew I'd better call before news traveled through the grapevine was Derrek. He would be mad if he found out Sampson knew something he didn't know.

"Hello."

"Jason, this is Colt."

"Hi Colt, how are you?"

"Oh fine, and you?"

"Good. Just a minute and I'll get Derrek."

"Jell-O, Colt." Came Derrek's voice a few minutes later.

"Ji Derrek, you and your Jell-O's. I was going to talk to Jason, but he went to get you."

"Hang on and I'll go get him."

"No, I wanted to talk to you."

"Oh, ok. What's up?" Derrek said giggling.

"Oh not much I just wanted to tell you something in person, before Sampson did."

"Why is that?"

"Because, I wanted to be the one that told you myself."

"Tell me what?" Derrek teased.

"Tell you about my weekend."

"Oh, so something has happened this past weekend?"

"Well, sort of. I spent the weekend with a guy I've known for a long time, but we have only been acquaintances. You've even met him, you know Max."

"Max? That guy you think is such a hunk? That tall skinny auto mechanic, that Max? I thought you said he wasn't interested in you!" Derrek protested.

"I was wrong obviously. We spent from Friday night to this morning together. And I wouldn't call him skinny."

"That's because you are both toothpicks. So what happened? Details man details!"

"Well, I met Sampson and Ron for a few drinks Friday at the Twenty-One at Ron's invitation. Before Ron ever got there I was gone, with Max."

"You're kidding? How did you manage that?" Derrek questioned.

"Max asked me to dance. We did and danced until we were hot, then we went out to the parking lot and I saw he had a new car and he let me drive his new Porsche. One thing led to another. I asked him to come to my house. He did and he didn't leave until this morning. He said he would call me this week."

"Well, that's great. Did you two do anything?"

"No, we sat around naked, slept in the same bed, showered together, but we didn't do anything. What do you think?"

"So you played cards and board games and got acquainted."

"Yea, we were bored stiff," I teased.

"Well the stiff part I buy. Did you play it safe?"

"Of course! And that was refreshing, too. He has a way of putting on a condom that is out of this world."

"And how is that?"

"Lots of lip action. Let's just say he's great in bed." I paused, and then said, "and out of bed too."

"Sounds like you are already getting feelings. Do not rush things!"

"I'm not. I've known him for a long time. He's always been a great guy. I've just never known him this way before."

"Well, still, just take 'er slow, okay?"

"I will. So, how are you and Jason?"

"Oh, fine. We've been relaxing and getting the yard into shape. It is a lot of work."

"But it's worth it. It's a beautiful yard." I complemented.

"Thank you for saying so. I like it. It does require lots of work."

"Well, I should let you go. I just wanted you to hear this from me before you heard it from Sampson."

"I appreciate it. Take care. Good luck on it."

"Thanks." I also needed to call Darrin. He and I had talked about using the direct approach before. He wouldn't appear to be interested, but in truth he would be pleased to know I took his advice.

"Hello."

"Darrin, Colt. I am surprised you are home. I was actually prepared to leave a message on your machine."

"Well, I can hang up and you can call back and get the machine if that's what you want," Darrin laughed.

"No, I guess I can just talk to you in person," I fired back. "I just hope your answering machine doesn't get jealous."

"Oh the comic. Not. This is one of those rare evenings I am home early. So dude, what's up?"

"I just called to tell you that I spent the weekend with a man. And I used your direct approach a couple of times."

"And who is this man that you finally came to your senses and were up front and direct?"

"Max, that mechanic I have told you about before." I said.

"That tall lanky dude you are so in lust with?" Darrin said.

"Yes, that would be him."

"I hope it turns into something. You were right about me finding Mat and being direct with him. Let's hope my direct approach works as well for you."

"I know. We'll see. I won't keep you. I just wanted you to know."

"Well, thanks for calling. I do have some paper work I need to do before Mat gets home. Good luck. Later tatter."

"Catch ya later. Tell Mat hi." I said.

"I will tell him." Darrin replied. "Keep me posted."

I needed to call Marshall as well. He would be the one person who would know exactly how much Max's visit meant to me.

"Hello."

"Marshall, Colt. I have news to share with you."

"You sound happy. What's the news?"

"I spent the weekend with Max. I had a wonderful time." I blurted out.

"Well Colt after all this time that is great."

"I know. He said he would call later this week. I sure hope he does." I said.

"Oh, I bet he will. I am happy for you." Marshall said.

"Thanks Marshall. It was a fabulous weekend with him." I said.

"I am sure it was. Sounds like he lived up to all the fantasies you have shared with me about him." Marshall replied.

"Yes, lived up to and surpassed." I said.

"That is wonderful. I hope this develops into something beautiful for you." Marshall said.

"Me too Marshall. I need to get going. I just wanted to let you know."

"Thanks for calling Colt. Keep me posted. Bye."

"I will keep you posted. Tell Tom hi. Later."

The first of the week drug by, I kept wondering if Max would really call. But my worries were wasted as Max did call to invite me over to his place. I was thrilled at the invitation. He did keep his promise. Driving to his house I was a wreck. When I arrived I discovered his house was similar to Marshall's. It was an older house built about the same time Marshall's was. He had restored the woodwork but hadn't gotten as elaborate as Marshall had.

After we toured his house, Max excused himself and left me in the living room. In a few minutes he called to me from his bedroom and told me he needed some help. When I walked into his bedroom he had candles lit everywhere and was lying naked in the center of his bed.

I undressed and crawled into bed with him. We went beyond just sex. He whispered to me as we hugged, "You just made love to me in a way no one has ever done before." It brought my level of emotions to a point they exploded onto my face. Max noticed, "I see the word love met with your approval."

The only answer I could muster was a nod. I gained my composure and was able to muster up a request, "As someone said to me not so many days ago mind if I spend the night?"

"I don't mind if little Max doesn't mind," he said.

"He will be fine until morning. I will just have to be up very early and get home to let him out." I responded.

Those first two days turned out to be two of many days we spent together over the next few weeks. The time we spent together always seemed to go by so rapidly. We were always touching each other or holding hands. The time we spent at work and alone seemed to drag by so slowly. We began to see one another every free moment we had. We found we shared many interests. We truly enjoyed each other's company. We enjoyed walks, just talking to each another, listening to music, dancing, television, going for drives and four wheeling.

I began to write Max a daily note. A note that generally contained dozens of reasons why I was glad we had got together. I also began to write him poetry expressing how my feelings were gushing out of me. He enjoyed reading my notes, *the dailies* as he called them and I always got a kiss, a hug and a smile.

The poems he said made him feel special. Those usually got a bear hug. From Max I got little notes taped to the visor in my truck, or hidden under the toothpaste or under my pillow. This relationship was very different from any I had previously. We were friends first and enjoyed each other before we became lovers. We did know each other before the emotional involvement. We had fun together, before we had emotions, before sex. We remained friends even after love and sex. We were truly living together, just in separate locations. We had the age-old problem of having to be at his place or mine. Carting clothes back and forth, taking the dog back and forth traveling between the two homes.

I never lost the desire of wanting to see Max even though we hadn't been together very long. That thrill inside when I did see him was always there, like every day was the first day we met. To wake up next to him in bed every morning was still like a fantasy. Each day we spent together was as exciting as the first. We both worked at keeping the fire burning. We tried to do something unique every day. There had been nights Max had to work late because he had trouble with someone's car. He had promised that it would be done that day and he always kept his promise.

I helped many nights to get a job done. I would run errands, go get parts he needed so he wouldn't waste time. He had been good to me as well. Many nights when I had to stay for a conference at school, or a meeting, or a class, Max fixed dinner for me. Sometimes he even took me to dinner. He was very considerate. When we both had a late night, we would take each other out, or order a pizza, or just sit and cuddle.

Max and I had this sixth sense we shared between us. We had many surprises for one another when they were sorely needed. We cheered each other up when we were down. It was like he could read my mind and I could read his. There were many times I was thinking about something I'd really like to do and Max would suggest the exact idea I was thinking about out of the blue. Or as often I suggested something and Max would say he was just thinking about that idea. There were many times we had suggested the same thing at the same time. He is truly wonderful. I not only have a lover but a friend. He truly is my friend, shoulder to cry on, and my companion. He said he feels the same way about me.

We discussed meeting one another's families. That dreaded moment when you meet the family of the man you are seeing. Max had a sister that lived in town and a brother that lived in state. Max's sister, Marie, was also a teacher at the high school level. Max just knew we would hit it off. I wanted him to meet my sister who lived just a few blocks away from me. My youngest brother lived in California and my other brother lived not far from me.

One night when I went by Max's place he was still working on a car in his shop.

"Max, I decided to just come by straight from work," I shouted as I walked into the garage.

"Babe, I am so glad you are here," Max said as he peered from under the hood of the car he was working on. Beside him stood a tall slender woman, with long brown hair, and as I approached Max said, "Colt, this is my sister Marie, Marie, this would be the man I have been telling you about, Colt."

"Nice to meet you finally," Marie said with a smile, "I hear you are a fellow teacher."

"Nice to meet you as well," I said shaking her hand, "yes, I teach elementary school."

"Well, I teach at an alternative high school, so we are at opposite ends of the spectrum," Marie said.

"I am almost finished here," Max interjected, "why don't I take you both out to dinner and you two can get better acquainted."

"I think that would be fun but I would need to call Matthew and let him know I will be late getting home first," Marie said.

"You know where the phone is sis, just do it." Max responded.

While Marie was on the phone Max explained she had car trouble when she left work and she had called him to come and rescue her. He had gotten her car started but asked her to follow him home so he could check the car out in the shop.

After Marie called home we left for dinner. We had a wonderful time. I did feel a strong connection to Marie. She was married and had two little boys. Her husband Matthew worked construction and had just started his own business. We all three talked for hours. Marie and I bored Max with our war stories about children, administrators, and parents that we had dealt with. By the end of the evening I felt I had known Marie all my life.

One night shortly after meeting Marie, my sister, Tess, had stopped by after work to drop off a movie she had borrowed. She had just arrived when Max pulled into the garage. Max came bounding up the stairs from the garage, I met him at the door and got the kiss, hug, smile that I always got before he realized someone else was in the room.

"Babe, you could have warned me you had company!" Max said embarrassed.

"Well, I didn't have much time. Tess, this is Max, and Max, this is my sister Tess."

"Well Max it is nice to finally meet you. I have heard all about you," Tess said shaking Max's hand.

"Oh, lord, what horror stories has Colt told you?" Max said concerned. "It is very nice to meet you as well."

"Tess I was just fixing dinner why don't you stay for dinner and you can get to know Max," I spewed out quickly.

"Yes, stay," Max encouraged.

"Well, let me run home and give my dog some relief and then yes, I will have dinner with you guys." Tess explained. "Then Max I can tell you the horror stories I have heard," Tess said with a laugh.

We had an enjoyable evening. Max and Tess seemed to hit if off. We ate dinner and talked. Tess discussed Max's business with him. They both talked about investments, finances, and the day to day running your own small business. I got my turn of being bored silly while they discussed finances and business. When Tess got ready to leave we walked her to her car. When she started the engine Max heard a noise and had Tess open the hood. He tinkered here and there and sent her on her way, pleased with himself that he had prevented a car problem.

In the next week we managed to also meet the parents. We spent one night at Max's parents for dinner. I was nervous as hell. Max had warned me that even though his parents knew he was gay, he had never brought anyone home he was dating before. He thought his mom would be fine but he wasn't so sure about his dad, he was retired from the service and had been a very stern father, and he had never really discussed the men he had dated with his parents. I hit it off with his mom instantly but I was very nervous around his dad. We ate dinner together and talked about Max's business and how Max and I had met.

Then Max and his mom got up to clean up the dishes and his dad asked me into the living room. I nearly died. However as we went into the living room, Max's dad talked to me about teaching and how he admired teachers and all the things they had to put up with. It was probably the best thing that could have happened. By the time we left that evening I was very comfortable with both his parents.

A couple of days later my mom had car trouble at work. My parents are divorce so she called me to come rescue her. I called Max to ask him if he wouldn't mind helping. He came to her rescue. We drove to my mom's work and Max had her car fixed in a flash. He told her she needed a new battery and if she would follow us to Max's garage he could put one in for her. She was so relieved to be rescued she said yes.

We drove back to Max's place and he put a battery in the car. When mom tried to pay him he refused, saying it was no big deal. So she insisted on taking us to dinner. During dinner mom chatted to Max about her car and would he be willing to work on it for her, tune it up, do regular maintenance work. She never trusted the dealerships and at least Max was someone she could talk to in person. The evening ended with hug for Max from my mom when she left to go home.

I decided Max needed to meet my dad. He was a very quiet person so we took Tess with us to take my dad out to dinner. As we were walking out Max did his routine, spectacles, testicles, wallet, cell, and keys, and I had to laugh. When I got into Max's car to go pick up Tess, on the seat was one of his little surprise notes. When I opened it said, *Babe, I am scared as hell to meet your dad. I'll do my best to strike up a conversation.* I put the note in my pocket and looked over at Max.

"I think you will do fine. We have Tess coming with us so there will be four of us to keep a conversation flowing," I said to try to sooth his nerves. "I was horrified to be alone with your dad and we did fine."

"I know, Babe, but I am just nervous!" Max said. We picked up Tess and then my dad. We went out to eat. Max and dad hit it off by talking about cars. Dad loved to tinker with cars and he and Max talked forever about cars. Neither Tess nor I had ever heard dad talk so much to someone he had just met. I was so relieved that Max was able to actually talk to dad. Other than my brother Chip, Max had now met my in town relatives.

So we had become a couple. We managed to meet some of each other's family. That had gone well. I wanted to do something to show Max how I felt. It was as if I had known him all my life but in reality, it had just been two months. I really wanted to ask him to marry me. I knew this was considered to soon to make those plans but I was ready.

He changed my entire outlook on life. He and I had talked about the fact we want to change careers but neither of us is sure what to do next. We seemed to be able to bounce off one another very well. The hugs, kisses, surprises, little notes, and lovemaking just continued to get better and better.

Talking came easy for us. We talk so much about things we want to do together I think we made enough plans already to last us the rest of our lives. When school gets out we have plans to go away for a few weeks and camp and have fun alone. The one topic we hadn't really discussed yet is being a couple, being "married". I think we both realize the other feels that way. It just has never been verbalized.

To celebrate two months of a relationship and surviving meeting one another's families, I decided to make a special dinner at my place for the two of us. I wrote Max a very special poem. The evening was unplanned except for dinner, one surprise, and the poem. Max arrived at my house from work like clockwork. I told him I was making a special dinner. He greeted little Max as he came in the door with a pat on the head.

"Babe, the table is certainly set fancy. You got something up your sleeve?" Max remarked as he walked into the dining room.

"Well, not exactly up my sleeve. It has been two months since we got together. I wanted to celebrate the occasion." The doorbell rang and little Max ran barking to the door. "Would you get that for me, Max?"

"Sure Babe." Max walked to the door and opened it to a deliveryman.

"I've a delivery for a Big Max?" The man said with some doubt in his voice.

"That's me," Max responded.

"Here you go sir," the delivery man said with relief.

"Thank you." Max opened the box as he walked back from the door. "Look Colt, a dozen white roses. Wonder just who these could be from?"

"Well, why don't you read the card?" I suggested.

"I don't have to, to know who they are from but I will. Let me see, says, *Happy two months, I'm falling in love with you, Colt.* I knew they were from you. Thank you Babe I'm falling in love with you too." He walked over and gave his now famous hug, kiss, and smile. I hugged him back and the doorbell rang again.

"This time Colt you go to the door." So, I did with little Max in tow. Yet another deliveryman was at the door.

"I have a delivery for Colt."

"That would be me." He handed me a vase filled with roses. "Thank you." I closed the door and turned around to Max. "Hum one red rose and five white roses! Wonder who these could be from?" I teased.

"Read the card and see." Max said.

"Like you said, I don't have to but I will. Says, *Good grief Babe, has it been two months already? I love you, Big Max.* Thank you big Max!" I walked over to him and gave him a hug and kiss. "So, where are we going to put these roses?" This must be love I thought. No man had ever sent me roses.

"For now let's put them in the living room. God, these are beautiful Colt. Thank you Babe." He kissed me again.

"These are beautiful too. They are a first. No man has ever sent me roses before. I am deeply touched. They answer a question I wanted to ask you tonight."

"What question is that?"

"I was going to ask you how you really felt about me. I mean, I know you love me, but I am to a point with you that I want more than spending time between our places. I want to be married to you."

"Married? Do you really mean that Colt?" Max said earnestly.

"No, I just thought it sounded good," I teased, "of course I mean it!"

"So, can I take that as a proposal?" Max grinned from ear to ear.

"Yes. Would you like me to get down on my knee?" As I spoke I got down on one knee, I took my ring from my finger and held it out, "Max will do me the honor of marrying me?"

"YES my answer is yes. There's a lot to talk about and settle, but, yes!" Max said emphatically. He took the ring and tried several fingers to find a fit. It slid onto his pinky finger.

"That is what I wanted to hear you say so badly." We stood there and embraced one another.

"I am sorry I can't get my engagement ring on my ring finger, but I know what it means." Max said.

"I know, it was spur of the moment, but I wanted you to have a ring." I said. Tears began flow down my face. When I looked up at Max, he had tears in his eyes.

"Don't we make a pair?" Max said.

"Yea, we certainly do. I need to finish dinner. There is another little surprise under your plate." I pointed to the table.

"What now?" Max walked over to the table to find an envelope under his plate. He looked at the ring again. "The daily," He said as he opened it and looked at me. "No, another poem! I stand corrected." He stood there, read it, walked over to the kitchen, and stood behind me. He put his arms around me and I got the hug, kiss, and smile.

"Is this really how you feel?" He asked.

"What do you mean?" I asked.

"The words, in this poem you wrote to me," he began to read it aloud.

"Wishes

A dream of a life time

Has finally come to be

One that brings the frills

And all the desires

In one man

That once were only thoughts

Now turned to reality

Bring happiness

A deep love that show

When I

See your smile

Hear your voice

Touch your face

Kiss your lips

Hold you tight

It makes me cherish the day we met.

Love, Colt

Those words, are they how you really feel?"

"Yes, they are. I took grain pains in writing that particular poem." I said. I felt a tear roll down my cheek.

"It's special. I am very touched. I feel honored." Max said as he wiped the tear away. "I see you are crying again." He said.

"They are tears of joy, trust me." I said.

"I believe you." He said. "The words echo how I feel as well. Colt, if I didn't look like you had spent hours fixing this dinner I'd say let's skip dinner, I'll take you out. Since you did, tell me how I can help?"

"You can take those potatoes and the salad to the table. Open the bottle of wine and pour it please."

"I will." Max said with a smile. I brought the rest of dinner to the table and we sat down to eat. Max picked up his napkin to put it on this lap and stared at it.

"Do you never quit?" He teased.

"What? Quit what?" I said innocently.

"This napkin it says, *'Marry me Max'.* That's what. I'm so touched."

"Well, I originally thought that the napkin might be the catalyst to open the conversation we have just had."

"It could have. But, I am already engaged now you know." Max smiled. He held up the ring to show me. We were in our own worlds. After dinner we carried the dishes to the sink and put the leftovers away. We cleaned up rapidly.

"Babe, what time is it?"

"By the clock it is seven, why?" I wondered why he wanted to know the time. I suspected that something was up.

"Oh, no reason. Why don't you get your jacket and come with me?"

"With you where and why?"

"Don't ask so many questions. Just do it ok?" Max pleaded.

"Ok. Do I need to take little Max out first?"

"Probably would be a good idea." Max responded.

"Ok little Max, make this a quick walk!" I took little Max out and big Max followed and we went for a short walk. I was really touched. Max was the only man who had ever sent me flowers. I wondered what he had up his sleeve now. Married! He had accepted my proposal. My mind was reeling. Max was looking at his engagement ring again. We walked back to the house and went in.

"Ready Babe?"

"Ready as I'm ever gonna be Big."

"Let's go. Let me check, spectacles, testicles, wallet, cell, keys, I have them all," Max said.

"Little Max, no long distance calls, no wild parties, and no loud music," I said laughing. We walked down the stairs to the garage. We got into Max's car and drove off. We headed for downtown.

"Give me a hint where are we going?" I pleaded.

"Oh just back to my place." Max quipped.

"Bullshit you would have brought little Max if we were." I protested.

"Maybe, maybe not. You'll have to wait and see." Max teased.

"Max those are beautiful roses. I am touched. Those roses are very important to me. Like the first night we were together. They are so significant to me."

"Somewhere in the back of my mind I remember you saying that no one had ever bought you flowers, in particular, roses. So, I remedied that."

"Yes, you did." I said.

"I love my roses as well. But this ring means so much to me." Max said holding his hand out to look at the ring.

"We can buy a real ring later. That is all I had to offer at the moment." I reasoned.

"No, this is my engagement ring. I am sticking with it." He smiled.

"That works fine for me. As long as you are happy with it, so am I. Come on where are we going?"

"I'm telling you you'll just have to wait and see."

"You're mean." I teased.

"I know." He grinned.

"I can't believe you said you would marry me. I am still feeling like that was a dream." I blurted out.

"Well, I accepted and I will marry you. Just name the day and time." He said. "Why don't you sit and think about what you want for a wedding to take your mind off this surprise." He suggested. He held my hand. I had even learned how to keep my hand loose enough he could shift gears and still hold my hand. We were definitely headed downtown. That much I could see. What he had planned still had me pondering. I squeezed his hand and kissed his cheek. He squeezed my hand and kissed me quickly. We held hands for the rest of the trip. We pulled into a parking lot and stopped.

"This is it kid. I thought we could just sit here and neck like the first night we spent together."

"No way, I can tell by the look on your face you are just teasing me."

"Am I?" Max said very seriously.

"Yes you are!"

"I am. I bought tickets to that play you said you wanted to see. That's what is up!"

"You are so special. You even listen to me when I am rambling on and on!"

"I try to Babe, I try to." We got out of the car and walked to the theater. As we walked through the door Max swatted me on the seat. I turned and scowled at him and he just laughed. The play wasn't exactly what I had expected. It was good though. We had made faces at each other, poked each other at funny lines, and had a good time. We even held hands for a long time. As the curtain went down we got ready to leave.

"Like it Babe?"

"I did. It wasn't what I had expected, but I did enjoy it."

"What would you like to do next?"

"Well . . ." I looked at him with a grin on my face.

"Besides that! We can do that when we get home."

"I would like to go home and dance in the living room alone with you."

"If that's what you want to do we will."

"It is." I said.

"Ok, let's go." As we walked back to the car we exchanged lines from the play and laughed. We drove home holding hands and being silent, listening to our music. We were greeted by little Max when we arrived.

"Hi Max, long time no see. How was your evening?" Big Max said as he petted little Max.

"Need to go out?" Little Max barked and ran to the door as if to say yes.

"I'll take him Babe. You go sit down," Max said.

"Ok. I'll pick out some music to dance to."

"Sounds good," Max said as he closed the door behind him.

"Make it a short walk!" I yelled at them. While they were gone, I mixed drinks, lit candles, and put on some soft slow music. I sat and thought about being "married" to Max. The front door opened and in bounded Max and Max.

"Quick enough for you? I thought you said you wanted to dance! What happened to all the lights?" Max asked.

"We can dance by candle light can't we? This has been a rather important evening so far. I thought this was romantic." I explained.

"Sir, may I have this dance?" Max asked.

"Certainly." I replied. We danced to many songs and had several drinks. We hugged and kissed. We talked about the two months that had just passed. Max showed me his engagement ring several times. We ended the evening in the same manner we had ended our first evening together, Max carried me up to bed and made love to me. I couldn't stop thinking about the evening's events, getting married!

"Max, you really will marry me?" I asked again.

"Yes Colt, I will. We have to decide what to do about your place and mine. One of them will have to be sold or rented out or something."

"I know. You love your place as much as I do mine. That's going to be a tough decision. You run your business out of your garage too. It seems logical to sell this place and move to yours."

"But Babe, that isn't exactly fair either. I was thinking. You want to change your career. I want to change mine. Maybe we should sell both places and buy one of our own. Invest some of the money into a business we could both work at."

"That doesn't sound bad to me. Selling the houses and buying a new one will be the easier part. What kind of business?"

"I don't know Babe. We can take our time looking into that. Decide that later. There's no rush. I've had the shop for ten years and you have taught for eighteen. You can teach a few more years and I can run the garage a few more years."

"But if we sell your house you'll loose the garage. What will you do about that?"

"Oh, I don't know. Let's discuss this later. Right now I love you and I want to be with you. That's all that really matters anyway. The rest we can work out day by day."

"Guess so. I do love you Max a great deal. In time we can get this together."

"The other thing we need to discuss is what kind of ceremony we want to have." Max said.

"You do read my mind. Part of me thinks in a church, part of me thinks at one of our homes."

"I know and that is what we have to discuss." Max sighed. I laid there astounded how much we thought alike sometimes. We held each other until we fell asleep.

The next morning when the alarm went off I got up and walked little Max quickly. When I went back into the house, I noticed big Max wasn't up yet. I went back upstairs and he was still sleeping, or so I thought. I went in to go ahead and brush my teeth and shave before I woke him up. I walked into the bathroom and took out the toothpaste. I found a little note attached to the toothpaste reading, *"Colt, To the man who has captured my heart, you name the day, the time, the place and I will be there to marry you! I love you, Max"* as I turned to go wake Max up, I bumped into him coming into the bathroom.

"I see you found the note," he said grinning proudly.

"Yes I did. How sweet!" I replied with a sigh.

"I mean that. You say when and where."

"I think we should make that decision together." I put my arms around Max and hugged him. He kissed me on top of my forehead.

"Do you have to go in to work today?" Max asked.

"Well, no. Yesterday I left extensive plans just in case."

"Go call in sick then. I've already cleared my day."

"Okay I will. "As I called in sick Max crawled back into bed. I joined him there.

"Well, Babe, what do you think? When shall we wed?"

"I don't know. It's June. School ending is such a bitch as it is. This month would be pushing it."

"True. But after you are out of school you will have plenty of time to do running around and getting this together."

"That's true enough. We still have to decide about the houses."

"I know. What do you think of the idea of renting one of them out for now?"

"You mean you'd live with me before you marry me?" I said jokingly.

"What are we doing now Babe? I mean the only difference is we go between two places all the time. I am tired of the driving back and forth."

"I am very tired of traveling between both places as well. Yes that sounds good but which place?"

"I don't know. There are pros and cons for both places. Let's get back to picking a date first."

"When is your ideal date?" I asked.

"This is going to sound silly, but for two gay men, I think Halloween is perfect." Max held his breath.

"You are kidding! I've always felt the same way!"

"Then that is settled Babe. Halloween it is. Now where do we move to? Your place or mine?" Max looked so serious, but I had to laugh at that line.

"I am sorry to laugh, but your place or mine sounds like we just met and are trying to decide where to have sex." I giggled.

"That is true." Max laughed. But he continued on with his thought, "I guess the real question is which one would rent out easier."

"Good point. Which one do you think has the best potential?" I questioned.

"I don't know. We could just run an ad in the papers for both of them and see which one rents first. Let that be the determination." Max paused for a moment.

"I like that idea." I said.

"And if mine rents out I have a solution for the garage. We could make it part of the lease that until further notice the shop space remains mine. That way I would be there during business hours to conduct business. That solves that problem. And even if we sell it we could make the same deal, only we'd have to rent the garage from the new owner."

"That sounds good. At least those two decisions are made."

"Yes. I am glad they are!" Max sighed. I rolled over next to Max and began kissing him. "I gather this means you don't want to discuss this any further?"

"For now we have basic decisions made. I have other things I would like to do since I have the day off work!"

"Oh really? What could those other things be?" Max asked.

"Do I have to draw you a picture? This isn't a banana pressed against your side." I pointed out. Max got the picture.

For the next few weeks, we spent time trying to rent out one of the houses. For the most part we had very little luck. No one wanted to meet the prices we felt fair in renting. One night while we were trying to decide what to do one of

Max's friends called. He was thinking of moving out of state, didn't want to sign a lease on his apartment for six more months, and wondered if Max knew of anyone looking for a house sitter, or a short-term lease. Well, that happened at the most opportune time for us.

Max told him to come on over and we could talk about the situation. When he arrived, he and Max discussed renting my place. Then they talked about cars and cars and cars. So for part of the summer we rented out my place. But that wasn't permanent.

We talked about our wedding and who to invite. We walked on the bike path, rode bikes on the path, used the pool, and got tan. One night while we were discussing our future plans Max got a call from his brother Steven. He was in town and he thought perhaps Max would like to meet him for a drink.

Max agreed and drug me along with him. On the way to the bar, Max told me Steven was a very logical thinking person so he wanted me to be prepared for anything. When we arrived Max introduced me as his boyfriend. Steven seemed to deal with that well. But when Max told him we were going to get married he just couldn't understand why. There were no gains to be had for two men to make some commitment to one another.

There were no children to be raised, no financial gains, and no laws that covered such an arrangement in this particular state. He just couldn't understand. I could see the logical side that Max had warned me existed. But I did like Steven. He was enjoyable to talk to and very generous, he insisted on paying for our drinks and taking us out for an after drink dessert.

We went camping once with my brother Chip and his girlfriend DJ. He and Max hit it off talking about racing cars, engines, transmissions, and car parts in general.

I worked on finding a minister and we created lists of guests to invite. We decided I should create the wedding invitations. I worked on them and put them together for Max to approve. I also wrote a wedding vow. I wanted Max to write one as well but he was stumped at what to write. So I shared mine with him.

"Let me read what you have Babe." Max said. "I can't believe you wrote the vow yourself. Let's see what it says." He read aloud what I had written, *"Wedding Vow: Max Michael I believe in the relationship we have established. At this point in my life I, Colt Gregor, stand here to make a lifelong commitment to you; I ask of you no more than I ask of myself; I give to you no more than I give to myself; I am here for you, as you for me; I tell you only that which is true; Our good times over shadow bad; Our love over comes negative; Our strength subdues hostilities; Time stands still for no one, and I now commit to work on a life long loving, faithful, honest, supportive, relationship, our life together. I vow to be your husband, symbolized by this ring. Will you accept this ring as a symbol of my commitment, my love for you?"* He paused.

He wiped a tear from his eye and said, "Yes, I do, this is great Colt. May I use this too?"

"You could. I'd prefer you wrote your own though, worded with your feelings and thoughts."

"I guess that makes sense. I'll have to think about it!"

"Here are the invitations I have planned. Tell me what you think," I handed Max the sample. He looked them over and then laid them down.

"How many of your friends have you told about this ceremony?" Max asked.

"Actually, up to now, none, why?" I pondered.

"Not even the gang, Sampson, Derrek, Darrin and Marshall?" Max asked.

"Believe it or not, not even Sampson, Derrek, Darrin or Marshall. I don't want to go through the teasing, the questioning, the quizzes, the jokes about Halloween, the gags about my being a romantic, who will be the wife, who will be the husband." I said.

"Well, I think you should tell them now. I think they could help us with a few things," Max responded.

"Like what?" I asked.

"Well, for one thing, I want Marshall to do the cake and plan the food portion of this event." Max replied. "And

Derrek can provide some of the tables and chairs we will need and Darrin can provide some novelty items for us. Sampson can help you with these invitations."

"Well, you do have a point. I guess I should get them ready for this and ask for their help," I responded. "But for now I am just going to tell them this is a Halloween party. Ok?" I pleaded.

"Babe they are your friends. If that is what you feel is best then that is what we will do." Max replied.

"What about your friends? Any one in particular you want helping with this process?" I asked.

"I think I have some ideas there. We can certainly make this less of a hassle on us if we have our friends help," Max responded. "I think I can get the place decorated and a good sound system to use from my friends."

"Would you be bothered if I didn't exactly tell Derrek, Darrin, Sampson and Marshall what was happening?" I asked.

"I still am not sure I understand why you would want to keep that information a secret." Max said.

"I would like to get this planned without all their teasing and their practical jokes. And the four of them can be very protective and bossy, but mainly I would like to hold out until the End of the Summer Party." I responded.

"Cutting that a bit close aren't you?" Max said.

"Yes but, if I just tell them all we are having a Halloween party, or better yet a Halloween celebration, I can put in ninety percent of the details to enlist their help, with just a few changes a month before the event." I said. "On our invitations I will say it is a wedding and that the reception will be a costume party. The gang won't need an invitation. That way a Halloween Celebration will be partially true."

"Babe aren't you afraid someone else will spill the beans before your party?" Max said with great concern.

"I think I can pull this off. My sister is about the only person they all four come into contact with and I can give her a heads up." I said.

"Ok Babe, they are your friends. My lips are sealed. I just hope you can keep a lid on this until you want to spring it on them." Max replied. He was always so supportive.

So we both contacted our friends and families and began to put the plans into place for a fall party that was actually a wedding ceremony. Derrek, Darrin, Sampson and Marshall were most willing to help create a Halloween celebration and they were putting together an excellent party. Tess was willing to keep the secret.

Daily life went on and Max's birthday came along. On the morning of his birthday I was excited. I woke up early and as quietly as possible I snuck out of Max's bedroom to walk little Max real quick. I tried to be very quiet and took

415

Max on his walk quickly. Normally I would have just put him in Max's yard, but today I didn't want little Max to bark and wake big Max. I wanted to start my surprise before he got up.

Max was still sleeping when we got back. I shut the bedroom door so little Max couldn't get in to wake big Max. I went back to the kitchen and quietly fixed a special breakfast. I had carefully hidden the supplies I needed in the spare bedroom so I didn't have far to go to get things.

I went and put on the shirt I choose to wear first just in case Max woke up. It was one of Max's old muscle shirts that was worn and full of holes. It was large enough on me that it covered the parts of my body I wanted covered. I felt it made me look seductive. I then took the banner I had made and taped it above the dining room table. I placed his birthday card on his plate. As I turned to go back to the kitchen, I was caught in the act.

"Babe, what are you doing?"

"Oh nothing much, I was fixing your breakfast."

"That's not your shirt, that's one of mine. I must say it looks good on you. I hadn't realized you'd gotten so tan!"

"I have been working on being tan. This baby blue just accents my skin is all." I modeled the shirt.

"What's this?" He pointed to the banner, "'*Happy 35th honey! Love you Babe*', you remembered my birthday! That's what all the commotion is about!"

"You thought I forget?"

"Well, no, but I didn't expect you to be up at the crack of dawn doing something. Now I know why you insisted I clear the day." Max said.

"I told you I wanted to spend your birthday with you. Except for a few little plans your wish is my command today. Your highness, what may I do for your oh royal one?"

"For one thing, give me a turn around so I can see you in that shirt."

"As you wish sire." I was glad to see the muscle shirt had the effect I wanted.

"That's better than seeing you naked! The holes are in strategic locations. It is just long enough to make one wonder what's under there, and just short enough to give a hint of what's there. Ooough, I like it! Is this supposed to be one of my gifts?"

"In a way, yes I wanted to look sensuous and appealing." I replied.

"Well Babe, it worked!" He walked over to me and gave me a hug, a kiss, and a smile. He began to laugh. "I thought you were supposed to please me today not me please you!"

"If it pleases you to do what you are doing, then I have accomplished my goal haven't I?" I remarked.

"I guess that is true."

"What do you wish me to do sire?" I bowed.

"Do we have enough time for you to follow me to the bedroom before you have to serve whatever you are cooking?"

"That can certainly be arranged me lord." I turned the burner on the stove to low.

"Then follow me servant." As we walked up the stairs, I was pleased with myself. This was exactly the result I wanted. We had a very compatible sex life but for his birthday I had wanted to be seductive and arouse him in a different way. I felt I was successful so far.

Max turned around as we walked and said to me, "Colt, I can't tell you what an effect seeing you in that shirt has on me!"

"Oh, I think I can tell just by looking at you!" We got to the bedroom and Max laid down. I stood there.

"Well, servant, don't just stand there, arouse me. Make passionate love to me!"

"You look aroused to me already."

With a poor British accent, Max commanded, "Does thou believe he was to speak, I said make love to me not chatter away!" With those commands, I made love to him. I was so into the role it was a very different experience. I stood back up and looked at Max. I bowed.

"Was my lord pleased?"

"Me lord is very pleased. Put that shirt back on. Let's see what it is you hath made for breakfast servant." I put the shirt back on and we went to the kitchen. I opened the lid to the skillet and unveiled Max's main course.

"Looks good, potatoes, eggs, and what else?"

"A little bit of green pepper, onion and cheese. It's a country breakfast of Marshall's."

"Then it ought to be good."

"If you'll take your seat me lord, I shall serve thou." I bowed again.

"I shall." He walked to the table and saw the card. "Aw the royal birthday greeting?" He stopped at his chair and looked at me. He pointed to the chair and cleared his throat. I went and pulled it out for him. He sat and read the card. I had intentionally bought two cards, one serious, one silly. "This is a surprise. A card that actually just says have a great birthday. I expected one of those joke cards at least."

"The day isn't over yet, now is it me lord?"

"Oh so the servant has some more plans up his sleeve does he? Well, in that shirt I guess they couldn't be up your sleeve, but well, you get the idea. Lord that does do something for your sex appeal!"

"So I'm not sexy usually huh?"

"Is the servant being insubordinate?" Max smiled, "You know what I mean. Yes, you are sexy usually. This is just a different kind of sexy." Max ate and we dropped the servant routine as we talked about our families and the week we were having.

After breakfast I cleaned up the kitchen while Max read the paper. We took a hot steamy shower together. We sat in the living room while Max thought about what he'd like to do. I was hoping he wouldn't want to do anything in the evening. That is the one place I had made definite plans. I decided to jump back into the role of a servant.

"Well me lord, hath thou decided what thou wants to do next?"

"I hath. I want to go downtown and rent a room at a fancy hotel and spend the afternoon there. I've never done that before."

"Yes sire. When would thou like to depart?"

"In a little while. I want you to wear that shirt, or at least take it with you. After all it is my birthday present."

"As you wish sire." I was beginning to get into the role of the servant. It was kind of fun to play out this kind of fantasy. Max seemed to be enjoying it. I had to figure out a way to subtly get him to come back to the house by six or so. I didn't want to give away my plans but I did need to have him home by then. Otherwise, it would ruin the evening's surprise.

"Servant, bring round the carriage, I am ready to leave." Max commanded, going back to the role of his royalness.

"As you wish sire. Which carriage would thou prefer? The one with the carrying capacity or the one with the smooth ride and lots of horse power?" I bowed as I spoke.

"The one with the smooth ride, I like those horses better."

"Yes sire. May I put some clothes on first me lord?"

"If you deem it necessary." He laughed. I put the muscle shirt on, and then dressed in jeans and a shirt over it. I didn't think going into a fancy hotel with that shirt on alone was a great idea. I went and got the carriage and returned to the door to get his lordship. We walked out to the carriage and drove downtown.

"Which particular establishment doest thou wish to enter?"

"Well, let me see. How about the Palace? It's supposed to be fancy."

"As you wish sire." I drove to the Palace and parked the carriage. "What room doest thou wish to rent?"

"The bridal suite I think will suit me."

"Yes sire." We walked into the hotel and I walked up to the front desk. "I'd like to rent a room please."

"Yes sir. We have a number of rooms available would you like one with a view of the city?" The clerk asked looking at me and then Max.

"I would like to rent the bridal suite, if it is available." I said.

The clerk looked at me with an astonished look and sharply replied, "Yes sir it is available. How long did you want the room?"

"Just for today."

"Yes sir." We went through the paper work of renting the room and the embarrassment of not having any luggage when the bellhop was called. We were shown to our room. After the bellhop left Max and I broke into uncontrollable laughter.

"Babe did you see the look on that clerk's face when you asked him for the bridal suite? I thought I was going to die right there. It was all I could do to control myself." Max laughed harder than before.

"I know. I had a hard time keeping a straight face. His underwear was in such a wad I could barely keep from laughing. I almost said his Royal Highness wants the royal sweet. Can you imagine that reaction?"

"He would probably have wet his pants right there! Babe if this is how the entire day goes, this is going to be the best birthday I have ever had!" Max continued to laugh.

Getting back to my role I said, "Me lord I hope it is the best ever. Would you look at this room! It's set up almost like a house. A living room and a bedroom. Let's go explore!" I was caught up in the room and lost my role.

"Is the servant giving his lordship orders?"

I caught myself, I bowed, "A thousand pardons, me lord. I merely meant to suggest that perhaps me lord would like to look around the suite."

"That's more like it. I want to see what the bathroom and the bedroom look like." We walked into the bedroom. There was a round bed in the center of the room. The bathroom had a Jacuzzi tub. It quickly brought to mind many things I would like to do to his lordship while we were staying here. From the look in Max's eyes I believe we were thinking the same thing.

"His lordship would like a bottle of champagne."

"As you wish." I picked up the phone and called room service. I ordered a bottle of champagne and they talked me into cheese and crackers as well. While we waited for room service, we lay on the bed and looked at the furnishings in the room. It was a nice place.

"Honey, uh I mean, your lordship, this is a nice room. I always wondered what the bridal suite looked like. Maybe in October we should come back here and spend the night?"

"It is an interesting room. Perhaps we could spend our honeymoon here. By then we may want to do something else." We heard a knock at the door. I got up to answer the door.

"Your order sir."

"Thank you." I tipped the man, and closed the door. I took the cart to the bedroom.

"Would your lordship like me to pour sire?"

"Only if you strip down to the muscle shirt first."

"As you desire." I stripped down to the shirt and opened the bottle of champagne. I poured Max a glass. "Here you go sire."

"You may pour yourself a glass."

"Thank you me lord. Most gracious of thou." I couldn't help but laugh at that one. "Any other wishes sire?"

"I'd like you to runneth me a bath. Not too hot, not too cold." I bowed and went to the bath to run a tub of not too hot water. I came back out and knelt at Max's feet.

"Servant, I wish to have my clothing removed." Without a word I took off Max's clothes. I stood in front of him awaiting my next command. "Servant, escort me to the bath." I walked to the bath with Max bringing the cart with me automatically. Max got into the tub and noticed the cart. "I see the servant hath read me lord's mind."

"I tried me lord. Hath I pleased thou?"

"Yes you hath. You would please me more if you would get into this tub with me!" I started to take off the shirt and was interrupted. "Did thou have permission to remove that shirt?"

"No, sire. I did not."

"Then do not remove it. Get into the tub at once as you are!" I did. We spent the rest of the afternoon role playing and making love. We both enjoyed the discovery of how much this little fantasy had enhanced our lives. It was amazing how new and different we felt together pretending as we were. We ended up taking a nap. When we woke up, I was in a panic. It was after five, and I still hadn't come up with a tactful way to get Max home. I went for the semi-direct tactic.

"Your lordship, I must make a humble request. We must get back to the castle. We need to check on the royal dog."

"We must? Is that a hint I am possibly holding up some plan of yours?"

"Yes me lord. I do have a plan that does make it necessary to return home soon. I beg your forgiveness."

"Thou arth forgiven. The day has been so much fun so far, I'm willing to go along with you." We got ready to leave. We took one last look around the room and checked out. The front desk clerk seemed relieved to see us go. We drove home laughing about the clerk and how offended he looked. As we pulled into the garage I was hoping the next part of the day would be ready and waiting. And that Max would enjoy what was waiting for him. I purposely let Max get ahead of me and walk into the house first. As I walked behind him I was relieved.

"SURPRISE!" In the living room stood most of Max's friends I knew he hadn't seen much of lately. I looked at Max to see his reaction.

"You little devil you! This is a surprise!" Max and I got engulfed by the crowd. I had taken the liberty to invite the gang so I had someone to talk to as well. Not to mention they all were asked to do favors for me, a prelude to our wedding ceremony. I did have a moment of panic that one of Max's friends had or would say something to Marshall, Darrin, Derrek or Sampson about our ceremony. I prayed that wouldn't happen. A buffet dinner was awaiting Max.

"If the birthday boy would come to the kitchen, we could begin to serve dinner." Marshall announced.

Max walked to the kitchen. "Did you cook all of this Marshall?"

"Yes Max, I did. I hope you enjoy your dinner. Happy birthday."

"What did Colt bribe you with?" Max quizzed.

"Nothing," Marshall said. "I owed him a favor. I was glad to do it though."

One by one the guests filled plates and found places to sit and eat. We didn't have enough seating in the dining room. Many people had to sit on the couches, chairs, the floor, the deck, around the pool and some even sat on the front lawn. I went through last.

"Thanks Marshall, I do appreciate this."

"Like I told Max, I was glad to do it. You haven't been this happy in many years. I'm so glad you and Max are together. Cooking is something I enjoyed doing."

"Hello Tom. I see Marshall has you working?" I said.

"Certainly does. It's kind of fun actually. You do look very happy. I'm glad."

"Thanks Tom."

There were many conversations as we all ate. Max was surrounded by friends. He seemed to be having a good time. As we finished dinner Sampson asked for everyone's attention. He tested out a new comedy routine on the crowd. His reception was great. He walked over to me when he had finished. Ron walked over with him.

"Well Colt, what did you think?"

"If you don't tell him he was fabulous he'll be crushed," Ron teased.

"It is great material. Is this a new routine or is this one you have performed before?"

"It's a new routine. Some of the material I have used before but not in this manner."

"Thanks Sampson. I appreciate you doing this." I said, Max walked up as I was talking.

"Yes, thanks Sampson. You are a very funny man. I don't know how you come up with this material." Max added.

"Oh I just use things that have happened to me in my life. I'm glad you enjoyed it."

While we talked Darrin went around handing out party favors, so to speak. He had brought some novelty items from his store to give to the guests. Attached to each one was a miniature business card from Ins & Outs. When he had circulated around the room he walked up to me.

"So you think everyone likes these little gifts?" Darrin asked.

"Oh I'm sure they do. All the important things, jumping penises, penis erasers, and emergency condoms they are all cute. Thanks. It adds to the party atmosphere."

"I told him I thought this was the best way to advertise the store," Mat added.

"You are probably right. I see you are helping pass out trinkets," I said.

"I like watching the looks on the men's faces. It's a riot," Mat said.

"I'm hoping it will add customers to the store too." Darrin said.

"I'm sure it will Darrin. It was a good idea to put a miniature of your business card on each gift. It makes its point." I said.

"I hope so." Darrin replied. He and Mat walked off and Derrek and Jason walked up.

"Colt do you want the band to play now?" Derrek asked.

"If they are here sure."

"They are. It is one of the first times they have done a private party. They are hoping to drum up some business." Derrek added.

"They are a decent band Colt, I've heard them before," Jason reassured me.

"I feel like an advertising agency tonight." I mused.

"Why is that?" Derrek asked.

"Well, Marshall cooked dinner. That supports the Fez. Darrin brought novelty items from Ins & Outs. Sampson did a comedy routine. Now this band. It's like an evening of advertisements!"

"Yeah, uh huh, it is. But it is still a celebration. Let me go tell the band to play." Derrek walked off. Jason was talking to someone else. I was left alone for a few minutes. Max seemed surrounded by people. Derrek introduced the band and they played many songs that got everyone quiet while they listened. The guests seemed to enjoy the live music. Max and I danced to a few songs. The evening was filled with gifts being opened, conversation, birthday toasts, and music. As the evening wound down the guests seemed to leave as a mass. All at once Max and I realized suddenly we were home alone.

"I must tell you Babe this is the best and most unusual birthday I have ever had. I know you must have been busy for weeks. Let me tell you it paid off! Thank you so much!"

"Hon, you are most welcome. What else would you like to do before the day comes to an end?" I asked.

"Babe I'm tired. I am ready for bed. Let's leave the cleaning for tomorrow."

"Didn't Derrek tell you? He has a cleaning crew coming over as part of your birthday gift." I said relieved.

"No he didn't. How thoughtful. Your friends sure did a great deal for this party. Marshall cooked for all those people and made a beautiful cake on top of that. Sampson's comedy routine was great. Darrin's gifts were a stitch. The band Derrek had perform was very good. They are quite a gang!"

"Yes they are. We've done many things for each other over the years."

"I'm sure you have. It shows."

"If you want to go to bed we can. The cleaning has been taken care of."

"Where is Max?"

"I almost forgot about him. I need to let him out. I'm sure he's probably in the bedroom already." We went up to the bedroom and sure enough there he was on the bed.

"Babe maybe he doesn't need to go out."

"I'll leave him. Don't be amazed if I get up in the middle of the night however."

"Oh, I bet he'll be fine. He went in and out with various guests tonight."

"We'll see." Max walked over to the bed to turn down the covers. An envelope flew out of the bed. He picked it up. "Ah ha, another birthday card! So that's what you meant this morning when you said the day wasn't over." He opened the card. "Here's the tacky one! *'A good man is hard to find, but a hard man is good to find. Happy Birthday! Hope 35 is the best year yet. I love you, Colt.'* I knew you'd get a tacky one!"

"I warned you. Besides it isn't tacky, it is the truth."

"This guy is a hunk, but I still love your body better."

"Especially in this muscle shirt?" I had stripped down to just the shirt while Max had fiddled with the card.

"Let's just say that shirt enhances your body."

"Does thou wish I wear it to bed?"

"Yes his lordship doth." We got into bed and cuddled. We ended his lordship's birthday cuddling close.

"It's going to be difficult to make your birthday top this celebration." Max whispered to me.

"It doesn't have to top this." I whispered back.

I was relieved that it appeared no one spilled the beans about our plans. I think actually Darrin helped distract that topic with his little party favors. All seem to be going fine. It was great to have summer.

At night Max and I would take long walks and sit by the pool. We enjoyed the warmth of the evenings and getting darker tans. We would come in from the pool and eat dinner and watch television or listen to the stereo. Some nights we met friends for drinks or went dancing. Many nights we were romantic and cozy at home alone.

I worked on plans for our wedding while Max was at work. We both talked about what we wanted to do. I was very happy. I still felt like this was a dream come to life. We again moved from Max's place to mine. We used the pool at the townhouse complex in the afternoons. Not as nice as a private pool but still a pool.

"It's been a beautiful day," Max noted, "It's so relaxing to lie here in the sun. You are getting dark."

"It is great to lie here in the sun. You're getting dark yourself. I'm enjoying the summer this year. You are making it the best one I've had in a long time."

"You are making this one of my best summers in years. I'll be glad when the house business is settled. Then we can decide what we want." Max sighed.

"I know. I'm about ready to go in, you?" I asked.

"Yes, I am. It's getting too late to be in the sun anyway," Max answered. We got up and went back to the house. Little Max greeted us at the door. We threw the towels on the couch and petted little Max. "Want a beer?"

"Sure," I said, "want me to start dinner?"

"Let's listen to some music and drink a beer first. I'll get the beer you put on some music." Max suggested.

"One we can dance to? Or one just to listen to?"

"One to dance to, one that moves."

"Comin right up." I replied.

Max came back from the kitchen, "Here's a beer." The music was playing in the background. Max and I danced to the first song. It felt so good Max pushed the repeat button. The same song played again. We danced again but this time we began to dance with seductive motions and rub up against one another. We tossed our swimming trunks across the room and danced together. The song repeated again and we kissed. We were caught up in the rhythm of the music. We began to make love to the beat of the music. As the song ended only to start again we lay on the floor holding each other.

"The song just got to me," Max explained, "and carried me right into making love to you spontaneously."

"I noticed. I enjoyed it. You can do that anytime!" I said.

"You did respond," Max said, "I love that about you. You respond to me without a lot of questions or resistance. You just let things happen."

"You respond to me too. I love you so much."

"The feeling is mutual Babe." We had rented out Max's house to some college students. They wanted to rent the place just for the fall semester. We still couldn't decide whether to sell the houses or just rent them. We hadn't found anything we wanted to buy yet. We were going to take our time looking at places to buy. For now we had one place rented for at least four more months. We would just improvise.

As the middle of August came along, I realized school would be starting soon and the panic hit me. I had warned Max at the beginning of summer I need a vacation right before school started. He had planned some days off so we could go away. I wanted to take him to a secluded place outside Orchard that Marshall had shown me when I first met him. We packed the truck with the camping equipment and left town on a Monday. Monday was mainly for my satisfaction. It would soon be a workday again. We got to Orchard and I drove Max to the little place in the hills I liked so much.

"Well, Max, what do you think?"

"Secluded place it's warm, out in the open. I like it Babe," Max answered.

"Do you really?"

"Yea, I do. Don't you little Max?"

"See that stream over there?" I pointed into it.

"I do. Why Babe?"

"It is really a blast to walk up. That road over there is great to four-wheel on. I think this is the greatest little place!"

"Well let's pitch the tent and go for a walk. I want to see all these things you've talked about for the last four hours."

"Ok, let's put up the tent."

We'd put the tent up several times over the summer. Somehow this time we got things messed up. I guess we were in too big of a hurry. The poles wouldn't go up the way we remembered them.

"Colt just let me do it. Go sit by the truck."

"What makes you think you can do it any better than me?" I snapped.

"Don't get smart, just let me try." He said calmly.

"Oh, all right!" I huffed off and watched Max. He tried several times but still the tent wasn't up right. He threw the poles down and sat on the ground.

"Damn thing! What are we doing wrong?"

"I don't know.   At this point, I don't care." I was angry.

"Just cool off that's part of the problem," Max responded.

"I will." I said.

"Let's sit and think for a minute. Calm down and think about how nice it is to be away." I looked at the poles and pondered what we were doing wrong. I messed with putting them together again.

"Colt just leave them for a minute."

"Ok, ok!" I sat down and tried to relax. Max found the problem. We were attaching the poles in the wrong order and he had the tent up shortly.

"There. See if you just relax a minute it gets easier."

"I guess. At least it's up." I was anxious to show Max why I liked this area so much. I wanted to go walking.

"I am still dumbfounded at how comfy you camp Babe." Max reflected.

"It is not comfy!" I said defensively.

"I didn't mean I don't like it, don't get your underwear in a wad again. I just never realized you could make a tent like a luxury tent. It's nice," Max said. He walked over and kissed me then the hug, then the smile. "You are so wired. Just relax and enjoy yourself."

That trio always calmed me down and his soothing voice was settling. I was able to relax and I finally responded to his comment about camping, "I like to have a few things along to make camping a little more comfortable. It's still camping."

"I know. So what did you want to do first?" Max asked.

"Let's walk up the creek. I'd like to do that first. It's late enough in the afternoon it will be warm. And the water should be warm. I'm sorry I got angry. Thanks for getting the tent up." I hugged Max and kissed him.

"It's ok. Everyone gets angry now and again. Let's go walk so you can burn of some of that excess energy. Want to take Max along?"

"Might as well. He'll enjoy the walk." While Max went in to find little Max's lead I stripped to tennis shoes. He stopped in his tracks when he came out of the tent.

"You going to walk up the creek that way?"

"Why not? Good way to sun the bod. There's no one out here. Marshall and I even walked up the creek in the buff before. We never saw anyone. If it will make you feel more comfortable I'll take cutoffs along." I said.

"Ok. I'll join you then. When in Rome do as the Romans do I guess." Max went back into the tent and returned with the backpack. We started walking up the creek and playing in the water. It was warm and relaxing. I was glad we had come here.

"Babe I can see why you wanted to come. This is so secluded. I am enjoying this. I'm also enjoying watching you walk along. It's kind of nice to be out walking in the buff. That's why you wanted to walk up the creek first isn't it?" He laughed.

"You do know me well. Just up ahead of us a little is a sandy area that is almost like a small beach."

"Oh, really?" Max winked as he spoke. We walked until we came to the little beach. We had taken little Max off his lead and he continued to walk. We had to call him back.

"Max, come here. Dad and I are stopping here for a minute," Max said, turning to me, "I thought we could sit and sun bath for awhile."

"You don't have to make excuses. We can stop. I think I can see why you want to stop." We sat on the sand. Max put his arm around me gave me the kiss, hug, smile.

"I know why I love you so much. As pushy as you can be you are always full of surprises, full of excitement and energy. I like this place. I do love you."

"I love you Max. You are always willing to try my ideas half-cocked as they may seem." Max kissed me again. Little Max returned and I put his leash on him. We tied him to a bush so he would stay close. We lay back in the sand. Max rolled on top of me. I had been correct about why he wanted to stop. It felt good to be in the middle of nowhere making love in the great out doors. We watched the sunset for a few minutes. It was beautiful.

"I suppose we should head back. It is beginning to get dark," Max suggested.

"We should. I'm hungry any way." We walked back to the tent splashing in the water little Max barking at us as we splashed. We built a fire put on cutoffs fixed dinner and ate. We fed little Max and cleaned up the dinner mess. Then we sat relaxing.

"Look at the moon. It looks so big out here. It's a full moon tonight," Max noted.

"It is beautiful. Want a drink?"

"Yes I do. We can sit here by the fire and drink ourselves into oblivion," Max said.

I walked back to the tent to fix a drink. When I came out with the drinks Max was sitting naked on the chair. I walked over and let the condensation on the glass drip on his stomach.

"Ough, that's cold. You are mean." Max giggled.

"Naked huh. And who was making jest at me earlier today for being naked?"

"Well, it seemed natural. It is so warm here. It feels so refreshing to sit outdoors naked. We can't do this at home," Max said in defense.

"I know. That's why I wanted to come here," I answered. I also stripped, and sat beside Max.

"Copycat!" Max cried.

"Lord. You sound like one of my students." I sighed.

"That's why I said it." Max said. We sat and drank beside the fire for hours. We had the freedom of being alone in the "wilderness" together. It was a great evening looking at the stars in the sky and talking. We finally went to the tent to sleep. The wilderness seemed to have the same effect on Max as it did on me. We just cuddled up to one another and held tight. We touched each other's bodies, exploring, but left it at exploring. In the morning we got up and had brunch in the buff.   Then got ready to go four-wheeling and exploring.

"I suppose you don't plan to put any clothes on to go four-wheeling?" Max asked.

"No, I don't. I thought I'd take cutoffs and a shirt in case it rains. Otherwise, I see no need to dress out here."

"Oh, ok. I'll follow your lead. Want to take the cooler and the booze along?"

"Yes. We can stop and eat somewhere have a couple drinks. After all we don't do this often. Maybe even lay in the sun."

"I'll pack if you'll make sure Max is ready to go," Max said.

"You got a deal." We did our respective duties and left. The road wasn't really rough but it was out in the middle of nowhere. Definitely a four-wheel vehicle trail however. We drove to a place where we could see out over the countryside. We found an abandoned farmhouse. We stopped to look around.

"This looks interesting. An old farm house let's see what has been left behind!" Max said excitedly.

"You just never know. Sometimes some real interesting things have been left behind!" We walked over to the farmhouse itself and went inside. It looked as if it had been abandoned, many years ago.

"Look at all the furniture! It's covered in dust. Ough, look, it's even turned into a nest by mice, or something." Max noted.

"Look in this kitchen. This old wood burning oven looks like it came from a restaurant!" I said.

"It is an old wood burner. I've never seen one this big. Wouldn't Marshall have a fit over this?" Max said.

"I bet he would. Look at Max sniff. I hope he doesn't drag up a mouse, or something else."

"Me too, look out there. There's a barn. Let's go investigate it." Max left the house and headed for the barn. I followed. We looked around the old farm. Most things were left in tact, rotted out from the weather, for the most part, but left in tact. Little Max came running up behind us. It looked like whoever lived there had just left everything behind and moved on. We got back in the truck and drove. We found a place where there was a pond. We stopped and had lunch.

"Let's get the blanket out and eat over by that rock," Max suggested.

"That's fine. It's so warm out. I am glad we came on this last vacation before school starts," I commented.

"I thought we agreed not to mention that word," Max reminded me.

"I guess we did. You thought I was bad when school was out just wait until I go back!" I warned.

"Oh, I can hardly wait."

"I'll get the blanket and you can get the cooler and booze please." I said.

"Good thing you added that please." We walked over by the rock and spread out the blanket. We ate lunch and fixed a drink. We sat in the sun. The warmth felt good. It was a cloudless day with the sun shinning bright. It wasn't hot but warm.

"Your little butt is getting tan," Max leaned over and hit my butt.

"So is yours wise guy."

"I've never had a tan behind before. Hope I don't burn it. I'd hate to think how uncomfortable that would be." Max said.

"Put your shorts on if you are worried," I suggested.

"Not right now. I like the idea of a tan butt. I will give it some more sun." Max replied. The day began to get very warm. We drove back to camp and took a siesta. When we woke up we took a walk along the creek in the opposite direction. We splashed and played again. In the evening we fixed dinner and sat out under the stars. We talked and enjoyed the solitude. We sat cuddled together on a blanket. We ran our hands over each other and just enjoyed touching and kissing. We left it at just cuddling and nothing else again.

Unfortunately the next morning we had to break camp and return home. Max couldn't be gone from the garage any longer than he had been. At least we had a few days away. As we left it started to cloud over and rain making it feel like our time camping was over anyway.

"I'm sorry we had to leave Babe. Looks like it would have rained all day." Max tried to console me.

"It probably would have been crummy all day. It's just as well we are headed back. I enjoyed the time away from home. Thanks for making time for us to get away."

"No problem," Max said as he kissed me. It had been the kind of camping trip I had always wanted to have in that part of the country. It was worth it even if it had been short.

From that point forward we were busy. Max seemed to have an unusual number of cars to work on. School starting was a few days away. Max had been working on his part of the vow. I had arranged most of our plans. We decided we were just going to have the ceremony at the townhouse. We found someone to perform the ceremony. I dreaded school. I always get so nervous the night before school actually starts. I had my classroom organized, nametags ready.

"Babe, will you sit down! I can't believe you. You have done this for eighteen years and you are pacing around like it was your first year of teaching."

"I warned you. It is like the first year of teaching. That first day is so important. You have all new kids and you have to set the tone for the entire year that first day. You have to have a real middle ground of not being too big a bitch, but not being too nice either. There are twenty to thirty some bodies whose names you don't know. There are the parents who are as nervous as you are, who come to see the new teacher. It's just a very stressful day."

"I'd never thought about all of that. You'll do fine. You have done this for years."

"I know. It is just difficult. I just get really uptight the night before it all starts. Let's go for a walk or something."

"How about if we go ride bikes. That should wear you down." Max suggested. We did go for a long ride. We raced with each other. I could see Max was trying to wear me out. He just didn't realize it was my mind that needed to be shut down. Not my body. We came back into the house and sat.

"Better? Are you tired now?"

"I'm physically exhausted. My mind is still running a hundred miles an hour. I have a hard time relaxing the brain."

"I'll be right back." Max walked upstairs and I heard cabinets open and shut in the bathroom. He re-entered the living room with towels, oil and a smile. "Let me see if I can't at least occupy your mind for a while. Take your clothes off and lay on the towels. I'll give you an oil rub down."

"That will help occupy my mind." I stripped and laid face down on the towels. Max striped as well and poured oil over my back and massaged it. He spread the oil down my body and massaged as he went. He flipped me over and repeated the process on the other side. His massage began to center in the middle of my body. I pushed him back and laid him on the towel. I gave him a massage. Then I let him finish what he had started to do when I pushed him back. It did take my mind off school and I actually slept that night.

From there my school year began. I met my new class, got to know the kids. They seemed like a good group. Max got busy at the garage. The first week of school went by smoothly. Max made it much easier. He took me to dinner he made sure we spent time having fun each evening. He even helped with some of the projects I brought home. He was surprised how many teachers I worked with knew about my life style. He was more astonished at how well they all accepted him as a part of my life, as the "husband" that he was about to become.

We continued to lay by the pool in the late afternoons and walk along the canal in the evenings. Fall was coming but Max had made it a summer of summers. We had spent time with each other's families. I had become very comfortable with Max's parents and his sister Marie and her family. We hadn't seen as much of Steven and his family. Max and mom seemed to be really getting close. Max enjoyed Tess and Chip's company. My dad was like Steven, we didn't spend much time with him, but he seemed to like Max. Life seemed to be moving along in a happy mode for us.

The end of the summer party had to be planned. Max felt it was best he wasn't there, at least this year. I agreed with him knowing that none of the others had ever brought their "significant other" to our little get together.

Besides I had to tell the gang I was engaged and we were going have a wedding as well as the Halloween celebration. I was astounded and proud of myself for keeping this a secret for so long. So I had some news for the party. I'd announce it after everyone arrived. Then all the jokes would begin, but they would also have such a short time frame before the wedding with all the things I was going to ask each one to do for me, they would also be very busy. I hoped that would keep their pranks to a minimum.

Interlude IV Zee Surprise

"Speaking of Max, Colt, what is the news I've been waiting all evening to hear?" Sampson asked.

"Yeah, what is this news you have kept from us?" Derrek asked.

"Well . . . . You all have things you are planning to be doing soon, and I guess, I fit in a way," I replied.

"God, guy, would you get to the point already!" Darrin protested.

"Max and I are engaged and have decided to get married and have a wedding." I finally said.

"You finally got what you wanted, huh?" Marshall said.

"That is great Colt, congratulations!" Derrek said.

"I guess that news was worth the wait, Colt. You are happy. Congratulations," Sampson said.

"You mean you got the man to agree to a ceremony? Will miracles never cease?" Darrin added.

A voice came from behind us, "Yes, he did. He has a real hard sell. He even proposed on one knee and gave me this ring."

I turned to see who was talking and it was Max, I shouted, "Max, what are you doing here?" Max flashed his "pinky" ring.

"Oh, I just thought I'd get Tom, Mat, Ron, and Jason together and crash this little private party of yours." Max said.

"I thought you were . . ." The other four said simultaneously, and laughed.

"Max called us all and told us to meet him and we'd surprise all of you," Ron said.

"We all wanted to know what you do at these parties," Mat said.

All five of us got out of the hot tub, walked over to our respective partner, and gave him a hug. It was remarkable to see the ten of us in the same place at the same time. We had all been together at Derrek's Fourth of July party and then at Max's birthday, but not alone. Max, as well as Mat, Tom, Ron and Jason realized how important this evening was to the five of us.

"Guess we'll have to start having ten here instead of five," I said.

"And perhaps we can start traveling from house to house in the future," Sampson said.

"I'd really like to be included next year," Max said as he kissed me.

"Me, too," Ron added as he hugged Sampson.

"Don't leave me out! I've wondered what these parties were like the past few years," Mat added as he swatted Darrin on the fanny.

"I've wondered what went on just like you, Mat. I'd like to be here, too," Tom said as he tickled Marshall. "But Marshall and I will be gone."

"I said I would fly back next year Tom, we can come together," Marshall added.

"It's unanimous," Jason concluded as he picked up Derrek.

"Let's go back up to the house and fix another drink," I suggested.

"There are five of us that don't have a drink," Max added.

"Yea uh huh let us go then," Derrek said. We all walked back to the townhouse and were greeted by little Max. He was startled to see ten walk in the door, in place of the five that left. He ran over and greeted Max first, then Marshall, and made his rounds.

"I think we should include all the kids next year, too. Bet they would enjoy the time together," Derrek suggested.

"Except Geoff, I doubt she'd enjoy all the dogs!" Tom said.

"It's doubtful," Marshall added. "She's not particularly fond of dogs."

"Oh, I think she could adjust. I think it's a good idea," I added.

"Well, I doubt I'd fly her out here from California." Marshall said.

"California? Why would she be there?" Max asked.

"Because Marshall and I are moving out there next month," Tom explained.

"Really?" Ron said.

"Is it moving time or what? Darrin and I may be moving to Arizona." Mat added.

"Haven't I heard all this somewhere before?" Sampson announced. "For the sake of our other halves let me try and summarize the news items of the evening. Marshall and Tom are moving to California. They asked if Ron and I would want to buy their house. Darrin and Mat are going to Arizona to open a new store. They may stay there. Derrek and Jason are taking an ocean cruise next month for first year anniversary. Colt and Max are engaged and going to get married and have a wedding ceremony, don't remember a date given. And last, but not least, Ron and I are taking a belated honeymoon trip this month to Hawaii, and are currently looking to buy a house. Did I miss anything?"

"I think that covers it," Derrek said.

"Except, our wedding," Max added, "It will be October thirty-first."

"Lord. I should have known the date!" Marshall sighed.

"I wasn't the one who mentioned it," I said.

"No, he wasn't Marshall, I was," Max defended me.

"Well, we all knew that was the day he's always talked about," Darrin explained. "Hey, aren't you two having a Halloween celebration that night? Boys I think we have been had!"

"Not really *had*, Darrin, let's just say kept in suspense for a time. Colt thought you would give him such grief about a wedding on Halloween he wanted to wait for this party to tell you."

"Well, I suppose we probably would have given him a great deal of grief," Marshall replied.

"I feel slighted, I could have come up with so many great one liners on that topic over the last few months," Sampson quipped. "How could you keep this a secret?"

"Well, I just wanted to keep this under wraps until tonight. Besides, by making it a Halloween Party, we avoid all the pranks you guys would have pulled."

"I thought we were having drinks," Jason reminded us.

"Sorry, I forgot. Coming right up," I said, "Max would you like to help me?"

"Oh, certainly," Max said.

"Let's just move past this point and back to the party for tonight. Just to be sure I remember correctly, it is specifically JD and Coke for Tom, Mat, Ron, Darrin, for Jason Gin and tonic, for Marshall a Manhattan, for Sampson Vodka Seven, for Derrek a beer and Max, you're on your own."

"Correct!" came from the group.

"On my own, thanks a lot," came from Max.

"Dude pranks, from us?" Darrin shouted.

"Yes pranks from you dear sweet innocent boys," I replied and quickly walked into the kitchen to mix drinks. Max walked back to the kitchen with me and we made eight drinks. It was like being a bartender at this point. Max got himself a beer. He and I stood in the kitchen to talk for a minute. It was such a wonder to see everyone together and such a relief to have our wedding announced.

"Max thanks for doing this for all of us. It's nice to see everyone all together."

"I have to admit I was being selfish. I mainly wanted to see what it was you guys did here. When I called the other four they had the same curiosity. So we made plans to crash your little party. Besides, I figured you would need help when you told them the Halloween party was actually a wedding. Having their significant other here helped keep that roar to a whimper."

"I'm glad you did. I think you saved me a great deal of grief." I got Max's hug, kiss, smile and then another more passionate kiss that was interrupted.

"You two can save that for later! Get in here with the rest of us and socialize! You have kept enough secrets for a while!" Sampson shouted.

"Coming!   Just wanted a minute with Max."   I answered.

"You had better not be cuming or we may all be embarrassed . . . . I'm just teasing you. We noticed you weren't out here." Sampson explained as we walked back into the living room and distributed drinks. "I wanted to propose a toast. To old friends, new beginnings, superb husbands, and husbands to be, cheers."

We all managed to clang our glasses, or bottles, together and drink to that. For a few minutes there was silence. We all looked at one another. Max got up and put on some music from an old album that held many memories for me.

"God, that brings back memories, doesn't it Colt?" Marshall said.

"Sure does. I was just thinking that as the song began to play. That song played in the bar nightly for the longest time. It was requested constantly." I said.

"I remember hearing that in the hotel." Darrin said.

"That's right, you worked in the hotel that was above the bar at the same time Colt and I worked there." Marshall said. "I almost forgot that."

"It's been a while back, dude." Darrin said.

"Reminds me of living back in my hometown wishing I could move away." Sampson said. "Far away and start a new life."

"I have the same memory!" Tom added. "Wanting to move from small town USA and start a new life."

"It's just an old song to me," Jason commented.

"I don't even remember it, but I like the song." Ron said.

"Reminds me of cruising the bars," Mat said.

"Of when I first started going out to gay bars for me," Derrek said.

"Of an old bar I used to frequent," Max said. "Guess I choose an album with lots of memories. I just like the music. The comment about old friends brought it to mind."

Derrek got up to get some more food, "Do you want anything Jason?"

"No, not right now," Jason replied.

Right behind him Darrin went to get food. They got into a discussion about business. Small business, verses the big corporations. Corporate buy outs, job security.

Ron, Sampson, Marshall, and Tom got into a discussion about buying the house. The asking price of the house, when they could come over to take a look at it, how many square feet, what kind of public service bills and when they would actually be moving. The things Sampson wanted to know about a house.

Jason and Mat were talking about music. The different kinds of music they liked. How their age difference had influenced their choice of music. Who was hot now and who was hot when Mat was Jason's age.

Max and I just sort of took it all in. This was different from any of the previous parties. But then, we were all single in the beginning. Then some of us were dating. Some weren't. This was the first time in the years we had this gig we all were involved with someone all at the same time. I listened to the many different conversations and enjoyed the touch of Max next to me.

"Hey everyone, listen up," Derrek interrupted the various conversations, "Darrin and I have a great idea. Next year at this time we think we should all meet in Las Vegas. Wouldn't that be fun?"

"Not a bad idea," Sampson concluded.

"If the old man will take me, I'd love to go," Ron replied.

"It's fine with me," Mat said.

"Good idea," Jason agreed.

"I like the idea," Tom said, "you honey?"

"Sure. It would be closer for us." Marshall agreed.

"Well, Max, Colt, what do you think?" Darrin said.

"We'll be there," Max said.

"It could be a weekend instead of a night." I added.

"Then it's agreed? Next year, end of the summer, Las Vegas?" Derrek asked.

"Let's drink a toast to the idea, to solidify it." Sampson suggested.

"To Las Vegas," Darrin said, "this time next year." We all once again clanged our glasses and bottles together. Las Vegas next year sounded fine.

Of course that led to conversations about what wild and wonderful things we could do in Vegas. Everyone had a story about something they had done there. The excitement was in the air. New drinks were made, more food consumed. Discussions about the pros and cons of driving, flying, or taking a train darted through the air. Ideas on things we could do as a group. There were suggestions of places to stay, one couple being responsible for making the reservations for everyone. Staying on the same floor as a group, like a convention of fags Darrin said.

From there we turned to a discussion of our wedding. It seemed like everyone was ready to pitch in and change party plans to wedding plans.

"Marshall I would like you to be my best man," I said unexpectedly.

"Colt, I would love to be your best man." Marshall replied.

"I am sorry, I didn't think. Darrin, Derrek, Sampson I love you all, but Marshall and I have known each other for a very long time. He was with me through my ugly first relationship. That is why I chose him."

"I think I can speak for all of us," Darrin said," we just want you to be happy. We are happy if you are happy."

"I agree," Sampson replied.

"Yea, uh huh, me too," Derrek said.

"I would like it Darrin if you would be my best man," Max said. "I feel like we have connected in a unique way."

"I would be honored Max." Darrin said seriously.

"Wow, what a night," Derrek said.

"Glasses everyone, another toast to the best men, Marshall and Darrin." Sampson shouted.

"Cheers!" Came from the group.

We continued to talk about the wedding, all the things that needed to be completed. We talked about so many possibilities I think it wore everyone out. Derrek and Jason said they were leaving and everyone else joined them.

"Now remember boys, you have a wedding to finish planning and then a trip for a year from now. We expect that you two can handle this," Sampson said as he and Ron left.

Hugs and congratulations were given as each couple left the house. It had been one hell of a night.

"Interesting party Babe," Max said. "Some final decisions were made tonight."

"I am sorry I didn't discuss my best man choice with you, it was an impulse of the moment." I said.

"I totally understood your choice. You noticed I joined right in and made my choice." Max replied.

"I am amazed you choose Darrin for your best man and not one of your friends." I said.

"Well, your gang is so much a part of this wedding. I knew they would be there for us. I do enjoy Darrin, tough as he pretends to be. He has a pretty romantic side to him and we both love cars." Max explained.

"Looks like we have plans for a year from now and some plans to complete for a little over a month from now," I replied.

"That sounds like what I heard. Guess we have been selected as the couple to handle reservations for Vegas. 'Colt's always handled the party in the past.' I liked that excuse."

"Sorry Dear. You kind of got stuck with that one."

"Oh, I don't mind planning the Vegas trip. Sounds like you have some plans to put in place with the gang for our ceremony."

"Yea, I have to do some planning with the gang."

"Perhaps that is where we should go on our honeymoon to check things out in Vegas, don't you think?" Max said.

"We could. I haven't been there as an adult. Be nice to see what it was like before next year." I said.

"Then we can set that up for our honeymoon and at the same time investigate for the gang's trip. It was funny to see them decide we should take care of the group Vegas trip. It will be nice to have all of us together again. Especially with Marshall and Tom moving and possibly Darrin and Mat, we will need to get together as a group to catch up with their lives."

"Yea we will. Let's leave this mess for the morning. I'm too tired to clean it up."

"It's mainly dishes. I don't think there's any food left. I'm ready for bed anyway. I love you Colt."

"I love you Max. Let's go get little Max and go to bed. Honey do you realize we will be husband and husband in little over a month?" I said.

"Yes, I am aware of that Babe. You getting cold feet?" Max asked.

"Not at all." I said. "You?"

"Hell no!" came his response. "See the ring? I wear it proudly and tell everyone it is my engagement ring."

I loved Max so, he was a wonderful partner. I was relieved, now the gang new. Not only did they know, two of them were going to be best men at the wedding. Over the next month, I would have to get things finalized for the wedding. The wedding, which thought still gave me a thrill.

Five Now Ten, *The* Wedding

People, food, chairs, music, clothes, would
I ever be ready? In fifteen minutes, I was supposed to stand
in front of my relatives and a group of my closest friends to
pledge my devotion to Max. Max, where the hell is he? I
hope he didn't decide to go for a walk now! I couldn't go
looking for him. I had no time. Hopefully he would appear
soon. Gees, will I ever get this over. Why did I want to do
something so stupid as to exchange vows in front of people?
Hindsight is twenty-twenty, whatever that saying is, oh well,
it was too late now.

   Our living room is jammed full of people. I can't go
out there until the ceremony begins. Right now I felt like I
was having a nervous breakdown. Man! Thank goodness for
Marshall, he had spent the morning decorating the house with
flowers, putting up chairs and turning our house into a chapel.
He also spent hours baking our wedding cake, adding detailed

frosting and two grooms sitting atop the cake. At least all of that was done. But Max, where in the hell was Max.

I felt someone putting an arm around my shoulder from behind me. It startled me and I jumped, it was Marshall walking up to me in my panic. "Oh, Marshall, you scared me."

"You okay? You look a little worried," he said as he pulled me close and gave me a comforting hug. "I know it's not Max's kiss, hug and smile, but it is as close as I can get."

"I was just thinking that perhaps this was a dumb idea after all. I mean, we are two gay men what difference does it really make?"

"Let me see, that would sound like Steven. You know better than that. We have been friends for years and that is all you have ever talked about, a wedding ceremony. And here it is. Your dreams come true. Sounds like the last minute jitters to me." Marshall patted me on the back.

"I just haven't seen Max in the last few minutes. Lately he has been going off on long walks. I just hope he didn't take off and forget the time. And yes, with Max's brother constantly reminding me that this is a pointless thing for two gay men to be doing I guess it is getting to me." I replied.

"Aw Steven is just so very practical. And Max, he won't forget. I think perhaps he is even more excited about this day than you are if that is possible." Marshall soothed.

"I guess you are right Marshall. I am just so nervous. I will be glad when it is all over." I answered. "I can't thank you enough for everything you have done for us today. For that matter, everything you have ever done for me. Particularly for being my best man."

"You are so welcome for everything. It was an honor to be asked to be your best man. Let me go and see if I can find Max. Perhaps he is with Darrin. In the mean time, relax. You don't have much longer to wait now." Marshall walked down the stairs into the living room and disappeared. About that moment Max came walking up the stairs.

"Max where the hell have you been, I was getting worried!" I blurted out without a thought.

"Colt I am offended! You thought I would leave you standing at the Alter." Max replied calm as could be, "I was talking to the minister about the ceremony and to Darrin about our rings." He came close and gave me a kiss, a hug and a smile.

"No, I didn't think that you would leave me standing at the Alter. I am just so wired. I needed just to be able to be with you before this all begins. So the minister has arrived?" I tried to make up for my shortness.

"Yes the minister is here and ready to begin. So can we just calm down and let this wonderful event unfold?"

"We can, what did you have to ask Darrin about the rings?" I panicked.

"I was just checking to see that he and Marshall had them here. They do." Max leaned over and gave me another hug, "Babe, don't you know it is bad luck to see the bride before the wedding?" He laughed

I had to laugh to he always had a way of making me feel better. Almost time. Would we ever get this over with? "Max aren't you the least bit nervous?"

"Colt, why? Those are all our closest friends, our families, I love you, you love me, don't you?" He frowned. "All we are doing is publicly announcing that we are in love and committed to stay that way."

"You are right, but I just worry I will screw up, or do something stupid. Or that one of our dear friends will do something very embarrassing since it is Halloween. What if one of them does some trick or treat thing like last night?" I spewed rapidly.

"Babe, will you chill. You are talking so fast I can barely understand you. I think at the best friends' dinner they all got out all their laughs. Sampson did the trick or treat gag which of you is the trick, which is the treat. Tom paraded out in diapers with a pacifier in the shape of a penis. Darrin got in his did you know you were going to marry royalty, the queen gag. Derrek had to throw in that you were the fag and I was the man. Marshall gave his older man speech."

"And then your friends gave me all the bullshit that you are really married to crank shafts and engine blocks and I will be a crankcase widow. I think when we decided to have that dinner it was the best thing we ever did. It will all be okay. I think it is time," I took a deep breath, "let's go." I said.

"You look so great in that tuxedo! Okay let's do it. Colt I love you so much." Max replied.

"You look pretty damned handsome yourself in your tuxedo. I love you deeply too." I replied with a kiss attached. Max turned and nodded to Marshall who was standing in wait to start the music at Max's nod.

We walked down the stairs and into the room and I wondered why we had chosen such a sad song to play. Kind of hit me all at once how sad the lyrics really were. I knew we mainly choose it because we had lost friends to AIDS and we had no guarantee we would escape this life without being in the same boat. But it seemed very sad to me at this moment in time. We walked in holding hands. I caught a glance of Max as we walked. He was beaming that smile I always got. He was such a wonderful man. I was never sure why he loved me, but I was certainly glad he did.

We reached the fireplace and turned to face one another. Darrin moved over and stood by Max, and Marshall moved over and stood by me. They were both handsome in their tuxedoes as well. My mind went blank. I had written this vow and at this moment couldn't remember a word. Lucky for me we had a minister there to conduct the ceremony. It gave me time to compose myself and get ready to say my vow.

"Colt and Max have gathered all of you here today, close friends and family members, to witness a pledge of their love to one another and to begin a union of two people." I lost track of the minister's speech until she said, "We will now hear the vows they have written for one another, Max we will begin with you," the minister said.

"Colt I, Max Michael, am here today to pledge to you my devotion, my love, my support, my understanding and encouragement to you and to our relationship. I will do all in my power to make you happy, to maintain our relationship to the highest standards. But more, I give you my unconditional love, to be with you through all that life has to send our way. I love you and want to spend the rest of my life being with you and only you." Max had tears in his eyes he was fighting back. I felt a cold chill go down my spine. My turn, oh lord.

"And now Colt, your vow to Max," the minister continued.

"Max Michael I believe in the relationship we have established. At this point in my life I, Colt Gregor, stand here to make a lifelong commitment to you; I ask of you no more than I ask of myself; I give to you no more than I give to myself; I am here for you, as you for me; I tell you only that which is true; Our good times over shadow bad; Our love over comes negative; Our strength subdues hostilities; Time stands still for no one, and I now commit to work on a life long loving, faithful, honest, supportive, relationship our life together. I vow to be your husband, symbolized by this ring. Will you accept this ring as a symbol of my commitment, my love for you?" I was about to cry.

"Darrin and Marshall the rings." The minister said. Darrin handed Max my ring, and Marshall handed me Max's ring. I took a deep breath.

"Colt, will you accept the ring, as a symbol of Max's commitment, his love for you," the minister continued.

"I do, with the deepest love in this world," I responded. Max placed the ring on my finger.

"Max, will you accept this ring, as a symbol of Colt's commitment, his love for you?" the minister continued.

"I do, with the greatest love in my heart," replied Max. I placed the ring on his finger. I grabbed him and gave him a kiss as if I had never kissed him before. I heard a sigh come from the group behind us and then applause. It was done! I was so glad. As we broke apart, we turned to the crowd. I began to cry, Marshall grabbed my arm, Darrin grabbed Max's arm, and I realized I hadn't let the minister finish the ceremony!

We both turned back to the minister who was quietly laughing. "With family and friends as their witnesses, and the powers vested in me, I pronounce Colt Gregor and Max Michael husband and husband. May they have a long and prosperous life together," the minister concluded. "And you may kiss the groom, again!"

"I guess this means we're hitched!" Max said with a laugh. He turned to our guests and shouted, "let's all have some champagne." Everyone stood and waiters came into the room with bottles of champagne and glasses. Marshall gave me a hug, as Darrin hugged Max, and then Darrin hugged me as Marshall hugged Max.

The minister turned to the room, "A toast to the newly weds, congratulations, to many happy anniversaries on this day."

"Cheers" was heard around the room. Max took me by the arm and we began to walk through the room of guests. The first person we encountered was my sister. She hugged Max and said, "So, I finally have a brother-in-law. Welcome to our family. It is good to have you become a part of our family."

Max began to cry, "Tess, thank you so much. I feel very much a part of your family. Since I started to date Colt your family has always been wonderful to me." As he spoke my mother walked up to him and hit him on the shoulder.

"Yes Max, welcome to our family!" Mom hugged Max. I felt a hand on my shoulder, I turned, and it was Max's mother.

"Colt, it is nice to finally have you as a son-in-law," she said as she kissed my cheek. I hugged her and began to cry.

"Thank you. I feel like apart of your family. I am so glad you are here."

"I wouldn't have missed this for the world." She turned to my mom and they began to talk about their "boys".

Max's dad was next, he came over and said, "Well boys looks like you are married now. Take care of each other and congratulations."

"Thanks dad." Max said.

"I plan to take excellent care of Max." I said to his dad.

"Congratulations gentlemen." Came from my dad. He shook Max's hand and then mine. At that moment there were so many people talking all at once I couldn't keep track. Congratulations from every corner of the room, hugs, kisses, tears, I was lost in the hugs and lost track of time. Max's closets friends all came by.

"Cut the cake already," Sampson called from the crowd.

Quickly Max and I made our way to the cake before anyone else could stop to chat. The cake was one that was more beautiful than I had remembered from earlier when Marshall had brought it over. The guests turned toward the dining room and Max began to speak.

"First of all," Max began, "we want to thank all of you for coming to our wedding. You make us very proud. I would also like to thank my parents and Colt's parents for making sure we both grew up with the belief that we could accomplish any goal we set our minds to. We wouldn't be here today if our parents hadn't given us such great guidance."

"Ladies and gentlemen, a toast to the grooms," came from Marshall.

"Cheers gentlemen!" Darrin added. Each person in the room tipped their glass toward us and drank.

"And so my husband, will you slice the first piece of cake?" Max asked me as he handed me a knife.

"With pleasure," I replied. I cut the first piece of cake and handed it to Max. He in turn cut the second piece of cake and handed it to me. I turned toward our guest and said, "Let him eat cake." Max pushed his piece of cake in my mouth and I pushed my piece of cake in his mouth. Our moms came to our rescue and began to cut the cake for the guests.

I realized my youngest brother was patting me on the back. "Colt I am happy for you. Max seems like a nice guy. From what Tess tells me he is a wonderful person. I hope you two will be very happy." Tab said to me as he reached out to shake Max's hand.

"Well Tab, I am so glad you and Tara could come out for the wedding." Max said.

"We wouldn't have missed this. Growing up with Colt, knowing his life style, this is not something I ever expected to have happen. He seems so happy and I am so relieved he found someone that cared as much for him, as he cares for you." Tab and Max moved away. They seemed to be in some deep conversation. I caught Max's brother headed my way out of the corner of my eye. He had such a difficult time with the idea of Max and I having a ceremony.

"Colt, congratulations, I was very touched by the ceremony. I must admit, I didn't think there was any point to the whole thing, but, I have changed my mind." Steven smiled. "It isn't the financial gains or raising children it's the idea of a ceremony for you both to share with family and friends."

"Thanks Steven. I am deeply in love with your brother, and although we live a different life style, we still wanted to share our love for one another publicly. I am glad you came." I was relieved he understood. He nodded and was taken away by my sister.

As they walked off I decided I wanted to be with my new husband. Time to play some music and danced with one another. I looked around the room to find Max. He was with my other brother, Chip. I walked over and stood behind Max. He and Chip were in a discussion about stereos. Only my brother could turn a wedding ceremony into a sales pitch for a new stereo system.

"I hate to interrupt you two, but Max, you owe me a dance. I just came to collect my debt." I winked as I finished my sentence.

"So I do Babe, so I do. Let's do it. Excuse us Chip." Max turned on the music we had selected. He walked me to the middle of the room and we began to slow dance. Max held me very tight. He whispered into my ear, "do you have any idea how happy I am at this moment in time?"

"If you are as happy as I am, then yes I do have a very good idea of how happy you are." I laid my head on his shoulder. "Look, I love this wedding band." I held it for Max to see. From behind me was a tap on my shoulder. It was Marie.

"May I cut in?' she asked Max.

"Only for a moment," Max winked at her.

"Colt, I just wanted to officially welcome you to our family. I know this is a crazy day, but I wanted the chance to just say I feel like you belong in our family and you are the best thing that ever happened to Max," she said with tears in her eyes.

"Thank you so much Marie. I feel very close to you. You have made me feel so welcomed already. I appreciate your telling me in person," I said as I choked back tears. At that moment my shoulder was tapped again.

"Your time is up sis," Max insisted. He held me tight and we began to dance again. "You still want to go change into Halloween costumes before everyone else does?" Max whispered.

"Yes, I do. I want to beat Derrek to the punch. I know him oh too well. Think we can slowly move our way to the stairs without attracting too much attention?" I whispered.

"Oh, I think we could do that. Most everyone is dancing or eating. If we just keep dancing in that direction, I think we can make it." So Max eased me toward the stairs. As we got close we very quickly slipped up the stairs and into our bedroom. We made it without getting caught. I closed the bedroom door as we walked into the room.

"Phew, we made it!" I sighed.

"Yes, we did, but I think we had better change fast. Everyone will be looking for us." Max walked to the closet to get our costumes. I began to wonder just how totally weird we really were. It was Halloween, after all, and it was our "wedding" so I guess, we could do what we wanted.

"Max, only you and I really know the significance of these costumes. This crew is going to think something totally different!" I giggled as we quickly changed.

"Let them think what they will. Dressing as a king and having you dress as the manservant is a romantic memory for me. They can all think whatever they want.

Besides gives them all something to talk about, something to ponder and try to read what they will into the costumes." Max replied.

"Oh, they will talk about it. Darrin will tease endlessly, Derrek will never stop asking why those outfits. Sampson will want to know the significance of the outfit. Marshall will be the only one who kind of knows why we have these costumes. It will be kind of fun." I explained. As we finished changing a knock came at the door.

"You guys in there?" Derrek said. "You can NOT start the honeymoon with guests in your house! Besides your reception has started now, remember?"

"Yes Derrek, we are in here, and coming out now." Max answered. He opened the door and we walked out.

"What in heavens name have you two done? Why are you dressed as a king and, well, uh, whatever?" Derrek interrogated.

"Well we did say the reception was a costume party now didn't we? I figured we would beat you guys to the punch. And whatever it is, I am dressed as a servant." I replied.

"But why a servant?" Derrek had to know.

"Personal reason." Max replied and walked out the door.

"How personal?" Derrek pressed.

"Trust me on this one Derrek, very personal. Just go with the flow, okay?" I suggested.

"You guys have some kind of kinky sex life I don't know about?" Derrek inquired in a determined voice.

Max laughed so hard he cried and walked down stairs. Derrek grabbed me by the arm. "You guys are into kinky, aren't you?"

"No Derrek, we are not. Chill man, just enjoy." I pushed past Derrek.

"Then why did Max laugh so hard? What are you two hiding?" Derrek continued.

I didn't turn back, I just kept walking. I got the crazy idea to catch up with Max and go into the old servant routine. I had enjoyed that so much this summer. It made Max so happy. As I caught up with Max, I saw he was talking to Marshall. "Me lord, what can I do for you? I am sorry I lost track of you me lord. Is there anything thou needeth?"

For a minute Max looked startled. Marshall winked, and said "I won't even ask. Costumes for the reception I assume. I suppose this goes back to Max's private birthday celebration. A king and his manservant, however, still works for a groom and groom."

Max got himself pulled together and replied, "Yes servant, go fetch me a drink, and do it fast you scaly wag."

"Yes master, by your liege." I walked off. As I walked to get Max a glass of champagne Darrin grabbed me.

"What the hell are you supposed to be dude?" Darrin grumbled. "This is your wedding day and you are dressed as a servant? I thought you would stay dressed as a groom for the reception, that is a novelty in itself."

"I know we could have stayed dressed as grooms. And I also know you guys very well. Max and I just decided to join in with the costume party and be something other than grooms." I explained and continued on my way.

"You really meant that the reception would be Halloween costumes huh?" Darrin said as he walked beside me.

"Hell yes! You guys would have turned it into a circus any way," I said, "so why not just beat you to the punch and join right in."

"You saying that we would have done something tacky at your wedding reception if you hadn't decided to stick with the Halloween celebration?" Darrin complained.

"Yes I am. The same guys who short sheeted the bed last night; the same guys who hid Max's Porsche the day before; the same jokers that pulled stunt after stunt at dinner last night? Nah, not you guys." I laughed.

"Aw, come on now dude. Like we do one little thing and you have us down as criminals or something." He also laughed. And as he did Mat walked up dressed in a harness, leather vest, leather chaps, stripped boxers and a riding crop.

"Oh, no, not your leather!" I nodded.

Darrin turned and burst into laughter. He laughed until he cried. "I didn't know you were going to wear those boxer shorts honey."

"Well I had to wear something under my leather chaps." Mat said. "I think I have missed something here, what the devil are you supposed to be Colt?"

"I am supposed to be Max's servant. And as I was saying to your innocent other half, Max and I just wanted to keep up with the parade of costumes we knew you guys would produce."

"We just all thought it would be a riot to wear the most bizarre costumes we could find and see what you would do. You did say a costume reception party. Guess you know us pretty well, don't you?" Mat sighed.

"I know you guys very well." I said.

"You asked for it by deciding to have a costume party reception on Halloween." Darrin teased.

"Ah yes we did, but think of the fabulous anniversary parties we can throw," I replied.

At that moment several guests got a glance of Mat, then me, and the entire room was moving in our direction, all asking the same question. What was the costume I was dressed in? And what was Mat supposed to be? At that moment I heard a tapping and looked over to see Max tapping a glass with his wedding band. Everyone turned to see where the noise was coming from.

"Dear royal guests, my manservant Colt, and my royal self King Max, decided to be the first to put on costumes for the reception, but I see we were not alone in that thought. So at this time dear royal guests let me just announce, let the changing into costumes begin."

Most everyone laughed. In walked Ron dressed as a clown, who was followed by Sampson in full drag. Sampson cleared his throat and the crowd turned to see what now. For most it was a total shock. There stood six-foot-one Sampson in heels, in a bright baby blue evening gown, huge bust, and bright red hair down to his shoulders. Kind of a skinny Mae West if you will and he had the very same attitude.

"Your lordship, his manservant, ladies, gentlemen, and queens, I have one announcement to make. It would appear our groom and groom have a more profound sense of humor than any of us realized. I am here to toast this union. If they are able to poke a little jest at themselves on their own wedding day, I suspect they have one of the most confident relationships I have ever known. So, a toast to the newly weds. May you have wealth, health, and above all, a great sex life. Cheers! Or as they say over the gums past the teeth, look out throat here it comes!"

With that toast, the mood of the room seemed to change. More of a festive party attitude prevailed. It felt good to me. This is what I wanted my wedding to be. From my deep moment of thought I heard my summons.

"Servant, have ye gone def? I said servant, come hither and bring me my drink!" Max was shouting. I turned and walked up to Max with his drink. He grabbed me and kissed me passionately. With that kiss, I wished we were on our honeymoon. Oughs and aughs sprung from the room. Max rejoined reality and stopped kissing me.

"If that is the treatment a manservant receives, then perhaps Marshall I should become your manservant," Tom yelled to Marshall.

"Perhaps you should try once and see what happens." Marshall yelled back.

Costumes seemed to come in every imaginable form and the reception turned into a Halloween party as planned. It was wonderful. I leaned back against Max and took it all in. He just put his arms around me and held me close. Yes this was the kind of wedding day I wanted. I put my left hand on his left hand and our rings clanged together. We both looked at each other and smiled.

I turned to Max. "Max this is what I truly wanted. Something wonderful to remember, something that celebrated our friends and us. I love it." I turned and kissed Max again.

"Babe, I agree. This is a day I will remember fondly the rest of my life. I agree this is more of what I wanted. A celebration that celebrates all of us, not just you and me." Max hugged me tight again.

"So, tell me Max, Colt, this the kind of thing that happens at a gay wedding?" Tab asked us from behind.

"I wouldn't know I have never been to one before." Max said, "but this is what I wanted to have. A day to remember all of our friends as well as to remember to celebrate the love I have for Colt."

"No clue," I added, "I have never been to a gay wedding either. I just know what Max and I wanted is truly unfolding as we watch. I will cherish this day forever. I hope you have your camera. These would make great wedding shots."

"I do and I planned to take many pictures. Perhaps it is none of my business, but is there significance to your costumes?" Tab inquired.

"Oh there certainly is. Can I share with him Babe?" Max looked at me with almost pleading eyes.

"I guess I don't mind. If you want to tell him, be my guest. I won't stop you." I truly couldn't imagine Max getting into all the details. However one never knew. I listened prepared for the worst.

"Well, for my birthday this summer as a joke Colt got into this role as a servant, and we spent most of the day role-playing. It turned out to be a very romantic day and so we decided this would be the perfect costume to wear."

"Tactful, very tactful," I whispered in Max's ear. I took a slight sigh of relief.

"I suspect there is more to that story but I get the idea." Tab replied. Tara walked up about that time.

"So boys, what is the point of these particular costumes?" Tara asked as she walked over to us. Behind her came Steve.

"Yeah, what is the deal here?" Steven said.

"Actually I would have to say it has more to do with romance than anything else," Tab interjected. "The costumes seem to have come from a private birthday celebration Colt had for Max."

"What do you mean?" Tara & Steven chimed in stereo.

"Let me try," Max said, "this summer on my birthday we got into a role playing mode, where Colt became my manservant for the day. I cherish that memory and so we decided to make that into our costume for our reception."

"So let me ask this," Tara said, "why a Halloween wedding with a Halloween reception?"

"Well," Max beat me to the reply, "we in all honesty just felt for a gay couple what better day than Halloween. Its festive, its fun, and we can celebrate how we feel about each other and our friends in a party atmosphere. Most gay individuals play the game of being straight at some point in their life and so Halloween, the holiday of costumes and pretending to be someone you are not, just seemed most appropriate."

"I just figured you choose Halloween for your ceremony because you were anti religion." Steven replied.

"No, for the fact it is a day of celebrations, with costumes and pretending. It just seemed like the perfect day to both of us for a gay couple to have as an anniversary every year." I explained.

"I guess it makes sense put that way." Tara retorted.

And in walked Jason, dressed as a sailor and right behind him was Derrek dressed as a pregnant nun. Oh this could create some sparks I thought. Shortly behind Derrek was Darrin. He, to my surprise, was dressed as prince. Not what I would have expected. The prince had Mat at his side, walking as if hypnotized or in a trance.

From Max's friends we had the court jester and his queen, the sailor and his um, lei, the sheik and his belly dancer, the king and his queen. No one could say they lacked imagination. We were missing a couple from the gang here. And as that thought crossed my mind, in they walked. Marshall was dressed as a groom with a knife in his back and Tom was Jack the Ripper. What a crew.

I turned to Tab, "get your camera, a Kodak moment has arrived. Pictures of all these costume will be our best wedding pictures."

"Hath the servant forgotten his place? I did not hear any request before that command was given," Max said, and then giggled. "Let the picture taking begin!"

I began to feel like we were in the bar scene from some movie, it was perfect. It was like the feeling I had as a kid getting up Christmas morning and seeing all the gifts and opening them, being surrounded by family and just being so happy to be alive and have so many new things to play with. I just watched the costumes parade by. My sister turned up as a gypsy. Tab and Tara turned up as Popeye and Olive Oil. Steven came as a vampire, a very convincing vampire at that, his wife came as one of his victims. Chip came as an old hippie.

Max's dad dressed like he was straight out of the roaring twenties. My dad was Groucho Marx. One of Max's friends wore a diaper and carried a bottle. My mother dressed as a bum, from her generation, but everyone thought she was a homeless person. Max's mom was dressed as little Bo Peep. There was a pumpkin, a cowboy, an Indian, werewolf, Merlin, a nurse, doctor, the MASH crew, a nerd, Aladdin with an Arabian knight and the usual witches, ghouls, ghosts, cats, mummies and Frankenstein.

Tess set up table with a crystal ball. Marie dressed as a genie. There were so many costumes I couldn't take them all in at once. Watching people celebrate, dance, and have a great time. It was wonderful. Once again, my thoughts were interrupted with awareness I was being beckoned.

"Manservant, answer me. You are sleeping on the job this eve!" Max was saying.

"Yes sire, your wish?" I answered.

"I wish that you were not so deep in thought. You worry me." Max sighed.

"Not to worry sire, I am just enjoying the evening. Looking at all the costumes, watching the people enjoy themselves. It is like being a kid again on Christmas morning." I turned to face Max and looked deeply into his eyes.

"Okay, as long as that is where you were. And speaking of Christmas morning, we have a table of gifts we need to go acknowledge," Max pointed in the direction of the table.

"Ah, yes, I see that we do." I said. We headed to the table and once again Max used his wedding band and glass to gain the attention of our guests. Marshall and Tom had opened the packages for us and put the cards from each package with the gifts. I held each gift for his lordship and he announced the name of the person on each card. We had some wonderful gifts

"What a generous group you all are. These are magnificent gifts. We thank you so very much. May I suggest that you all try out these marvelous treats provided by Marshall from the Fez," Max said to the guests. "Eat, drink and be merry!" We circulated through the room talking to as many of our guests as possible. Congratulations were given and hands were shook, kisses exchanged. An amazing evening had unfolded.

"You know it is our honeymoon now. Think we could say our good byes and leave without too much hassle?" Max asked.

"Doubtful, it is still early. Let's make the rounds together again, speak to our guests and then we can slip away." I suggested.

"Okay, I can handle that. No long conversations, okay?" Max begged.

"Agreed" I complied.

So, we went around the room again. We spoke to guests we had missed before, got congratulations, hugs, kisses, lots of advice. Everyone seemed to sense we were merely being polite, performing a duty of sorts.

One thing we had done was pack the car so we could just slip away. Little Max would be watched by Marshall and Tom. They were staying at our house while we were away. We had our tickets to fly to Vegas. Someplace I had never been as an adult and someplace Max enjoyed a great deal. We would fly out in the afternoon.

All we had to do now was check into the hotel for the night. We had decided to go back to the honeymoon suite, this time, on our honeymoon. Freak out another clerk. Then in the afternoon Marshall was going to meet us and take us to the airport. He and Tom were going to spend a few days here and use Max's car. They would fly back to California next week.

We decided to announce to the guests we were leaving. Max grabbed a bouquet of flowers to throw into the crowd. He clanged on is glass again to get everyone's attention.

"Lords and Ladies, we would like to thank you all for attending our wedding. At this point, Colt and I are going to begin our honeymoon. But please, stay and enjoy yourselves as long as you would like. We would like to give one big thanks to Marshall, Darrin, Derrek, and Sampson for all the work they did to pull off this wedding. Colt will toss the bouquet into the crowd." Max said.

A crowd gathered just in front of us. I took the bouquet, turned my back to the group and tossed it into the crowd. We were amazed that the person who caught it was Sampson.

"So old man, looks like you are going to have to marry me!" Ron yelled.

While the group teased Sampson, we slipped away changed back into our tuxedos and then went to the garage. When we got into the car we found a large card taped to the steering wheel. Inside we found a number of bills clipped together. The card read *"Congratulations on your marriage. May you have many happy years ahead of you!"* Then scrawled in what looked to be Marshall's handwriting was

"We figured you two would need some gambling money. So, here is $1,000 for you to blow. We love you, THE GANG. PS, if you win big, you have to split it with us!"

"That was sweet of them. That's a chunk of money," Max said. "Leave it to them to have to put a gag at the end, split the winnings with them!"

"It is a great chunk of money. They all know I don't gamble. Guess they figure I might if I just had money given to me to blow." I replied. "I am not so sure that is a gag at the end however!"

Max started the car and we drove off back to the Palace. On the way down I replayed the visit we made there this summer. The look on the desk clerk's face was priceless. It would be wild if he were the person who was at the desk tonight. What a riot that would be. I chuckled to myself.

"And just what are you laughing about over there?" Max asked.

"Oh this summer. Remember? I was thinking about that desk clerk and how uptight he got. I laughed thinking about what if he was the same person at the desk tonight?" I laughed again.

"That would be too funny. Especially since we have the room reserved and it IS our honeymoon and we do have bags this time. Would be fun." Max laughed too.

We went high class, let the valet take the car, and went to the front desk. To my disappointment, it was a totally different person at the front desk. Max walked up to check in. "We have a reservation, Michael is the name."

"Ah, yes sir, the bridal suite. Would you just sign the register here? Did you want that on your credit card?" The clerk looked over at me and smiled. "That way when you are ready to check out you can just leave your key in the room, and any calls or room service will just be billed to your card if you want."

"Yes place the bill on my credit card." Max answered.

"Do you gentlemen have any luggage?" The clerk inquired.

"Yes, we do, over there," Max pointed.

"I will ring for the bellhop. This your anniversary or your honeymoon?" The clerk asked.

Max and I looked at each other in amazement, but I had no trouble spewing out, "Honeymoon."

"Congratulations." The clerk replied. "It is good to see family have the guts to actually rent the bridal suite and celebrate their relationship. My lover and I did several years ago when we got together. I have never forgotten that night."

"We hope to have the same experience. Thank you." Max said.

"You gentlemen enjoy your evening. If there is anything you need, don't hesitate to call down. I'm Bill," he said.

"Thank you Bill, I'm Max, this is Colt. We appreciate your kindness."

"Yes, thank you. Makes out wedding day even a little more special." I added.

"Did you have a wedding today?" the clerk asked.

"Yes, we just got married." Max said.

"Wonderful, congratulations." The clerk said.

We walked to the elevator and up to the room. When we walked in a rush of the events of this summer came over me. Definitely a romantic place to be for a honeymoon, the memory from this summer was a good one. The bellhop put the bags down and turned to Max.

"Is there anything else I can do for you sir?" He asked.

"No, that will be all. Thanks." Max handed him a tip as he spoke.

"Thank you sir. You enjoy your stay." The bellhop replied as he left the room.

"Well does thou have that same shirt packed away in the royal honeymoon bag?" Max asked.

"Yes, thought ahead sire. Tis in the bag." I answered and just automatically started to walk off and change.

"Halt!" Max commanded. "Doest thou have my permission to leave this room? Change here before my very eyes servant."

"Yes sir," I replied and bowed. Then I stripped. Found the garment and put on the "sex" muscle shirt. Then I walked over to Max. "And your lordship's next desire?"

Max smiled, took a deep breath and said, "That you promise you love me for the rest of your life, that you never ever leave me."

"I don't ever want to Honey. I love you so very much, so very much." I embraced Max. We just held each other tight for a few minutes. I was just in awe to be hugging this man and with the realization of what we had just done, that he was my husband. I was carried away with the feeling of love and excitement and sexual desire.

"His lordship senses a very strong desire from his manservant. Me thinks you could be interested in a sexual encounter?" Max laughed. I got the standard kiss, hug and smile that I had never grown tired of receiving.

"You think? You only think? Perhaps you should examine the situation closer. Perhaps if you made a physical inspection of your servant you wouldn't have to just think." I replied.

"I don't just think, I am certain," Max replied as he began to undress himself. At the moment there was a knock on the door. I ran to the bedroom as Max answered the door.

"Bill would like you to have this bottle of champagne," the bellhop said handing the bottle to Max.

"Well, tell him thank you," Max replied and again tipped the bellhop. Max pulled the card off the bottle and read it to me, *"May you have a long and prosperous life together."* That was so sweet of him."

"That was," I said returning to the room in my sleazy muscle shirt. My return reminded Max what he was doing when we were interrupted by the knock at the door. As he disrobed I was in deep though, thinking of the first time we had ever been together. It still amazed me this man was in love with me. He could have been with anyone he wanted.

I had a question to throw at him that was a very serious one for a honeymoon night. But I had to ask now. "Max, I have a very important question to ask."

"Ugh, I don't like sentences that start with Max, that have the important question part and tone of voice. You have me worried, but fire." Max frowned, looked puzzled and almost scared. He stepped back a step and looked at me.

"I want so badly to make love to you, but without the safe part." I just blurted.

"That is it? Not nearly as bad as I had imagined. I feel the same Babe, but do we want to take that chance? You know both our doctors advised we wait at least a year, and then be retested, and then, maybe we could consider dropping safe sex." Max rationalized.

I was more emotional, "At this point in my life I would rather take the chance. I love you so much and every time we make love, I want so bad to just make love, not have to think if I have any open sores in my mouth, stop this, avoid that, put on condoms. It is not like making love, it's like practicing some stupid ancient ritual. I just am so tired of having to have safe sex."

"Babe, you know how bad I want to say yes. You could so easily seduce me and I wouldn't stop you. But, I have to keep reality in place. What *if*, heaven forbid, one of us turned up HIV positive? Then we would be right back at the same place we were when we met. Running from HIV, praying we didn't break a condom or get a cut or, or, or. This is so difficult! You have thrown a tough one at me." Max paused. He walked over to me and held me tight. He stroked my back, he kissed my cheek. Finally he whispered, "Colt, the what if scares the hell out of me. If one of us turned up positive, and the other didn't, it could totally destroy our relationship."

"And on the other hand, if one of us turned up positive and the other one didn't and we never had real sex, real love making, it would haunt me the rest of my life. The thought of never ever having made love to you in a natural and normal setting would devastate me. I am willing to take that chance Max. I love you too damn much." I employed. Max had tears in his eyes, I kissed him.

I continued with my argument, "I have had enough regrets in my life. The boy in seventh grade who tried to seduce me I turned down. Not leaving my bad nine-year relationship sooner than I did. Not taking charge of my career when I was younger. Not being more forward. Not taking advantage of some prime sexual encounters I could have had. Sexually have I saved myself. And for what, well, for this very moment in my life! I don't want to loose this prime time in my life with someone I am so deeply in love with, oh man of my life, my husband, me lord."

"Colt, oh Colt, you can be so damn moving. I guess you are right. I would be so upset if one of us did turn up positive and we had never ever made love naturally. Oh, this is a tough one. Can we just lie beside one another for a while? Can I think this through just a little?" Max looked so perplexed.

"Of course you can. I just had to tell you how I felt. It just hit me this is our wedding night and I would like to totally make real love ala natural to you. I am willing to take the risk." I sighed. "But, I will go with whatever you decide." We walked to the bed and lay down. We held one another very close. I got into a deep thought about our life together and what if one of us was positive. If it were me, yes, the old total guilt trip of what had I exposed Max to? If it were him, the total fear of his death and being alone again. Wanting to be HIV positive right along side of him. And what if he did die, he couldn't do that to me.

"Max, don't ever die on me and leave me alone." I sighed.

"Colt, don't you ever die and leave me alone." Max began to kiss my neck and stroke my face. My response was to stroke his back and kiss his neck. It was all so beautiful, he was so wonderful. I ran my hands over his body. He ran his hands over my body. We kissed passionately. It wasn't until we were laying next to each other holding tight that the realization hit me that we had just had unprotected sex.

"Max, thank you. I won't ever regret this. I certainly hope you won't either." I was now concerned Max would at some point regret what we just did.

"Babe, it felt so good, I don't ever want to have safe sex again. Now that we have broken the rule, let's just not ever have safe sex again. I don't think I can go back now. That was too beautiful." Max gave me his kiss, hug and smile. I was in heaven. No more safe sex.

"That is one hell of a wedding present Max. That was a bigger commitment than our wedding ceremony. I love you." I got tears in my eyes.

"I love you too. It is a gift that felt I needed to give to us. Just never go away." Max held me tight. I was so relaxed so happy it was just the most wonderful love making of my life. I felt a few tears from Max run down my chest. We needed to be celebrating I thought and Max read my mind. "Hey, let's put that bottle of champagne to use!"

"Good idea," I smiled. Max opened the bottle, there was a loud pop as the cork came out and flew across the room. Max poured us each a glass of champagne. "To my wonderful husband Colt, may we have many many happy years of marriage."

"And to my fabulous husband Max, never leave me my husband." Max brought his glass to mine and we clanged our glasses together. We polished off the bottle of champagne as we chatted away about our plans for the future. I felt so happy and yet so tired. I didn't want the evening to end, but the champagne was destroying my ability to stay awake.

I awoke to the sun shining into the room. Max was still asleep. The memory of having unprotected sex rushed into my memory, and for a brief moment, I got a sinking feeling in the pit of my stomach. Then the memory of Max saying we would never have safe sex again filled my thoughts. Then the memory how it felt to make love naturally brought a warm feeling inside. I looked back over at Max. He was so handsome. I moved closer to his body and began to lick the back of his neck. His body jerked, but then fell back against me.

"You trying to rape me or what?" Max whispered as he rolled over to kiss me.

"I was thinking about it." I replied. I kissed Max back. He pulled me on top of him and we lay there face to face, my body directly on top of his body. I stared into those deep brown eyes. "You regret last night?"

"What do I have to regret? That I finally made real love to my husband? No, I don't have any regrets. And I meant what I said I never want to have safe sex again. We broke the rule, let's never go back." Max said. He was so confident and firm in that statement.

"You'll get no argument out of me." I said.

"I didn't think that I would." Max gave me a big kiss and we laid back holding on to one another. Just taking in the moment of our first morning of being married.

"Oh, I don't want to leave this room for days," I whispered in Max's ear, "I just want to stay here and make love to you over and over again husband."

"I agree, but someone I know insisted we take a honeymoon out of town. And since that someone was so insistent we leave home and go away, I suggest we do exactly that my husband." Max winked as he finished.

"Yes, yes, I know that someone was very insistent. Wonder where he is now? Probably still looking for his spectacles, testicles, wallet, cell or keys." I laughed. "Want to shower together husband?"

"Husband, now that has a nice ring to it. Naturally I want to shower with you. Guess we should get with the program."

We laid there for a few minutes just holding each other. Then we got up, showered and enjoyed the time together. We dressed and checked out. The valet got the car and we were off. We went back to the house to check on Marshall and Tom and get our things together for Vegas. That was something I was looking forward to doing. I hadn't been to Vegas as an adult. As a child we had just driven through Vegas once, never really stopped. And I just wanted to see what it was like before we all meet there next fall for our annual bash.

When we got home Marshall and Tom were out running some errands. They had left a note they had taken the truck, but would be back in time to take us to the airport. We went up to our bedroom and checked to see that we had everything we had planned on taking with us. Got Max and went for a walk. It was a very warm day for the first of November. We discovered a few smashed pumpkins along the canal as we walked. We both seemed to be in a world of our own, taking in the trees, clouds, sunshine and the people we passed as we walked.

The trees had turned but not all the leaves had fallen yet. There were enough on the ground we could shuffle through them. I kicked some leaves at Max, he kicked some back. Little Max ran through them ahead of us. We just were both lost in our own thoughts able to walk side by side with out a word but in total communication with one another by looks. We were happy and as in love as any two people could be.

When we got back to the house, Marshall and Tom were back. They were in the living room waiting for us.

"Good morning boys." Marshall said as we walked into the house.

"Morning," Tom said.

"Morning Marshall, Tom." Max said.

"Yes, good morning." I said and walked over to Marshall. I gave him a hug. "Marshall, thank you so much for everything. I can not tell you how much I appreciate you flying out here early and doing the many things you did for Max and me."

"Colt, it was my pleasure. I have never seen you so happy in all the time we have known one another. Besides, Darrin helped me with everything."

"Well, we do appreciate the things you both did, you too Tom." Max said.

"You are welcome." Marshall replied.

"Not a problem." Tom said. "You boys ready to go the airport now?"

It was time to head to the airport and start the official honeymoon and in turn, the official or perhaps I should say the royal, marriage. I held out my hand and looked at that gold band one more time. Max placed his left hand on my left hand and we looked at our bands. Husbands, that had such a nice ring to it, we were finally married.